KERRI ANDREWS is Senior Lecturer in English Literature at Edge Hill University. She has published widely on women's writing, especially Romantic-era authors, and is a keen hill-walker and member of Mountaineering Scotland.

Further praise for *Wanderers*:

'Through the life stories of 10 wandering women, Andrews explores "the previously unacknowledged breadth, depth and distinctiveness" of their writing, and reveals a rich "female tradition of walking" . . . After writing this book, Andrews too finds her paths "companioned" (to use Nan Shepherd's word) by other women-wanderers, part of a rich cultural heritage that her fascinating research has revealed.'
– *The Guardian*

'Think of famous walkers and it's men like Wordsworth and Keats who likely spring to mind. But that's only half the story.'
– *Country Walking Magazine*

'In giving voice to female walker-writers, *Wanderers* fills out some big blanks in the history of walking, from an 18th Century pioneer to walkers of the present day . . . In Andrews's sensitive portrayals there's a sense of identification with her subjects. This may be as close as you'll get to the inside of Nan Shepherd's head.' – *UK Hillwalking*, Top Picks of 2020

'Although *Wanderers* does show its readers that there have, historically, been barriers to women's freedom to walk, its great achievement is to remind us of the prize worth challenging convention and facing th[...]is.'
– *The Pilgrim*

'Enchanted by Andrews's accessible, engaging, rigorous work, I opened this book and instantly found that I was part of a conversation I didn't want to leave. A dazzling, inspirational history.' – HELEN MORT, author of *No Map Could Show Them*

WANDERERS

A HISTORY OF
WOMEN WALKING

KERRI ANDREWS

FOREWORD BY KATHLEEN JAMIE

REAKTION BOOKS

Published by
REAKTION BOOKS LTD
Unit 32, Waterside
44–48 Wharf Road
London N1 7UX, UK
www.reaktionbooks.co.uk

First published 2020, reprinted 2021
First published in paperback 2021, reprinted 2021 (four times),
2022 (three times), 2023
Copyright © Kerri Andrews 2020
Foreword © Kathleen Jamie 2020

Printed and bound in Great Britain
by Clays Ltd, Elcograf S.p.A.

A catalogue record for this book is available from the British Library

ISBN 978 1 78914 501 4

Contents

This book is dedicated to two people

First, Adam Robinson. Thank you for saying you would walk beside me through this life, my companion on the path for which there can be no map

Second, our son Fhionnlagh, who has grown inside me as this book has done, and for whom all paths are open

Foreword

As humans, walking defines us. We are the two-legged apes. We walk, and we talk. We are the thinking minds – thinking in language, more often than not. The rhythms of our walking and of our thinking are one.

So why is it so difficult for half of the human race simply to walk? Why can't a woman ramble around, unaccompanied and unburdened, exploring the world she was born into, while turning her own thoughts in her mind? Such a harmless occupation! It doesn't seem too much to ask, to be able to walk outdoors, even in daylight, without fear. Of course we know why not. But of course we walk anyway, despite fear and derision, and always have.

Wanderers discovers a history of women walkers that spans three hundred years. The ten walkers within this book are also writers and noticers (because to walk is to notice). Each chapter explores the life and work and walking of a woman, from delightful polymath Elizabeth Carter (b. 1717) to contemporary authors such as Rebecca Solnit and Linda Cracknell. There is of course Dorothy Wordsworth, noticer-in-chief of hill and dale; there is Nan Shepherd of the mountains, and the city *flâneuse* Anaïs Nin. Here are women simply glad to be alive and moving, enjoying their own bodies – and also women power-walking their way out of ghastly marriages. For some women, walking and health amble hand-in-hand. For others, walking fosters creativity: Virginia Woolf paced out her novel *Mrs Dalloway*, as a pedestrian on the streets of London.

The book is brought to us by Kerri Andrews, whose company is just as intelligent and lively as the women she 'companions' along the way. Heaven knows how many miles are covered – an astonishing number. But miles don't really matter. What matters is that all women who can, should feel encouraged to get out there and claim our birthright. We should all be able to enjoy our walking free from fear, in what is, after all, our world too.

Thanks to this book, we know that even in solitude we never walk alone. A fine female tradition is at our backs, encouraging us along.

Kathleen Jamie

Setting Off

The summer had been glorious, with weekend after weekend of sunny weather, and I had been in the mountains for most of them, climbing and counting Munro after Munro (mountains more than 3,000 feet in Scotland). I was closing in on my hundredth and wanted to choose somewhere special for my century. What could be more memorable than a day spent on the Aonach Eagach? The name thrilled me the first time I heard it. The English translation – 'the notched ridge' – feels tame in the mouth compared to the muscular angularity of the Gaelic. The route is legendary in Scotland as one of the most aerated ridge walks in the country, its narrow arête linking two Munros high above Glencoe near the west coast. Tackling the ridge takes commitment, as there are only two safe ways on or off – the beginning and the end; people have died trying to escape elsewhere.

My husband, Adam, and our friend Ewan selected a promising looking weekend in August for our attempt. Ewan had been up before – had indeed 'compleated' all 282 Munros – and we were grateful to have his experience to draw on. We left a car at the walk end before driving 12 miles up Glencoe to the start, under the rocky cliffs of Am Bodach.

The climb was steep but simple, the scenery rapidly becoming outrageously grand as we came level with the rocky faces of the Three Sisters, while Bidean nam Bian, the highest mountain in the area, towered above us. The cloud level was lower than the forecast suggested, and before we reached the top of Am Bodach we were enfolded in fog. There we were to stay for the rest of the day, which proved both a blessing and a curse. Had it been clear, we should have seen that the knife edge on which we were to walk sat on a barely angled blade of rock 3,000 feet high – but it also would not have been raining. When the drizzle started – that fine, soaking mizzle at which Scotland excels – we should have turned back, but our blood was up, and the thrill of tackling the difficulties ahead was too tempting to resist.

The first challenge came immediately with the tricky down climb of Am Bodach and its rocky slabs. The gradient was only moderate but the moisture made the rock slightly greasy, and even though the cloud obscured what lay beyond, we knew it was no place to fall. It quickly became apparent that we three had very different scrambling techniques: Ewan, the much more accomplished mountaineer, preferred to 'face in' to the mountain, keeping his body close to the rock and his centre of gravity inwards; Adam and I were more instinctive, and found facing out more comfortable. Oriented like this, we could see holds and distances more easily, and we could use our legs as brakes, but if we lost control, there would be nothing to hold us to the rock. Ours was the more risky technique, though it proved more effective on the slabs where holds were several feet apart and tricky to see. We climbed down relatively easily while Ewan struggled, having to feel for holds and reluctant to rely on guesswork for sure ground.

Eventually all three of us stood on a narrow path, which undulated pleasingly towards the first Munro summit of Meall Dearg. We strolled along, the ease of the walking proving something of an anti-climax after the tense drama of the first scramble. Without much effort, we found ourselves at the summit cairn, where we sat and ate while contemplating what was to come. The route from Meall Dearg to Stob Coire Leith is little more than a rocky tightrope, the height of which changes constantly: it would take us five hours to cross the next 2 miles. For the most part, the scrambling was exhilarating – a constantly shifting three-dimensional puzzle for which the only solution lay in correctly aligning and realigning your body with the rock, moment by moment. It is work that demands total unity between mind and body and utter concentration, work that is at once exhausting and deeply satisfying. That is, until the Crazy Pinnacles.

Cruelly positioned near the end of the Aonach Eagach – if, like most, you tackle the ridge east to west – the Crazy Pinnacles are the most exposed, technically challenging section of the whole route. Over the course of the day, we had passed and repassed a couple of other parties attempting the ridge, including a father and son. Earlier, as we struggled on a particularly thorny down climb, I had decided to let them overtake us again, rather than hold them up. So it was that we were behind them as they approached the beginning of the Pinnacles. I'd been warned by an experienced mountaineer to 'if in doubt, stay high', but looking up at their jagged toothiness, this seemed like insanity. There was no path, no route over the extremely exposed rock that I could see – just a vast drop that disappeared nauseatingly into the fog below. My fears were evidently shared by the pair ahead of us, who spurned the first Pinnacle for a down climb off the rock. We watched them descend, then vanish. Assuming they knew what they were about, we decided to follow. My husband, the fittest of us, went ahead, but a yelp warned us that all was far from well. Hauling himself back, he collapsed in a gasping heap before explaining how he'd followed a path only to find himself hanging by his arms above a sickening drop. The previous pair must have jumped, at incredible risk and from a great height, onto the slender path below.

Upwards was the only safe option for us, and it was with enormous relief that my husband – again running on ahead – reported the discovery of the sketchiest of paths above. Taking it involved making a sequence of extremely exposed moves, however. As Adam swung his limbs out over the abyss ahead, I experienced the most intense fear of the day. Instead of the pleasurable tingle of adrenaline across the skin that had been with me for most of the walk, this sensation was primal. If he fell, I would be unable to help in any way, and my gut writhed as he spun around a tricky chimney with just two limbs anchoring him to safety. Just moments later, it was my turn, but having seen my husband's manner of climbing the crux, I opted to keep my centre of gravity low, and hauled myself up on my elbows and knees. At that moment, I cared nothing for dignity or torn clothing, and was simply grateful to be close to the rock.

And then it was all over. After the Pinnacles, the route becomes a clear path climbing with malignant steepness, though no difficulty, towards a minor summit, before rising again to the second and final Munro of Sgorr nam Fiannaidh. Brains and bodies were so utterly depleted by this point that we hardly registered that it had begun to rain in earnest. Soaked through and barely in control of our limbs, we began our descent towards the Pap of Glencoe, with Loch Leven and the Rough Bounds beyond becoming visible as we finally dropped out of the clouds towards Ballachulish below, and bed.

SEVEN YEARS EARLIER I climbed my first ever mountain. I'd been invited on a walking holiday to Wales with some female friends. We were going to climb Snowdon. I'd never been to north Wales, had never seen a proper mountain, and I had no idea what to expect.

While the others – Jenny and Sarrawat, along with Sarrawat's boyfriend Matt, and Matt's father and brother – chatted away as we set off from the car park, I was busy looking at the hillside that was visible below the grey skirts of the low cloud. Under the murk, I could just see the path winding upwards at an angle that made my palms clammy. After the first five minutes, our field of vision was reduced to just a few metres by the thick fog, but this suited me fine: if I couldn't see it, it couldn't scare me. Nonetheless, I quickly began to struggle. The men, exuberant and fit, seemed to race ahead, while I could only manage a trudge of 20 metres or so before needing to rest. It didn't take long for the men to lose patience with me, and they told me that if I wanted to wait for them, they would come and collect me on their return from the summit. I was hurt, their apparent concern for my comfort really securing their own. They didn't wait for an answer but disappeared into the mists above. I tried not to cry, but I was bitterly disappointed to have failed, and to have been assessed and dismissed as too weak to bother with. But as my head dropped, I felt Jenny and Sarrawat sit down next to me. The men had gone, but they had decided to stay, and they told me that we were all going to make it to the summit, however long it took. I wept then in gratitude – for their kindness, their friendship, for their gentle and genuine support. They put me at the front, which, with the benefit of experience, I now know meant that I would have control of the pace. We soon settled into a pattern of short gains and long rests, my breath rasping within moments each time we set off. It felt like an unending torment, the fog making everything look the same, and having existed mostly inside my own head for hours, trying to find the strength to keep my legs pumping, I was startled to see what looked to be hundreds of other people; and it was the summit cairn – the summit! – that they were buzzing around. The three men who had been in our party had obviously had their fill of the busy top and were sat some way from the worst of the hubbub. They were keen to be off, but Jenny, Sarrawat and I took our time at the peak, where I relished the complex emotions that took the place of the earlier unending pain. I was certainly elated, and exhausted, but I was also conscious of a profound gratitude. Alone, I would have given up. The men left me to fend for myself. It was the company of women that got me to the top.

THIS IS A BOOK about women who have, over the past three hundred years, found walking essential to their sense of themselves as women, writers and people. The history of walking has always been women's history, though you would not know it from what has been published on the subject. Since Jean-Jacques Rousseau's *The Reveries of a Solitary Walker* appeared in 1782, walking has been acknowledged as central to the writing of many famous male authors: William Wordsworth, Samuel Taylor Coleridge, Thomas De Quincey, John Keats, John Clare and others. These writers gained readers in their own time, and have continued to enjoy admiration since, not only for their literary accomplishments but their physical feats: De Quincey estimated that William Wordsworth walked 180,000 miles in his lifetime on what he understatedly described as 'serviceable legs beyond the average standard of human requisition'.[1] De Quincey himself is supposed to have walked an average of 70–100 miles every week, and Keats covered 642 miles in around two months while touring the Lake District and Scotland in 1818.[2] So closely were Romantic writers' reputations tied to their pedestrian exploits that walking has come to be held as the ideal means by which a poet can experience 'the spontaneous overflow of powerful feelings' William Wordsworth considered necessary for composition.[3]

Many have followed: Leslie Stephen, Henry David Thoreau, Friedrich Nietzsche, Emmanuel Kant, Robert Louis Stevenson, Edward Thomas, Werner Herzog, Robert Macfarlane. When these men write about their walking, they look back to earlier male walker-writers; even the most recent accounts of walking, such as Robert Macfarlane's *The Old Ways* (2012), refer mainly to other male walker-writers (with just the one exception in Macfarlane's case: his championing of Nan Shepherd's prose poetry about the Cairngorms, *The*

Living Mountain). So utterly has writing about walking been dominated by men that Rebecca Solnit has described it, with some bitterness, as a kind of club, 'not one of the real walking clubs, but a kind of implicit club of shared background', where the members 'are always male'.[4] The 2014 reissue of the popular anthology *While Wandering: Words on Walking* rather proves Solnit's point: the 'words on walking' are male-authored more than 90 per cent of the time; of around 270 entries, just 26 are written by women. Also underlining the validity of Solnit's claim is Frédéric Gros' *A Philosophy of Walking* (2014), which calls exclusively on examples of male walkers; the sole mention of a woman walker occurs, in passing, on the penultimate page. The universality of the title belies the fact that the book itself explores a philosophy of *male* walking, both in terms of subject-matter and in the pronouns used to describe the person walking – a generalized individual who is labelled throughout as 'he'. While this is possibly an unfortunate effect of the book's translation from French – with its gendered nouns – into English, it hammers home the apparent, and seemingly overwhelming, masculinity of walking. In describing Gros' book in an article for the *The Guardian*, Carole Cadwalladr notes that 'it's an examination of the philosophy of various thinkers for whom walking was central to their work – Nietzsche, Rimbaud, Kant, Rousseau, Thoreau (they're all men; it's unclear if women don't walk or don't think).'[5]

WOMEN MOST CERTAINLY DO WALK. And they write about their walking, and their thinking, and have done for centuries. Elizabeth Carter, a clergyman's daughter from Deal, began a lifetime of roaming as a young girl in the 1720s. Fearless and bold, and an aspiring vagrant, Carter covered thousands of miles of the Kent countryside, frequently alone, but sometimes with a friend, seeking out isolated corners for the quiet contemplation of the philosophical questions she would explore in the published works that later brought her fame, fortune and a reputation as one of the pre-eminent scholars in Britain. Carter wrote about her walks in jolly and chatty letters to her dearest female friends, where she turned sometimes unfortunate misadventures into comic episodes of derring-do. She was rarely deterred by anything the mercurial British weather could throw at her, and particularly relished the extremes of the eighteenth century's harsh winters (what has since come to be known as the 'Little Ice Age'). As a young woman, for instance, she wrote in high spirits to a friend in Canterbury how

> In proportion as my sister has mended, I have recovered my spirits, I am now nearly as gay and wild as ever, and want to be flying all over the face of the earth, though this weather something cramps my genius, for I cannot meet with any body romantic enough to take moonlight walks in the snow, and travel as people do in Lapland. If I was happy enough to be in Canterbury, what excursions should you and I make through trackless paths, and enjoy a season that less whimsical folk shudder at.[6]

'Whimsical' and 'wild' are apt words selected by Carter to describe herself – a woman who longed to be truly itinerant, and aspired to be taken up by a local magistrate for appearing to have no fixed home – and they are words that pepper

Carter's writing about her walking. Freed first by a liberal-minded father, and later by her literary wealth, from any need to conform to traditional notions of female propriety, Carter's most ardent wish – one frequently realized – was to bound 'from rock to rock like a wild kid' all the days of her life.[7]

Elizabeth Carter was in no way unique for relishing the contemplative space created by the rhythms of walking, or finding in pedestrianism rich matter for her literary works. Though it is William who enjoys the greater cultural recognition, his sister Dorothy Wordsworth was herself an accomplished and ardent walker who stepped out on an excursion almost every day of her early adult life, and she wrote extensively about the thoughts, memories and creative insights in which her walking played an integral part. She undertook walking tours, initially in the company of her brother and their close friend Samuel Taylor Coleridge, but later Dorothy Wordsworth walked with other women – her sister-in-law Mary Wordsworth, and Mary's sister Joanna Hutchinson. All three women wrote accounts of their experiences on these trips, though Dorothy's are the funniest, the most vibrant and the most rigorous in exploring the meaning of walking for her as a writer, as a woman and as a human being. Yet where William Wordsworth's prodigious ambulations added to his prestige as a poet, Dorothy's were considered by some to be detrimental to her appeal as a woman:

> The greatest deductions from Miss Wordsworth's attractions, and from the exceeding interest which surrounded her in right of her character, of her history, and of the relation which she fulfilled towards her brother, were the glancing

quickness of her motions, and other circumstances in her deportment (such as her stooping attitude when walking), which gave an ungraceful, and even an unsexual character to her appearance when out-of-doors.[8]

De Quincey's description is indicative of some of the cultural reasons which have tended to circumscribe women's walking in general, not just Dorothy Wordsworth's in particular: unfeminine (or, in De Quincey's terms, 'ungraceful' or 'unsexual') physical traits, and indeed unfeminine levels of physical activity, were subject to criticism – proper women were not supposed to be physically strong. When walking, De Quincey suggests, Dorothy loses her sex, even her personhood. If she is not a woman, what is she?

What is clear when reading Dorothy Wordsworth's journals and letters, however, is that neither these cultural prejudices, nor her supposed 'stooping attitude when walking', were insuperable barriers to her performing pedestrian feats to match her brother's: on one fine day in 1794, Dorothy walked with William 'at her side' for 33 miles, from Kendal to Keswick via Grasmere, 'through the most delightful country that was ever seen'.[9] Days later Dorothy Wordsworth wrote to her great aunt Crackenthorpe to counter the latter's criticism at hearing of her niece's 'rambling about the country':

So far from considering this a matter of condemnation, I rather thought it would have given my friends pleasure to hear that I had courage to make use of the strength with which nature has endowed me, when it not only procured me infinitely more pleasure than I should have received from sitting in a post-chaise – but was also the means of saving me at least thirty shillings.[10]

Dorothy Wordsworth's response demonstrates that walking was not only of physical benefit to her, but was a matter of personal, and perhaps moral, 'courage'. To walk was to make use of God-given physical gifts, and was, in a shrewd nod to received ideas of feminine domestic economy, financially prudent. While the reference to physical pleasure might have disconcerted the conservative sensibilities of great aunt Crackenthorpe, Dorothy's defence of her ramblings indicates the centrality of walking to her physical, emotional and indeed spiritual well-being.

There have been many other such women. A contemporary of Dorothy Wordsworth and her sisters-in-law, Sarah Stoddart Hazlitt, is known now almost solely as a result of her marriage to the famous essayist William Hazlitt, but she was, on occasion, an avid walker, covering extraordinary distances over two walking tours around the central belt of Scotland during a months-long residence in Edinburgh. Even more remarkable was the fact that she often walked entirely alone. The solitude was apparently a comfort to her, and provided some relief from the sordid horrors of colluding in her husband's adultery with a prostitute in an Edinburgh brothel so that they might obtain a swift divorce: William desired to marry a barmaid from London with whom he had become infatuated. Distraught at having perjured herself before a judge about her knowledge of William's activities in Edinburgh, Sarah sought solace not only in isolation, but in the extreme physical strain under which she placed her body during her walking tours. During her first, from Stirling to Edinburgh via the central Highlands, Glasgow and West Lothian, she covered 170 miles in eight days and proudly recorded each day's distances in her journal (the longest ran to 32 miles). Here she noted her satisfaction, and perhaps also relief, at the extent of her physical tiredness:

> I was very glad to get into my own lodgings, and literally wash the dust from my feet: indeed I made a thorough ablution, and the comfort of that, and clean clothes, after being choked with dust, is more refreshing than can be imagined by those who have not under gone the previous ordeal: it invigorated me so much that I seemed to have nearly overcome my fatigue.[11]

It is perhaps understandable that there should be a significant feeling of release in experiencing bodily, rather than emotional, exhaustion. And it is not too much of a stretch to imagine Sarah, as she washed her feet of road dirt, feeling at the same time cleansed of the moral grime of complicity in her husband's infidelity. She certainly seems to have found comfort through having and recording such physically trying experiences; even when she had to remain in Edinburgh on divorce business for weeks on end, she roamed dozens of miles through and around the city each week, criss-crossing and circling it repeatedly, carefully documenting the details. Though the journal is the only record of Sarah's walking, and though it covers just three months from mid-April to mid-July 1822, and though it was never published in her lifetime, its existence is evidence that walking, and writing about that walking, were fundamental to her ability to survive a period of extraordinary personal pain.

At around the same time that Sarah Stoddart Hazlitt and Dorothy Wordsworth were walking around Scotland, Ellen Weeton was also seeking an escape from personal difficulties through pedestrianism – in her case, the confined life of a governess, and later the extremely unpleasant realities of an unhappy marriage to an abusive husband. She tramped across parts of south Lancashire, the Lake District, the Isle of Man and Wales, walking up Snowdon alone, among other accomplishments. Like Stoddart Hazlitt, Weeton recorded her reflections upon her experiences in a journal, though unlike Stoddart Hazlitt, Weeton also documented many of her walks in her correspondence. Over the course of these accounts, Weeton's confidence as a woman walker grows, as does her sense of personal achievement and fulfilment. In 1812 she undertook a largely solo tour of the Isle of Man and, while her correspondence demonstrates that she harboured some anxieties about attack when she was out alone (a worry unlikely to have been experienced by the majority of male walkers then or since), prominent above all else is joy at what she was able to accomplish. This is most especially true of her account of her walk on 5 June 1812, in which Weeton covered a total of 35 miles. On a mountain road, sought out for no other reason than that it offered 'scenery and prospect',

> Often and often, as I went on, did I turn to feast my eyes on the beauties spread out at my feet. The air was serenely clear; England, Ireland, Scotland, and Wales were all perfectly distinct . . . I could . . . mark the mountains in

Cumberland and Westmoreland; Skiddaw, Saddleback, Helvellyn, Coniston, and several others. I felt a pleasure in looking at them, for there had my feet trodden, and some of my happiest days been spent! . . . Oh Ann! if you knew the pleasure I feel in running wild among such scenery, you would not wonder at my temerity, or at my undergoing so much fatigue to obtain the gratification.[12]

Walking, for Weeton, meant freedom – it was 'running wild', without restraint or control – and it brought her evident and enormous pleasure; more importance is placed by Weeton upon that pleasure than upon the cost of showing 'temerity', or eccentricity regarding social mores. It is also worth noting that Weeton, like Sarah Stoddart Hazlitt, considered as exclusive the sensations experienced as a result of walking: for Sarah, the refreshment in the simple act of washing her feet cannot 'be imagined by those who have not under gone the previous ordeal'; and Weeton's friend Ann would have to 'run wild' herself in order to fully comprehend her friend's emotional state.[13] If walking is 'not only [a] means of traversing space, but also . . . of feeling, being and knowing', then Stoddart Hazlitt and Weeton in their accounts can be seen to have gained access to new ways of understanding themselves, to new ways of thinking about their relationship to the world.[14] Furthermore, their accounts express a desire for their new-found knowledge to be shared – for others to have access through walking to the ways they have found of 'feeling, being and knowing'.

Harriet Martineau, in contrast, knew what it was to be unable to walk. For five years from 1839 to 1844 she was confined to her bedroom by a mysterious condition that left her fearing for her life. Cured by mesmerism, she measured the return of her health by the increasing number of miles she was able to cover: first a few hundred yards, then a mile or so, but quickly 3, 5, 10 miles. A move to the Lake District followed, and with it an earnest desire to become, like Dorothy Wordsworth and her brother William, entwined with the complex social, geographical and literary histories of the area. Unlike the Wordsworths, who were born to the Lake District, Martineau arrived in her forties, and she was keen to make up for lost time:

> Now, on my recovery, I set myself to learn the Lake District, which was still a *terra incognita*, veiled in bright mists before my mind's eye: and by the close of a year from the purchase of my field, I knew every lake (I think) but two, and almost every mountain pass . . . Of these joyous labours, none has been sweeter than that of my first recovered health, when Lakeland became gradually disclosed before my exploration, till it lay before me, map-like, as if seen from a mountain top.[15]

Once Martineau had built herself a Lake District home, she embarked upon a pedestrian voyage of discovery, exploring the contours and outlines of the fells with her feet and inscribing the landscape into her memory. In this passage, she figures herself standing above the Lake District, its mysteries now fully revealed to her. It is not conquest that enables her to take up this position, however, but learning, and it is walking that has enabled Martineau to know the place through both body and mind.

More women writer-walkers would follow in the twentieth century. Virginia Woolf recorded in diaries and letters the centrality of walking to the composition and development of several of her novels, to her confidence as a writer and as a person: for Woolf, walking underpinned how she understood her place in the world. Nor was she afraid of exploring the unsettling oddness of that place, an oddness which appears to have been intermingled for her with what she saw as an essential strangeness about the act of writing. Such peculiarities seem to have become apparent to Woolf primarily when she walked, which was often, though not always, alone, and often, though not always, in London. In the midst of writing *To the Lighthouse* (1927), Woolf asked of herself, in an eerie and haunting account of an evening walk in the city,

> What is it? And shall I die before I find it? Then (as I was walking through Russell Sqre last night) I see the mountains in the sky: the great clouds; & the moon which is risen over Persia; I have a great & astonishing sense of something there, which is 'it' – It is not exactly beauty that I mean. It is that the thing is in itself enough: satisfactory; achieved. A sense of my own strangeness, walking on the earth is there too: of the infinite oddity of the human position; trotting along Russell Sqre with the moon up there, & those mountain clouds. Who am I, what am I, & so on.[16]

For Woolf, both writing and walking enable, through different (though clearly related) mechanisms, access to profound and unsettling questions about identity, about the nature of self, and the essence of our purpose as human beings on this earth. This introspection is facilitated by the physical act of walking, and its results are to be recorded in writing. But, as Robert Macfarlane and others have noted, walking makes possible movement that is simultaneously inward and excursive: it prompts both 'sight and thought', a duality evident in Woolf's entry about her experiences in Russell Square; while the questioning inner 'I' of Woolf's journal is both a definite, wondering (and wandering) presence, it is also an unidentifiably small fragment of a much larger, frighteningly unknowable, whole – the edges of which are glimpsed by Woolf as she walks through the London night.[17]

Anaïs Nin was also a city walker, and pedestrianism was a crucial means of accessing 'the creative sources' of 'being'.[18] For Nin, though, the importance and function of walking shifted throughout her life. If at various times it served as solace and as creative wellspring, it also served to demonstrate to Nin her fundamental solitariness even as she strolled the crowded streets of New York and Paris. 'I often have the feeling of being alone on a mountain top', she wrote in her diary as a teenager, 'detached from other people, as I observe them.'[19] Walking was also, at times, a punishment, a treatment Nin forced upon herself in order to cure everything from depression to peritonitis. A thin and weakly child cossetted by relatives in America, 'where the supreme idol was health and hardiness', Nin writes how she 'tortured' herself with 'ice-cold showers' and 'long walks' into wellness.[20] Ultimately, though, the toil and loneliness of walking became sources of strength for Nin as she began to pursue with seriousness her ambition to be a published writer. 'I am tired of writing just for myself,' Nin wrote – to herself – in her diary in 1927:

I know I could make others cry and make them infinitely, desperately alive. I know I say what they wish to say and cannot say. And some, if my writing reached them, this writing that I have done walking alone, would know that there are several of us walking alone, and that it is good to know it.[21]

Through literature, and through walking, Nin saw an opportunity to create an imaginative community connected not only by their shared ideas, but by pedestrianism. On foot, Nin and others like her would be able to 'walk through enchanting stories' together, so that Nin's walking had the power to transform isolation into fellowship.[22]

Nor was Nin alone in finding walking to be a transformational experience; Nan Shepherd, writing in the years between the World Wars, was also sensitive to the essential strangeness of the experience of walking, of journeying into oneself at the same time as walking through, and into, the larger world. Shepherd walked over, between and even in company with the mountains of the Cairngorms massif, and sought, through her walking, different kinds of 'knowing' both the place and herself:

One cannot know the rivers till one has seen them at their sources; but this journey to the sources is not to be undertaken lightly. One walks among elementals, and elementals are not governable. There are awakened also in oneself by the contact elementals that are as unpredictable as wind or snow.[23]

Through walking in these mountains, in this place, Shepherd suggests in her account, the disconcerting yet innate connection between human beings and the earth is made evident – the act of walking here 'awakens' the otherwise unknown parts of us that claim kinship with mountain, or river, or sky.

In 1995 Cheryl Strayed undertook the sort of long-distance walking with which men have more often been associated. While John Muir's walks across the American West have long been a touchstone for (often male) writers considering the diverse landscapes of this vast continent, Strayed's extremely personal account of a woman's suffering and redemption experienced over hundreds of miles on the Pacific Crest Trail offers an alternative view of the relationship between person, pedestrianism and the natural world. Having struggled with addiction, loss and the collapse of her marriage, Strayed discovers the strength as she walks to accept how she has come to fail so badly. But the trail is a powerful agent of change and, over the course of three months of walking alone, Strayed finds both body and mind transformed by the rigours of hiking day after day in a brutal and brutalizing experience that overwrites all that has gone before. Initially hesitant about her physical abilities, her status as a solo woman walker and whether she has the skill to live in the wilderness for weeks at a time, she grows in confidence. Told of two men coming down the trail behind her, she resolves 'to meet them as the woman who'd left them in her dust instead of the woman they'd overtaken', and surges forwards with power and strength so that they cannot catch up with her until she permits it.[24] Writing consciously as a *woman* walker, Strayed contemplates the relationship between women's external and internal realities – including periods, vulnerability and confidence – and the ways in which women come to understand the world through which they walk. Her book is a love-letter to the brutalities and beauties of the American landscape, and articulates how the physical suffering of repeated walking can help move us back into ourselves.

Most recently, Linda Cracknell has sought to demonstrate how walking helps connect women with a shared history, and how it helps keep alive older ways of being. Roaming throughout Scotland on drove roads, old byways and former post paths, Cracknell is attentive to the ways in which earlier footsteps reverberate through the years. On Wade's Road, for instance, cut into the Highland turf to facilitate the movement of British redcoats throughout Scotland after the Jacobite rising of 1715, Cracknell finds 'a new busy-ness', a 'new company' on the path which resounds with 'the tread of Jacobites, Hanoverians, drovers, shoemakers, road-builders'.[25] Cracknell's paths ring with the voices of earlier women-walkers who passed there. As she travels across Scotland, Cracknell encounters Dorothy Wordsworth at the Birks of Aberfeldy, Jessie Kesson on the hills above Loch Ness and Alexandra Stewart in Glen Lyon, near Cracknell's home in Aberfeldy. Each woman's walking, Cracknell demonstrates, is valuable for its articulation of ways of life that have passed, or are passing. Stewart, for instance, had little patience with modern walkers whose speed left them inattentive to the landscape through which they travelled, and to which she herself was keenly attuned. 'There was always something to watch, some association to remember, changes in light and sound and fragments of poetry and local lore to think about,' she writes. [26] 'A well-stored mind is its own good company,' she notes, 'and long hours spent walking were not time wasted as they could be to mechanized armies nowadays who can't enjoy what they are passing because they've timed themselves to be somewhere else as soon as possible.'[27] So too for Cracknell, who is interested in how our bodies 'mark out time, with no need for a calendar or a watch', but with the feet instead: one-third of an hour was known as a '"mileway", because that is the distance that can be covered. Moving at walking pace perhaps determines our human sense of time more than we now realise,' she writes.[28]

THE WORKS of these women writer-walkers offer new insights into the role played by walking in human creativity, and demonstrate that while women walked at times for the same purposes as men, the experience of being on foot has frequently meant markedly different things for women. The meaning of walking has also changed for women writers over time, and has played different roles for women from different backgrounds – whether working class or middling class, British or American, city stroller or country walker. For all this richness, though, there has tended to be little discussion of women's walking as a cultural or historical phenomenon, and less of how women's experiences as human beings might have shaped their walking and writing, or how their walking or writing might have shaped their experiences as human beings. This is to the detriment of our understanding of what walking has meant, and what it might mean, for us all.

An important aspect of this problem is a failure to consider or acknowledge the effects of material circumstances on women's ability to walk, or write, or reflect. Dorothy

Wordsworth's opportunities to walk, for example, came to be substantially circumscribed by her domestic duties in her brother's home; Ellen Weeton, as a governess and as a mother, was also limited in her opportunities to walk by responsibilities at home. In contrast, William Wordsworth could head off on a walking tour, or walk over to Keswick to see Samuel Taylor Coleridge, or go for a stroll, whenever he liked, because the most pressing household duty, childcare, was managed by the women of the household, at the cost of their own walking. Rebecca Solnit articulates the cultural gendered assumptions on women's ability (practically, physically, securely) to walk:

> Legal measures, social mores subscribed to by both men and women, the threat implicit in sexual harassment, and rape itself have all limited women's ability to walk where and when they wished. (Women's clothes and bodily confinements – high heels, tight or fragile shoes, corsets and girdles, very full or narrow skirts, easily damaged fabrics, veils that obscure vision – are part of the social mores that have handicapped women as effectively as laws and fears.) ... Even the English language is rife with words and phrases that sexualize women's walking.[29]

Solnit brings her argument to a powerful conclusion by inviting her reader to participate in a thought experiment about the consequences of history's repeated failure to acknowledge the stringent limitations placed by society on female pedestrians. Walking, Solnit begins, has been generally accepted as

A mode of contemplation and composition, from Aristotle's peripatetics to the roaming poets of New York and Paris. It has supplied writers, artists, political theorists, and others with the encounters and experiences that inspired their work, as well as the space in which to imagine it, and it is impossible to know what would have become of many of the great male minds had they been unable to move at will through the world. Picture Aristotle confined to the house, Muir in full skirts . . . If walking is a primary cultural act and a crucial way of being in the world, those who have been unable to walk out as far as their feet would take them have been denied not merely exercise or recreation but a vast portion of their humanity.[30]

This thought experiment is provocative, and illuminating: could the dozens of men famed for their writing about walking have wandered so freely if they had been subject to the restrictive social attitudes held towards women alone in public; if, for instance, the term 'streetwalker' had the same connotations for men as for women? If the answer to these queries is 'no', then the question we need to ask is no longer 'did women walk?' but 'how did they manage to walk so much?' And if walking is central to an individual's 'humanity', understanding how walking is experienced by different people will enable a better comprehension of our shared humanity. For the most part, though, the writers of our history have focused on the experiences of men – a group of people with the time and leisure to walk, who have been authorized by social conventions to be mobile and alone, who are encouraged, even expected, to be physically active. An understanding based solely on the accounts of such individuals can only ever be, at best, partial – not least because men's experiences have been assumed to be *humanity's* experience.

THIS BOOK, then, sets out to offer an alternative view of the literary history of walking by making visible the previously unacknowledged breadth, depth and distinctiveness of ten women's writing about walking. I make no claim to comprehensiveness. Instead, I urge interested readers, once they are finished, to explore the Appendix, where they will find more examples of women who walked. There are many more besides.

While the influence of male walker-writers, from Jean-Jacques Rousseau, to William Wordsworth, to Leslie Stephen, to John Muir, can undoubtedly be felt in the works examined here, also in evidence are alternative perspectives and experiences, different ways of understanding the walking self and its place in the world – and a sense of a female tradition of walking. Unusual views of familiar places are to be found, as well as different priorities: Nan Shepherd eschews the commonplaces of men's writing (such as the 'self-exaltation of the mountaineer's hunger for an utmost point', as Robert Macfarlane describes it) for a more slanting approach to both mountains and walking which demonstrates, in place of 'self-exaltation', an 'implicit humility' in her 'repeated acts of traverse which stands as a corrective' to more typically male priorities;[31] Dorothy Wordsworth, Sarah Stoddart Hazlitt and Cheryl Strayed write of female spaces and from distinctly female perspectives; while Linda Cracknell's evocation of the perambulatory lives of Jessie Kesson and Alexandra Stewart demonstrates the creative power of recognizing and drawing on a female tradition of walking. Ultimately, the vitality, variety and significance of the different ways of walking, of seeing, of *being*, articulated by these women require us to re-evaluate our walking history, because that history has always been written by women.

ONE

Elizabeth Carter

As you desire a full and true account of my whole life and conversation, it is necessary in the first place you should be made acquainted with the singular contrivance by which I am called in the morning. There is a bell placed at the head of my bed, and to this is fastened a packthread and a piece of lead, which, when I am not lulled by the soft zephyrs through the broken pane, is conveyed through a crevasse of my window into a garden below, pertaining to the Sexton, who gets up between four and five, and pulls the said packthread with as much heart and good-will as if he was ringing my knell. By this most curious invention I make a shift to get up . . . My general practice about six is to take up my stick and walk, sometimes alone, and at others with a companion, whom I call in my way, and draw out half asleep . . . Many are the exercises of patience she meets with in our peregrination, sometimes half roasted with the full glare of sunshine upon an open common, then dragged through a thread-paper path in the middle of a cornfield, and bathed up to the ears in dew, and at the end of it perhaps forced to scratch her way through bushes of a close shady lane, never before frequented by any animal but birds. In short, towards the conclusion of our walk, we make such deplorable ragged figures, that I wonder some prudent country justice does not take us up for vagrants, and cramp our rambling genius in the stocks. An apprehension that does not half so much fright me, as when some civil swains pull off their hats, and I hear them signifying to one another, with a note of admiration, that *I am Parson Carter's daughter*. I had much rather be accosted with 'good morrow, sweet-heart,' or 'are you walking for a wager.'

Elizabeth Carter to Catherine Talbot, 1746

Elizabeth Carter was born a parson's daughter and became one of the most celebrated intellectuals – male or female – of the eighteenth century, but she also treasured the desire to be mistaken for a vagabond. She was indeed a 'rambling genius', a woman with an exceptional mind whose greatest pleasure was wandering the Kent coast near Deal, where she lived for most of her life. But Carter's desire for walking was so strong that she might well have been said to have been possessed, not so much by a *genius loci*, but a *genius peregrinus*. Carter found walking both soothing and useful. On foot and in the wilds, she was able to exist, at least for a time, without scrutiny or concern for social niceties, and she relished the escape that walking provided. She also found in the contemplation of her own, brief life and the ancientness of the land she walked stimulation for her intellectual pursuits.

It has long been assumed that women in the eighteenth century (and, indeed, in the years since) did little or no walking more arduous than genteel strolls around well-tended gardens. Women, it is often repeated, had too many concerns about their personal safety to be able to wander freely. In the eighteenth century, though, walking for pleasure was rarely undertaken by many men, either. Instead, walkers tended to be those who needed to move. In the Scottish Borders near my home, for instance, the old Herring Road that crosses the high moorland of the Lammermuir Hills from Dunbar to Lauder was trodden for years by women hauling creels full of fish from the North Sea to market. People in the Lake District and the west coast of Scotland walked 'coffin roads' to take their dead to burial, while the inhabitants of the Pentland Hills south of Edinburgh walked 10 miles each Sunday to church, and the same back. Drovers, fishwives, servants, tinkers, soldiers, gypsies and beggars all across the British Isles were to be found on foot during the eighteenth century and beyond, though vagrants who could not give a good account of themselves were subject to legal penalties.

Elizabeth Carter was unusual in her love of walking not simply because she was a woman, but because walking for pleasure was itself fairly unusual: those with the means typically travelled by horse, either on horseback or in some form of carriage. Although she mentions in her letter to Catherine Talbot above the dangers of receiving insults because of her sex, this is not what Elizabeth Carter feared when out walking. Instead Carter was afraid of being unable to fully escape her social respectability, of never quite being able to step outside her class. The wilds were where she felt she belonged, and it was on foot that she could come closest to them.

Carter's love of pedestrianism was not the only thing that set her apart from her contemporaries: her independent nature was evident from an early age, as was her especially fine intellect. First becoming a published poet aged seventeen in 1734, over the next twenty years her talents (as a poet, and her astonishing facility with languages) earned her the reputation as 'the most highly regarded learned woman in England'. Her greatest work was published in 1758, a translation from the Greek of *All the Works of Epictetus*, one of the most influential Stoic philosophers of the Classical world. Carter's edition of his writings 'remained the standard scholarly text until the beginning of the twentieth century'.[1] Greek was just one of nine languages in which she became fluent. By the end of her life in 1806 aged nearly ninety, Carter was revered as one of the most influential intellectual figures of the Enlightenment era.

She was born, though, the daughter of a provincial curate, the Reverend Nicholas Carter, in Deal, among what Norma Clarke has described as 'a changing, often numerous household' that in later years included a step-mother (Carter's own mother died when she was ten) and six boisterous siblings.[2] For all the business of the family home, however, Carter had complete independence to run her life as she saw fit, and she enjoyed the use of her own library and private quarters. She also ordered her time according to the rhythms of her walking and her scholarly pursuits, which often involved late nights, early mornings and little sleep.

Details of her walks are mostly found in the copious letters she sent to her friends, which were frequently filled with humorous accounts of the varied scrapes into which she managed to get herself, and others. In a letter to Catherine Talbot in 1744,

Carter described the ways in which she mercilessly tormented the poor unfortunates who happened to live within walking distance of her home:

I am at present engaged in a very eager, and I may add a violent pursuit of health. I get up at four, read for an hour, then set forth a walking, and without vanity I may pretend to be one of the best walkers of the age. I had at first engaged three or four souls to their sorrow in this ambulatory scheme, and 'tis not to be told the tracts of land we have rambled over; but I happen to be too much volatile for my suffering fellow-travellers, who come panting and grumbling at a considerable distance, and labor along like *Christian* climbing up the hill *difficulty*, till at length they quite sink into the *slough of despond*. (Have you ever read 'Pilgrim's Progress?') I often divert myself by proposing in the midst of my walk to call at places a dozen miles off, to hear the universal squall they set up, that I intend to be the death of them. Terrible are the descriptions that they give at our return, of the mischiefs occasioned by my impetuous rapidity, though I protest I do not know of any harm I have done, except pulling up a few trees by the roots, carrying off the sails of a windmill, and over-setting half a dozen straggling cottages that stood in my way.

My sister has desired to be excused going with me any more, till she has learnt to fly, and another of our troop sent me word last night she could not possibly venture, as our last walk had absolutely dislocated all her bones; so I have nobody to depend on now but my youngest sister, who is as strong as a little Welch horse; so she trudges after me with great alacrity, and promises never to forsake me if I should walk to the North pole. As we daily improve in this peripatetic way of living, I propose to do myself the pleasure of breakfasting with you some morning in Oxfordshire, from whence I shall proceed to dine with Miss Ward in London, drink tea with Miss Lynch in Canterbury, and dream of you all the same night at Deal.[3]

The letter rapidly moves from the factual to the fantastical, but in doing so gives a glimpse of Carter's capabilities as a walker, as well as an insight into her sense of humour. It is clear that walking is far more than a pleasurable diversion, but a 'way of living': one that brings health, companionship and a self-worth that is centred on being in company with other women.

This letter is typical of Carter as a correspondent – playful, light-hearted and whimsical. Carter relished solitude, but also enjoyed the company of other women on her walks, when it could be had. This was a rare treat, however, as few of Carter's friends lived nearby or came to visit her in Deal. More frequently, Carter walked imaginatively with her friends, either taking their literary works with her, or holding their conversation in her thoughts. Thus Carter rarely went walking without a woman by her side, either in physical, spirit or bibliographic form. 'I longed for you extremely the other night at Reading,' Carter wrote to the Shakespearean scholar Elizabeth Montagu in the spring of 1759: 'To ramble by moonlight amongst the ruins of an old abbey; you will be sensible this wish expresses more than a thousand speeches, if you consider how few people one would chuse for companions in such a scene.'[4] Carter's affection for the women in her life was often expressed through her desire to walk with them, whether or not that desire would ever be satisfied (and Elizabeth Montagu was, unlike Carter, a relatively unwilling rambler, given to timidity if taken away from people or civilization). Friendship was also articulated by Carter's frequent recommendations of walking to people including Catherine Talbot and Elizabeth Vesey, who, like Carter, suffered from frequent bouts of ill health. To Vesey, Carter wrote solicitously to enquire

> Do you ever take me along with you, my dear Mrs. Vesey, in your solitary rambles? It is but fair you should, consid-ering how often you share in mine. I hope your eyes will be strengthened by the repose which you so very rightly give them, and will furnish you with amusement, when the weather is too bad to admit of your walking. Walk, however, as often as you can, for I am persuaded it will be of service to your health and spirits.[5]

Walking helped bind Carter to her friends, and they to her, both emotionally and intellectually. For Carter, walking was much more than exercise (though the physical work of her tramping was a great attraction), it was fundamental to her intellectual pursuits. Carter typically read before she walked, and frequently took books with her on her strolls; walking seems to have enabled a kind of mental digestion that prepared Carter to write herself. Even when old age and infirmity began to limit what Carter and her friends could do as walkers, Carter's mind still required the physical movement of the body to order itself:

How should I love to ramble with you in search of every ves-
tige of our Saxon ancestors, in the spot where they first took
possession of a distracted kingdom, which they afterwards
raised to so much dignity and glory. *History* should be of our
party, and restore every monument to its original form: while
Imagination on the other hand, should point to the desolated
remains, and inspire every soothing charm of poetical and
sentimental melancholy.[6]

The power of Carter's fancy conjures here images of a
lost civilization along with the presence of a dear but absent
friend, suggesting a search for a more intimate kind of contact
with history and companions than can be obtained either
by reading books or friendly letters. The irony is that such
powerful imaginings of community are brought into being
by Carter's solitary walking: walking with actual company
would require no such exercise of her intellectual or creative
faculties. It is by writing of such solitary walks to her female
friends that Carter is able to create and inhabit the sororal
community she craves.

A lifelong haunter of the Kentish coast, Carter found the
sounds of the sea most conducive to her patterns of thought,
and the most evocative of her friends. In contemplating
the elemental noises of water acting on the coast, Carter
took pleasure in exploring the relationship between her own
fleeting life, the timelessness of her surroundings and the
presence of her friends. She told her friend Elizabeth Montagu
about one of the solitary rambles in which she sought out
such scenes:

I took a walk the other morning, which I believe you would
have admitted to be in the true sublime. I rambled till I got
to the top of a hill, from whence I surveyed a vast extent of
variegated country all round me, and the immense ocean
beneath. I enjoyed the magnificent spectacle in all the freedom of absolute solitude. Not a house, or a human creature
was within my view, nor a sound to be heard but the voice
of the elements, the whistling winds, and rolling tide. I
found myself deeply awed, and struck by this situation. The
first impression it gave me, was a sense of my own littleness,
and I seemed shrinking to nothing in the midst of the stu-
pendous objects by which I was surrounded . . . I continued
my speculations on this elevation, till my thoughts grew
overpowered and fatigued, and I was very well contented
to descend to humbler exercises and employments.[7]

Carter finds greatest pleasure in the 'freedom' granted
to her by being the only human in company with the wild.
Her encounters with the sublime landscape provided another
means for her to access the sorts of spaces where she might
be rid of her social standing, where she might exist simply
as a human. While there is a bleak loneliness inherent to
Carter's description of such locations, there is companionship
too; if walking in solitude and nature gave rise to feelings of
isolation, it was the sharing of that experience that enabled the
exploration of their significance and provided the impetus for
her to write. Elizabeth Carter needed walking combined with
study, solitude with friendship, for her creativity to flourish.

Balancing the various elements that made life rich for
Carter – the intellectual and the physical, the social and the

solitary – was crucial to her well-being. This balance was largely achieved and maintained through walking. Like many people of higher social status, Carter for many years split her year between her country home in Kent and London. Although the precise timing varied, it was generally accepted that winter was the season for the 'Town', while summer was for the country – even in the eighteenth century London was a smelly and uncomfortable place to be when it was hot. Although of modest birth and far from wealthy, Carter's literary successes rendered her reasonably well-to-do and provided her with the leisure time to join the fashionable in London, where theatre trips, morning calls, strolls around the parks and evening gatherings were the routine of the moneyed.

Carter's migration tended to happen in late December or early January, though she also visited friends in the city at other times of the year. While in London, it was Carter's habit to immerse herself in the sociable world of her intellectual female friends, spending evenings with different groups and enjoying conversation that contributed to the development of her literary works. If Carter attracted not the least attention at home, this was not the case in London. Surrounded by strangers in a society governed by a much stricter, and more elaborate, behavioural code, Carter had much less liberty to ramble according to her will. Finding herself in London one summer, she wrote to Catherine Talbot both to celebrate and lament her situation. 'I am not so happy as to be running wild in the nettle groves of Enfield,' Carter observed, 'But am panting for breath in the smoke of London. This is sad confinement for my active genius, however I read, write, sing, play, hop and amuse myself as well as I can: and every afternoon walk as if I was bewitched, to keep myself in health.'[8] Carter certainly enjoyed the delights of London life, and had, since she was young, relished a dance to excess: as a young woman, she wrote to a friend to tell her, 'I have played the rake most enormously for these two days, and sat up till near three in the morning,' despite which 'I walked three miles yesterday in a wind that would have blown me out of this planet, and afterwards danced nine hours, and then walked back again.'[9] It is an exhausting description of a youthful life lived wholly on foot, but in later years Carter began to find the social rounds of London life more wearying than any of her windswept Kentish rambles. Writing to Elizabeth Montagu after a particularly trying couple of days, Carter described how she was

> So excessively tired with my raking on Wednesday night, and a long walk which I was obliged to take the next morning, that I was really incapable of writing. It cannot, to be sure, enter into the imagination of your country women what fatigues we fine ladies are fated to endure in the exercise of a London life.[10]

Carter talks of her conduct as a sort of dissipation: her 'raking', or rakishness, is a humorously exaggerated description of her sociable late night. It is the description of being 'obliged' to go for a walk that is particularly striking, though – it is rare indeed for Carter to need compulsion to set her astride. For Carter, though, balance was essential. With her equilibrium disturbed, she was no longer capable of enjoying even that pleasure which was most fundamental to her – walking.

Most of the time, Carter managed her routine very carefully. While in London, even with 'a very extensive circle of friends' eager for her company, and even though Carter enjoyed dining 'out every evening', she habitually returned 'to her rooms no later than 10 o'clock' each night.[11] This, Norma Clarke has observed, enabled Carter to balance 'the solitude she required for her extensive reading and thinking with an inveterate sociability she both desired and believed to be a moral virtue'.[12] During her months at home in Deal, Carter used regular walks to help keep her life evenly poised between the scholarly and the active. As Norma Clarke has written, 'A balanced existence, in which long hours of hard, serious study were broken up by gardening, cooking, care of friends and family and – above all – long walks across rough country or along the shore, represented her ideal.'[13] This was the case regardless of the weather, for Carter entertained a particular fondness (sometimes well disguised) for truly stormy weather, even into her later years. Writing to Elizabeth Vesey in 1779 from Deal – when Carter was in her early sixties – about their mutual friend Miss Sharpe, Carter described one such ramble:

Miss Sharpe returned to this place last week, and I thank God her health is much better. In a walk we took the other day she was almost drowned and blown away. It was a beautiful morning, and we sallied forth, and were a mile from home, when the sky loured, and quite a storm of wind and rain came on. It acts with particular force in this unsheltered country. She hoped to secure herself by an umbrella, but this was but of little use against the driving wind and rain, unless she could have converted it, like a Lapland witch,

into a sieve. We were both very wet, but by the precaution
of changing our clothes as soon as we got home, caught
no cold; and to Miss Sharpe it is quite an adventure to
talk of, never, I believe, having been wet by a shower of
rain before.[14]

Poor Miss Sharpe – having only just begun to recover
her health, she is nearly killed off by Carter's overenthusiastic
misadventure. Carter's wry humour, though, reassures the
reader that Miss Sharpe, far from coming to harm, has gained
by her ordeal. There is something slightly pitying, however, in
Carter's observation that Miss Sharpe may never have been
soaked through by the weather before; for Carter herself, the
sharp airs and unimpeded storms of the Kentish coast are
highly sought and frequently felt pleasures.

Not that Carter was always in such good humour with
the weather, especially if it was not behaving as she considered
appropriate for the season. In July, when her friends elsewhere
in the country were basking in the summer's warmth, Kent
was, to Carter's mind, being unfairly scoured. 'In a tolerable
sheltered situation,' she complained to Elizabeth Vesey,

I believe this weather must be delightful; but in this open
exposed region we are so agitated by all the winds of heaven,
that whenever I walk out I am obliged to secure my hat and
cap in a very powerful manner to avoid the awkward distress
of having them blown to the Goodwin Sands.[15]

Well-timed weather, however, was one of the chief delights
of Carter's life, and it required little more than the local byways

to be accessible for her to take herself off. As the paths cleared following the equinoctial gales of the autumn, Carter wrote to Elizabeth Montagu in 1769, 'I design to travel over hill and dale, as far as my feet can carry me.'[16] Occasionally, though, other factors intervened to affect Carter's ability to walk in the wild weather she adored, including social conventions. Writing to Elizabeth Vesey, Carter described how 'the weather is sometimes so bad when I set out, that it is prudent not to expose myself to the censure of being out of my wits.' Her solution was to be out 'before it is light' to avoid any disapproving remarks.[17] Twenty years earlier, when she was perhaps more vulnerable to such external pressures, Carter wrote to Catherine Talbot describing the joys of the spring storms of 1747 she longed to enjoy:

> I did not at all need your good wishes that I might be insensible to the inclemency of the sky, for I should be very sorry to lose such a pleasing set of horrors; whistling winds and driving snows, I consider as the proper and becoming ornaments of winter, and I cannot help looking upon a fine day in that season with some kind of dislike as a very unnatural thing . . . I should certainly have [been] rambling up and down the face of the earth in the last blowing snowy weather, but on my talking one evening something about walking out, there was as much astonishment and outcry in the family as if I had seriously told them I was going to hang myself; and so to avoid the scandal of having abso-lutely lost my senses I was obliged to content myself with quietly sitting by the fire-side, and listening to the storm at a distance.[18]

Carter eagerly anticipates the power of such inclement weather full of 'pleasing horrors' – which are eminently preferable to 'unnatural' good weather. Perhaps for the only time in Carter's letters, though, her plans are thwarted by the concerns of her family. At all other times in her accounts, Carter has complete autonomy over whether, when and where she walked, so it is possible that the storm of this day was more than usually severe. However, for someone of Carter's physical bravery and determination, who was quite frequently 'wet by a shower of rain' and worse – and relished it – this was a sore trial indeed.

Carter found walking fundamental to living a rich and fulfilled life. Without it, whether because of exceptionally poor weather, ill health or the kindly meant but trying interference of the occasional friend or family member, she grew frustrated and restless. As a result, 'long, energetic walks' which allowed her to work off her boredom were essential to the maintenance of both physical and mental well-being.[19] Walking was Carter's preferred cure for everything from ennui to grief: stuck in a coach for longer than she was comfortable, Carter wrote to tell Catherine Talbot how 'The activity and spirit of a seventeen miles' walk was quite necessary . . . to enliven me after the stupidity of a tiresome journey';[20] and following her father's death in 1774, Carter vowed that 'as soon as the last sad ceremony is over, I will walk, and am persuaded I shall be the better for air and exercise.'[21] Walking, for Elizabeth Carter, was a most cherished panacea.

Carter's love of walking was well known to her family. Her nephew and early biographer Montagu Pennington recalled his aunt Carter's ardent love for walking in his *Memoirs* of her, published shortly after her death in 1806. He writes with admiration how

> She used to walk to breakfast with her sister Pennington, who lived about five miles away from Deal, without being tired, even when the weather was bad; and would sometimes return to Deal on the day which she had appointed, through a deep snow, when the roads were impassable for a carriage, and without suffering either from the wet or fatigue.[22]

The aunt Carter of Pennington's remembrance seems to have something of the witch about her as she floats through snow storms without the least harm. Carter herself, however, considered her person to be rather more vulnerable to everyday hurts than her nephew allowed. For the most part, these are the standard hazards of walking experienced by most who set off on foot – sunburn, the loss of the way, blisters, the weather – but occasionally Carter experienced anxieties peculiar to a woman walker. In 1763, while in Europe touring the fashionable watering holes with her friends, Carter was prevented from disappearing alone on a walk because 'a set of villains lurking about the woods renders it unsafe for me to walk alone.' A guard would have accompanied her, she wrote to Elizabeth Vesey, but 'I should lose all freedom of rambling and of thinking.'[23] Walking, it seems, could not be properly enjoyed without 'freedom' and 'thought', and these were banished for Carter by the company of men. A female companion, however, could be a boon. In 1743 Deal became overrun with a particularly high-spirited group of sailors. The festive tendencies of such men would have been well known to Carter, having lived for so long in a port town, but this group's celebrations must have been unusually raucous, as they warranted comment in one of Carter's letters. Writing to Catherine Talbot, Carter informed her that

> I am at present a little disappointed in being debarred the
> delight I used to take in rambling about by myself, by a
> set of rakish fellows from some ship who infest this place,
> and are a great disturbance to me. So I dare not walk now
> without a companion of true Amazonian bravery, who
> fears nothing but apparitions and frogs, from which I have
> promised to secure her, if she will defend me from what
> I am most afraid of, May-bugs and men; so by the strength
> of this alliance we both proceed in great safety.[24]

Although it is evident from this letter that solitary rambling remained Carter's preferred kind of walking, she writes too of finding comfort from combining forces with this 'Amazonian' woman. There is no need for a chaperone, or a chivalrous knight, or any other traditional masculine guardian of women's safety, because the women themselves are capable of protecting each other. With the sailors as much a terror as insects, though, and a guardian who is afraid of amphibians, neither danger nor protector are to be taken quite seriously in Carter's whimsical description.

Only rarely did Carter feel compelled to seriously consider her personal safety. For the majority of the time, her letters demonstrate that the only status she was conscious of as a walker was her class; her gender was, largely, incidental. On excursions with other walkers, Carter thought nothing of leaving her companions to take alternate routes, such as the high summer's day in 1750 when her party took a sailing trip up the coast and had to find their way back on land. With the others preferring to be conveyed in a coach 'by sixes and sevens as far as Sandwich', Carter decided to walk the whole way back with 'a couple of guides to instruct me in the road'.[25] Elsewhere in her letters, if Carter did make mention of her gender, the circumstances were more likely to be humorous than fearful, as on the occasion when she and her walking companion fell foul of some wild horses on their path. Carter recounted the story in a letter to Catherine Talbot:

> Many a hill and dale have I travelled over since I left you last night. The weather was too fine to be neglected, and I was unwilling to lose the enjoyment of the last beauties of autumn, so my peripatetic companion and I have set a compass which, if we had gone through the air, might have measured some seven or eight miles, but it would be difficult to compute its extent upon earth. We met with some hospitable people who refreshed us with tea upon the road, which gave us an opportunity, in our way home, to enjoy the bel serano of this charming moon, which, upon a fine green plain near the sea-side, made our walk extremely pleasant. But alas! it did not continue so all the way, for in a narrow lane we were met in very furious fashion by some wild horses, who had run away from their owners, and my companion set up such an outrageous scream for me to jump over a five-barred gate, to avoid them, as quite confused and stupefied me . . . I escaped however with whole bones, but made a woeful figure, for . . . I had neither a pin

or a plait left in my gown, and after walking a few paces
discovered I had lost my apron and my ruffles.[26]

Carter's writing here and elsewhere demonstrates that she was
aware that the freedom to walk as she chose was contingent
most especially on a social status which granted her certain
protections. Unmarried and of independent means, it was not
necessary for her to consider whether she conformed to notions
of 'ladylike' appearance or behaviour: entertaining no suitors,
requiring no financial protection, occupying no defined place
in society, Carter was able to sidestep patriarchal norms.

As Carter aged, however, her body, which had been so
strong and with which she had walked many thousands of
miles across Kent, began to fail. According to her nephew,

Walking, or any great exertion, became too much for her;
and though she was willing to take exercise, and felt the
necessity of it, a growing heaviness and indolence, increased
by pain, constant, though not violent, often prevented her
from regaining some share of strength.[27]

While ill health increasingly limited Carter's walks, she
continued to ramble when she could until very late in her life.
Aged nearly seventy, for example, she was still able from time
to time to fully enjoy 'rambling about', and continued to take
'solitary walks' to favourite haunts nearby.[28] Even as an old
woman, Carter could, on occasion, be found walking in the
sorts of wild weather that had delighted her when younger,
and she remained impervious to the doubtful glances of 'less
whimsical folks' who would 'shudder' at the 'trackless paths'

she longed to ramble.[29] A lifelong wanderer whose love of walking never faded, 'the keeping up the struggle against the languor of constitutional disorders, and the indolence of age' by keeping afoot was worth the effort, even if ultimately the struggle was in vain.[30] Perhaps because she had lived a full life of adventure and experience – a life spent almost entirely as a walker – Carter at the last had no 'dread' of death.[31] Instead, she was happy to reach the conclusion of her long journey 'to a country planted with trees of perpetual verdure', among which she would wander entirely content.[32]

IT WAS WHILE I was writing about Elizabeth Carter, her adventurousness and the importance of her female friends, that I happened to go for a hike in the Scottish Borders with my friend Cathy, a former colleague from my first academic post with whom I had reconnected by chance in Peebles years after we had last spoken. Since that reunion, we had taken a number of walks in the local area, Cathy's knowledge of the hills far exceeding my own. It was one of the first sunny days of spring, and the sunshine was hot on our backs as we set off along the farm track. I'd driven past the area many times but had never noticed the possibility of a grand circular walk in the hills above the river. We followed the fast-moving Caddon Water 2 or 3 miles up its course with the high Borders hills looming above us, their flanks dappled with pale green and dark brown where patches of winter grass yielded to heather. It was the end of the academic semester, and Cathy had had a particularly stressful few months, so we spoke of work, laughed about its idiosyncrasies and felt ourselves lightened by the good cheer and the gently moving air. The fields below us were filled with lambs, some of them just hours old.

Our way took us over the Caddon and up a sharp climb above the river before the track doubled back to reach higher still to a hill pass. Cathy and I talked of Elizabeth Carter as we approached the high point, and the experiences that had formed our own love of walking. We spoke of our friendship, and the important role walking together had played in the shaping of that relationship. All conversation stopped, though, as we reached the pass, for here was a symphony of hill sound. Above us a skylark sang with the most heartfelt ardour, its ceaseless music pouring over us like a cloudburst of melody. It was accompanied by a host of curlews: one provided a bassline ostinato, while others added modulating counterpoints. A peewit's high-pitched calls lent an eerie descant, and the wind susurrated among the moorland grass. Silently, two hares bolted up the hill ahead of us. They, unlike us, had not been bewitched by the siren song. It was long before either Cathy or I moved, and longer still before we spoke. But there was no need of speech. It was enough, instead, to be companionate with each other, and to relish the privilege of being allowed the company of the wild high moor.

TWO

Dorothy Wordsworth

I rise about six every morning and, as I have no companion walk with a book till half past eight, if the weather
permits . . . sometimes we walk in the mornings . . . after
tea we all walk together till about eight, and then I walk
alone as long as I can in the garden; I am particularly fond
of a moonlight or twilight walk – it is at this time I think
most of my absent friends.

Dorothy Wordsworth to Jane Pollard, 23 May 1791[1]

In December 1799 Dorothy Wordsworth walked 70 miles
with her brother William from Sockburn in County
Durham to Kendal in Westmorland. They were walking home,
back to the Lake District where they had been born, and from
where Dorothy had been exiled, away from her siblings, since
she and her brothers were orphaned in 1783. Over rough
paths and hill tracks William and Dorothy walked towards
the place where they planned, at last, to share their lives: Dove
Cottage in Grasmere, found by William just weeks before.
Their journey across the Pennines was arduous, with snow
showers and frozen roads combining to weary their feet, and

the short days of midwinter forced them to walk for miles in the dark. But they were together, walking strongly 'side by side' over the hills and covering large distances at speed, something they would do for years to come.[2] They arrived at last in Kendal, having covered 17 miles the previous day in under four hours, a 'marvellous feat of which D. will long tell', William wrote. Having bought furniture in Kendal, the pair very sensibly took a post-chaise for the final leg of their journey to their new home, arriving in Grasmere as the sun set between the mountains.

By the time Dorothy Wordsworth and her brother were setting out to walk home, walking for pleasure had become much less unusual than it had been when Elizabeth Carter was vagabonding across Kent. Over the last twenty years or so of the eighteenth century, pedestrians in the Lake District and, increasingly, Scotland, had worn paths to famous views, historic sights and mysterious monuments in more and more distant parts of Britain. By the time of Dorothy Wordsworth's death, mountaineering had become a relatively common pastime, with Wordsworth herself doing much to pioneer what would soon become a popular sport: she made one of the first recorded climbs of Scafell Pike with her friend Mary Barker and a guide in 1818.

However, the ability to walk for pleasure remained, as it had for Elizabeth Carter, contingent upon a certain level of financial freedom, and a degree of social status. For Dorothy Wordsworth, the freedom to walk was hard won. Orphaned early, at twelve years old she was sent to live with relatives or friends all over the country. Sometimes she was happy: with her maternal uncle William Cookson in Norwich, for instance, where she lived for a few years the life of a young lady; or with old friends the Hutchinsons in Stockton. At others she was miserable, especially while living with her cold and severe grandmother in Penrith. Always, though, her existence depended upon the benevolence of others: until her early twenties Dorothy Wordsworth lived by someone else's leave, and even then only for as long as her benefactor's circumstances permitted. While her brothers were able, because of their sex, to go to university, or to sea, or to travel through Europe, Dorothy Wordsworth, as a young and unprotected woman, had to accept whatever place her extended family offered.

When she arrived at Dove Cottage, Dorothy Wordsworth was doing much more than moving to a new house. The building represented permanence, independence and freedom, and it offered the chance for Dorothy and William not only to recreate something of the familial home lost to them both since early childhood, but the opportunity to spend their time as they wished. And they wished to walk. Dove Cottage was, quite simply, 'a dream made real'.[3] With no one to impose daily duties upon them, the siblings were free to do as they wished with their time: they gathered plants for the garden when it suited them; if they were tired, they slept; and if they preferred to walk than to tend to the house, then off they went. Dorothy, long a keen and capable walker, rambled almost every day in the first few months after arriving in Grasmere, and roamed widely over the local area. Frequently these walks had a practical element: while the Wordsworths had a home, they had little money. So it was on foot that Dorothy would collect the post, gather firewood, obtain woodland plants, visit neighbours – but Dorothy rarely returned by the direct route.

Instead she preferred to saunter in quiet and secluded places, learning all that she could about the less frequented ways of her new home. Such wanderings would be the pattern for much of Dorothy's adult life until a long decline into senility confined her to a bedroom at last.

Dorothy Wordsworth recorded details of her rambles around Grasmere and beyond in a diary begun during her first spring at Dove Cottage: having walked with William and their brother John at the start of the men's journey to Yorkshire, Dorothy resolved to document her daily activities in order to 'give Wm Pleasure by it when he comes home again'.[4] She was grieved by their parting, enduring a 'flood of tears' after giving her brother a 'farewell kiss', perhaps because previous separations had been so long and painful. But walking provided her with a mechanism through which to comprehend and manage such strong emotions.[5] Two days later, for example, she set off after tea to Ambleside, 4 miles distant, to collect the post. 'Rydale was very beautiful with spear-shaped streaks of polished steel,' she wrote, and, 'Grasmere was very solemn in the last glimpse of twilight.' The latter, she thought, 'calls home the heart to quietness', a quality valued by Dorothy because she 'had been very melancholy in my walk back. I had many of my saddest thoughts & I could not keep the tears within me. But when I came to Grasmere I felt that it did me good.'[6]

Walking was, for Dorothy, a means of experiencing both her new-found independence and her new home. Throughout June she made use of the long northern days to walk alone to Ambleside late into the evening, frequently returning home after ten o'clock, after the midsummer sun had just set. Although Dorothy typically enjoyed company when walking, she distinctly preferred solitude for these late evening wanderings. Returning from Ambleside on 2 June 1800, Dorothy was accompanied by her acquaintance, Mrs Nicholson. 'This was very kind,' Dorothy wrote in her journal afterwards, 'but God be thanked I want not society by a moonlight lake.'[7] This was perhaps because she already knew intimately most of the ways around Grasmere and had no reason to fear a familiar path on a moonlit night: throughout her journal, Dorothy Wordsworth writes of walking over and again favourite paths, and of turning aside at particular points to savour especially loved sights and sounds. Becoming acquainted with her new home meant, for Dorothy, walking and knowing it in every mood and every light.

Walking was an important way for Dorothy Wordsworth to explore and experience the beauties of Grasmere at particular moments, but as she retrod again and again her favourite paths, memories began to accumulate along the way, lending new and powerful meaning to her favourite walks. In her diary for January 1802, two years after arriving at Dove Cottage, she wrote,

> William had slept very ill, he was tired & had a bad head-
> ache. We walked round the two lakes – Grasmere was very
> soft & Rydale was extremely beautiful from the pasture side.
> Nab Scar was just topped by a cloud which cutting it off as
> high as it could be cut off made the mountain look uncom-
> monly lofty. We sate down a long time in different places.
> I always love to walk that way because it is the way I first
> came to Rydale & Grasmere, & because our dear Coleridge

did also. When I came with Wm 6½ years ago it was just
at sunset. There was a rich yellow light on the waters & the
Islands were reflected there. Today it was grave & soft but
not perfectly calm. William says it was much such a day as
when Coleridge came with him. The sun shone out before
we reached Grasmere. We sate by the roadside at the foot
of the Lake close to Mary's dear name which she had cut
herself upon the stone.[8]

Recorded here is a constellation of interconnected
memories and associations evoked by varying combinations
of light, the time of day, the company, the time of year and,
most importantly, the act of walking the same route over and
again. While it is Dorothy holding the pen, the memories
and sensations she records are a peculiar mixture of her
own independent recollections and her brother's, as well as
fragments from their shared experiences. Here 'we' slips into
'I', and back into 'we', making it difficult to disentangle which
feelings or memories belong to which individual. The act of
retracing this route makes indistinct the boundaries between
the siblings, and brings multiple pasts into the shared present.
As Lucy Newlyn has written, 'They saw their memories as gifts
– tokens of love – to be offered to each other, in reparation
for the years they had spent apart.'[9] Making and exchanging
memories, especially by retracing the same paths over and
again, helped create the shared past of which the siblings had
been deprived.

Much (though by no means all) of Dorothy Wordsworth's
walking was of this kind, over familiar ground; retracing was an
important means by which powerful imaginative connections

with absent friends, previous selves, past experiences – so important in her writing – were enabled. As Rebecca Solnit has observed, 'To walk the same way is to reiterate something deep; to move through the same space the same way is a means of becoming the same person, thinking the same thoughts.'[10] One such familiar walk was the journey back from Keswick to Grasmere: the Wordsworths' dear friends Robert Southey and Samuel Taylor Coleridge shared a house in Keswick, and there was much traffic between the two towns as a result. Although a common journey for Dorothy and William and for Coleridge, Coleridge's imminent departure from the Lakes for London in 1801 transformed the walk into a repository for all Dorothy's memories of him:

> Poor C[oleridge] left us & we came home together. We left Keswick at 2 o'clock & did not arrive at G[rasmere] till 9 o clock . . . C had a sweet day for his ride – every sight & every sound reminded me of him dear dear fellow – of his many walks to us by day & by night – of all dear things. I was melancholy & could not talk, but at last I eased my heart by weeping – nervous blubbering says William. It is not so.[11]

Coleridge had been the Wordsworths' walking companion since 1797, when all three lived in the peaceful seclusion of Somerset's rolling Quantock hills. There the three friends undertook hundreds of excursions, and covered, in all likelihood, thousands of miles. They walked together not only in the Quantocks, but later Germany and then the mountains of the Lake District along physical paths which also ran through time, threading together periods of intimacy, collaboration, distance and, for Coleridge, addiction. To travel the route between Keswick and Grasmere was to travel in, with and to fellowship, and to walk this path was to inscribe on the landscape the value of that friendship. In Dorothy's account, these earlier journeys became superimposed upon the Wordsworths' own return, so much so that the presence of these previous experiences became emotionally overwhelming. Curiously, while this walk enables Dorothy to imaginatively link herself with Coleridge – to recreate in this location all their shared walks – it closes down the connection with her brother, whose assertion that Dorothy's emotional response is due to 'nerves' is dismissed with the uncharacteristically blunt contradiction, 'It is not so.' Unusually, this walk does not serve to enhance the bond between the siblings: Dorothy alone is haunted by Coleridge's absence.

While this incident seems to have been traumatic and lonely for Dorothy Wordsworth, rewalking or retracing routes often proved comforting, calling forth from memory and imagination earlier times in the companionship of those who were now absent. When William went again from home in early March 1802, Dorothy seems deliberately to have sought out a walk resonant with memories of previous excursions there with her brother:

Wm has a rich bright day – It was hard frost in the night – The Robins are singing sweetly – Now for my walk. I *will* be busy, I *will* look well & be well when he comes back to me. O the Darling! here is one of his bitten apples! I can hardly find in my heart to throw it into the fire. I must wash

myself, then off – I walked round the two Lakes crossed
the stepping stones at Rydale Foot. Sate down where we
always sit I was full of thoughts about my darling. Blessings
on him. I came home at the foot of our own lake under
Loughrigg.[12]

The walk is described by Dorothy in such a way that the
reader is left with the impression that she and her brother
have always, and will always, be sat together near the stepping
stones. Even though William is physically absent, something
of him is brought into this place in this moment through
Dorothy's imagining of his presence – indeed the imperative
of 'we always sate' makes it impossible for Dorothy to be there
entirely alone.

Dorothy would make use of this kind of imaginative,
sympathetic walking following the death of her brother John
Wordsworth, the captain of the *Earl of Abergavenny*, which
was wrecked in Weymouth Bay in February 1805. A visitor
to Dove Cottage whenever he was able, John normally parted
from his siblings at Dunmail Raise, the high mountain pass
between Grasmere and Patterdale. Four months after his death,
Dorothy wrote to her friend Lady Margaret Beaumont. In the
letter, Dorothy describes the new and shifting resonances now
to be found in retracing this walk:

My Brother [William] is at Patterdale . . . there being a pass
from Grasmere thither. My Sister [William's wife Mary]
and I accompanied him to the top of it, and parted from
him near a Tarn under a part of Helvellyn . . . Near that
very Tarn William and I bade him [John] farewell the last

time he was at Grasmere . . . We were in view of the head of
Ulswater, and stood till we could see him no longer, watching him as he *hurried* down the stony mountain. Oh! my
dear Friend, you will not wonder that we love that place.
I have been twice to it since his death. The first time was
agony, but it is now a different feeling.[13]

When parting from Coleridge, Dorothy was overwhelmed
by 'melancholy'; in this account, she experiences 'agony'.
Both sensations arise from the combination of circumstance,
memory, imagination and the repeated overlaying of new
experiences along familiar routes. Dorothy's responses are
not fixed, though – the accretion of meanings, resonances
and recollections continues each time these paths are walked,
creating each time the possibility for new connections, new
configurations of meaning. Dorothy does not go into the
nature of the 'different feeling' evoked upon retracing this
route a second time, but it is represented as being some distance
from the former 'agony'. On this walk, in this place, Dorothy is
able to access all the layers of sensation and memory that have
accumulated, enabling, eventually, a restorative imaginative
connection with the brother who will never return over the
mountain pass to Grasmere.

Dorothy Wordsworth was unarguably bonded to the Lake
District hills, but she also ventured further afield from time
to time, undertaking ambitious pedestrian tours until she
was approaching fifty years of age. She kept accounts of these
journeys, which included two tours of Scotland (1803, 1822)
and one to the Continent (1820). In her journals of these walks,
Dorothy documented not only the itineraries of her party

and her own walking, but the encounters with people and landscapes which proved emotionally and creatively significant. These accounts make evident how important walking was as a source of imaginative connection between Dorothy and other people, and demonstrate that the sensations and thoughts recorded in her writing were evoked by the physical labour of placing one foot in front of another. Configurations of place and company were certainly of great importance in making walking meaningful for Dorothy, but it was walking itself that enabled specific and important kinds of understanding about herself and the ways in which connections with other lives might be sustained. As Robert Macfarlane has noted, 'walking is not the action by which one arrives at knowledge; it is itself the means of knowing': walking was the means by which Dorothy Wordsworth knew herself, and the means by which she knew others.[14] At the beginning of her first tour to Scotland in August and September 1803, made with William and 'dear dear' Coleridge, the travellers set off in a jaunting car (a conveyance with two wheels and reversed seats, pulled by a single horse), though they frequently abandoned it and William (the designated driver) to walk instead:

> We walked cheerfully along in the sunshine, each of us alone, only William had the charge of the horse and car . . . I never travelled with more cheerful spirits than this day. Our road was along the side of a high moor. I can always walk over a moor with a light foot; I seem to be drawn more closely to nature in such places than anywhere else; or rather I feel more strongly the power of nature over me, and am better satisfied with myself for being able to find enjoyment

in what unfortunately to many persons is either dismal
or insipid.[15]

The experience of walking here leads Dorothy Wordsworth
inside herself as much as it takes her 'along the side' of this 'high
moor', but being pedestrian was important both in developing
Dorothy's knowledge of herself, and her understanding of how
she related to other people. As she and William began the fifth
week of their tour (Coleridge left the party not quite two weeks
in: the reasons for his departure are reported differently by the
three), Dorothy encountered an impoverished woman on the
ferry across Loch Lomond:

> The ferryman happened to be just ready at the moment to
> go over the lake with a poor man, his wife and child. The
> little girl, about three years old, cried all the way, terrified
> by the water. When we parted from this family, they going
> down the lake, and we up it, I could not but think of the
> difference in our condition to that poor woman, who, with
> her husband, had been driven from her home by want of
> work, and was now going a long journey to seek it else-
> where: every step was painful toil, for she had either her
> child to bear or a heavy burthen. *I* walked as she did, but
> pleasure was my object, and if toil came along with it, even
> *that* was pleasure, – pleasure, at least, it would be in the
> remembrance.[16]

Dorothy's knowledge of, and empathy for, the woman she
encounters derives entirely from walking. Here she overlays her
material and physical circumstances and this 'poor woman's',

revealing as she does so the striking and pitiable differences between them. Yet what evokes the sincere and poignant sympathy is the knowledge that the two women move in the same ways: they have the same physiology, the same biology and, perhaps, the same body. Even as Dorothy outlines the differences shaping *why* they walk, she is aware that *how* they walk is identical.

Dorothy's encounter with this woman, and her reaction to it, is also indicative of the importance of the material circumstances of women's lives to their ability to make use of their bodies as Dorothy did. Rebecca Solnit observes that 'there are three prerequisites to going out into the world to walk for pleasure. One must have free time, a place to go, and a body unhindered by illness or social restraints.'[17] Dorothy herself observes that the 'poor woman' has none of these things, while she has them all; the enforced wandering of this woman, compelled by circumstance rather than borne of any desire to walk, is further complicated by the woman's obligations to others through her status as a wife and as a mother: titles that Dorothy Wordsworth would never bear. However, what is also at stake here is the ability to reflect upon the experiences accumulated through walking; Dorothy will also have the 'pleasure' of 'remembrance', a process which itself requires free time, a place for contemplation, and a body that was well enough for walking to have been enjoyable. As much as Dorothy's account reveals a kinship between herself and 'the poor woman' as walkers, it also indicates the considerable differences: Dorothy has the means (time, money, leisure) to articulate the meaningfulness of this experience, while the anonymous woman, burdened by her domestic functions, remains silent.

The encounter with the 'poor woman' was one of many experiences to fall Dorothy Wordsworth's way because she was a woman walker. Her status as a female pedestrian frequently enabled connections that might have been unavailable to men, or to which men might have been less alert. The unique benefits of being a *female* pedestrian can be seen in the parallel accounts made by Dorothy and Coleridge during their walks around Glasgow early on in their journey through Scotland. The day after their arrival, the party took a walk to the 'bleaching-ground' on what is now Glasgow Green on the north bank of the River Clyde at its final major meander. In one of his notebooks, Coleridge observed that he was

> most pleased by the [two] great Washing-Houses & Drying Grounds/ – Four Square Cloysters, with an open Square, & the Cauldron in the Middle/ each Woman pays a ½^{py} for her Tub & ½, sometimes in scarce times 1^d for a Tub of hot water/ a penny to the Watcher – so that the poorest person who can get Cloathes to wash may earn their living.[18]

Interested in facts and figures, Coleridge's reads like a government report. In contrast, Dorothy's journal captures lived human experience:

> In the middle of the field is a wash-house, whither the inhabitants of this large town, rich and poor, send or carry their linen to be washed. There are two very large rooms, with each a cistern in the middle for hot water; and all around the room are benches for the women to sit their tubs upon . . . It was amusing to see so many women, arms,

head, and face all in motion, all busy in ordinary household employment, in which we are accustomed to see, at the most, only three or four women employed in one place. The women were very civil. I learnt from them the regulations of the house; but I have forgotten the particulars. The substance of them is, that 'so much' is to be paid for each tub of hot water, 'so much' for a tub, and the privilege of washing for a day, and 'so much' to the general overlookers of the linen, when it is left to be bleached.[19]

While it would seem from Coleridge's account that he, too, spoke to women who were washing their clothes on the Green, Dorothy places importance on the fact that the women were 'very civil' to her, and that she 'learnt' from them – details which alter the exchange from fact-finding to an encounter. Where Coleridge is authoritative, Dorothy is humble, a student of the women who have both enlightened and amused her.

Such incidents occur at various points in Dorothy's writing about her walking, from her admittance to the private areas of the homes in which she rested with her brother and Coleridge on their trek through the Trossachs – areas usually overseen, and populated, by women – to her conversations with girls and women on the road; Dorothy's accounts of these moments in her walking offer unusual perspectives of scenes and people rarely recorded by male pedestrians. Perhaps the most extraordinary of all these experiences is one which occurred on Dorothy Wordsworth's second tour in Scotland during 1822, undertaken in the company of her sister-in-law, Joanna Hutchinson. With writing that flits between present and past tenses, Dorothy's literary style lends a moving immediacy to the distressing, yet companionable moment she and Joanna shared with two bereaved local women:

> Joanna passes me – and a shower that has been threatening in front of us falls in heavy drops. I shelter under a Bank, Joanna passes me, fearful of the damp, and when it was nearly over I followed, and found her standing within the threshold of a cottage with the mistress of the house, who looked melancholy, and I perceived a tear on her cheek. Three or four very pretty children were crowded together beside them. Joanna said to me 'There is a corpse within', and the mistress desired me to enter. I did so, leaving my companion in the outer room. A chearful fire was in the centre of a small black apartment, and at one end lay the body of a child covered with a clean linen cloth. The mother of the child (the mistress's sister) seated at the end of the bier. The house was very small, yet *another* woman, nursing *her* child, was of the family, and there were at least *four* belonging to the mistress herself. Cakes were baking on a girdle . . . the sorrowing mother, seeing no one else at liberty, suspends her last duties to the dead to turn the cakes, and goes back again to her place. While I was seated by this humble fireside, musing on poverty and peace, on death and the grave, the mistress of the house repaired to an inner room, and brought out a basin of milk, which she courteously offered me. I begged some of her warm bread . . . The shower was over, and giving a few halfpence to the little-ones we departed. We could not have presented money to the good woman of this cottage for what she had given us: we should have felt it almost like an insult offered to human nature.[20]

It was typical for walkers to pay for the incidental hospitality they received on the road, so it would be expected that Dorothy and Joanna would offer coins for the milk and bread, but this does not seem to be what Dorothy means when she talks about not being able to 'present money' for what had been 'given' to them. Rather, it is the experience of meeting these women that Dorothy has in mind, for which no money could be equal. Hospitality was understood as a transaction, however, and Dorothy and Joanna demonstrate their sensitivity to the situation by offering money to the children. Dorothy and Joanna have been allowed to participate in an intimate moment of familial mourning because of their sex, and because they were women on the road.

It was not always so harmonious for the two female pedestrians. While Dorothy was a strong and capable walker, Joanna Hutchinson appears to have been much less robust, and her relative weakness was a source of frustration to Dorothy at times. Dorothy's 1822 journal is full of descriptions (and complaints) about Joanna's slowness on the road, which is explicitly contrasted with her own vigour and strength – the sort of physical vitality for which she was criticized as unfeminine. Of their walk to Inverary in Argyll, Dorothy wrote,

> We set forward side by side at a very slow pace – sunshine and gentle breezes. I push on leaving my companion – sit by the wayside to enjoy the pleasing scene. The Lake very calm – hardly to be heard . . . Sometimes a fisherman's boat, with funereal sails, is seen at a distance, and sometimes we hear the sound of oars on the water . . . Joanna passes me – and a shower that has been threatening in front of us . . . falls

in heavy drops. I shelter under a Bank, Joanna passes me,
fearful of the damp, and when it was nearly over I followed,
and found her standing within the threshold of a cottage . . .
We separate often – no more rain. How quiet the road! . . .
The lake so very still I cannot hear it, or any sound of water
except at intervals rills trickling faintly. Joanna is far behind
– I hasten on, for the burst of Inverary.[21]

This stream-of-consciousness style is not typical of
Dorothy's writing, and the frequent breaking up of the prose by
punctuation – dashes, dots, abundant commas – suggestively
mirrors the pacing out of the route on foot. Dorothy's laconic
prose, with elisions and abrupt transitions from thought to
thought and from scene to scene, also parallels the experience
of walking with a shifting gaze. The reader, as a result, seems
to fall into the rhythm of Dorothy's walking, something which
brings a pleasurable immediacy to the text – the reader pauses
when Dorothy does. These rhythms, and these descriptions,
though, are specific to Dorothy's experiences: Joanna's walking
is made up of a different pattern of pauses and rests which are
only represented in Dorothy's prose if they overlap hers. Thus,
the final dash in this passage embodies both the literary and
physical separation of Dorothy's and Joanna's experiences:
Joanna is left 'far behind' in both senses as Dorothy, with a
dash of both body and pen, drives for the glories of the view of
Inverary, taking only her reader with her, and leaving Joanna
far behind.

If Dorothy's physical strength helped distance the two
women, their gender repeatedly brought them back together.
Walking towards the end of their tour in the high hills in

southern Scotland near the source of the Clyde, Joanna and Dorothy shared an experience likely to be had only by women pedestrians. Finding themselves without transportation at Elvanfoot, surrounded by rugged moorland, Dorothy and Joanna undertook to walk to Moffat, some 15 miles away. There they planned to secure transportation, with an alternative being to stop at the Toll-bar – the barrier across the toll road where the toll is to be paid – 6 miles distant, should Moffat prove unreachable. Soon after the women set off from Elvanfoot, they encountered a 'big strong old man', described by Dorothy as a 'tramper', from whom they asked directions. Almost immediately Dorothy regretted her actions, as she considered the fragility of her position as a woman walker:

> I instantly felt that I had been imprudent in speaking to him; but collecting myself I answered 'No, we are only going thither to wait for the coach'.
>
> Poor Joanna went on, not raising her eyes from the ground . . . her looks shewed plainly what she had been suffering, and she exclaimed, 'How could you be so imprudent as to speak to that man in this lonely place?' . . . It seemed I had never been in a place so lonely. While we were trudging on side by side, Joanna . . . fancied she espied a man hastily crossing over the side of a hill, *towards* us, though at a considerable distance. After this, I believe she never once looked behind, but went on at a speed for *her* almost supernatural.[22]

It is significant that it is at this moment that Dorothy chooses to describe the two women as 'trudging on side by side'.

Throughout the rest of the journal, the walking rhythms of the two women are completely at odds, but here, in the face of their shared perceived danger, their walking is united.

Having walked away from this 'tramper', the two women came to a homely farmhouse at the Toll-bar where they were able to lodge,

> but before we were well settled, or had got the accident which led us thither fully explained, the door was opened suddenly, and two travellers came forward . . . The men had a rattling wild air and demeanour which would have completely upset us had they overtaken us on the road . . . You may judge we were anxious that the house should be cleared of them, especially as we were convinced that it must have been one of these men whom Joanna had seen, and that they had hurried forward to overtake us; and we even *suspected*, from the tenor of their discourse, that they *had heard something* about us.[23]

Here both women are 'convinced' of their danger and both 'suspect' these men. There is no distinction made between Joanna's or Dorothy's subjectivities; instead the two women are bound together by their status as women walkers.

Being a woman meant that there were, periodically, restrictions to Dorothy Wordsworth's walking, especially after her brother William's marriage to Mary Hutchinson in 1802. The wedding was followed swiftly by the arrival of the first of their five children. Even before the marriage, Dorothy Wordsworth would sometimes stay at home while her brother walked, occupied by a domestic task. She was, she wrote to her friend Jane Marshall in September 1800, 'left' at home one day by William and their brother John 'to make pies and dumplings, and was to follow them when I had finished my business', though the parties missed each other.[24] Always heavily involved in the maintenance of the family home, as the years passed Dorothy was increasingly occupied by household tasks and, later, childcare, though at times she was able to combine her love for her brother's children with her passion for walking. Her brother's firstborn, John, was taken for a wild winter walk by his aunt, 'wrapped in flannels' so that 'no cold touched his Body', leaving the child 'delighted with the wind against his face', but there were limitations: with John and his infant sister Dora to bear, Dorothy struggled to walk just a few miles, as she lamented to her friends.[25] For a woman capable of walking alone 40 miles in a day, this must have felt inhibiting indeed, but the biggest trial was the curtailment of her walks with William. 'Some chance time Mary and I have walked with him', she wrote to Catherine Clarkson, but where the women had 'always' to 'make a point of taking John out', William was unfettered by the responsibilities of childcare. Dorothy Wordsworth's life as a woman walker was both enriched and restricted by her sex.

While Dorothy Wordsworth walked in companionship and with pleasure alongside others, the strongest sympathetic and imaginative connection in her accounts is with her brother William. It was through walking that the bond between the two, which had been so painfully stretched during their separate childhoods, was restored, and it was through walking that the bond was maintained and nourished over the decades of their shared life. Even when she could not walk with her brother physically, Dorothy accompanied him imaginatively. As a young woman confined by her sex and material circumstances to Britain, Dorothy Wordsworth sat with maps of the Alps in order to follow with her fingers the ways taken by her brother's feet a thousand miles distant and on a cut-price Grand Tour of Europe. When, thirty years later, Dorothy was to have the chance to stand at last upon the ground that William had trodden as a young man, that younger self seems often on the path before her. Dorothy's journal of this 'Tour to the Continent' undertaken in 1820 records a strange series of intermingled retracings of routes and selves that perhaps amount to a form of haunting: Dorothy's imaginative journey through the Alps, traced with fingers along the routes walked by William, is overlaid with the physical reality of walking there with him decades after.

The most significant moment in Dorothy's journal is the description of the group's ascent over the Simplon Pass, a high mountain route connecting Switzerland and Italy which William had walked in 1790. The experience had proved transformative for William as a man and as a poet, and its importance to William's poetic imagination leads, in Dorothy's writing, to a collapse of sorts between past and present selves, and between William's and Dorothy's individual subjectivities. Walking the Pass of Simplon becomes, as a result of Dorothy's creative and emotional responses, a node through which she is able to move imaginatively as well as physically:

> Our eyes were often turned towards the bridge and the
> upright path, little thinking that it was the same we had so
> often heard of, which misled my Brother and Robert Jones

in their way from Switzerland to Italy. They were pushing
right upwards, when a Peasant, having questioned them
as to their object, told them they had no further ascent to
make – 'The Alps were crossed!' The ambition of youth was
disappointed at these tidings; and they remeasured their
steps with sadness. At the point where our Fellow-travellers
had rejoined the road, W. was waiting to shew us the track,
on the green precipice. It was impossible for me to say how
much it had moved him, when he discovered it was the very
same which had tempted him in his youth. The feelings of
that time came back with the freshness of yesterday, accompanied with a dim vision of thirty years of life between.
We traced the path together, with our eyes, till hidden
among the cottages, where they had first been warned of
their mistake.[26]

Assisting the overlaying of experiences, and of selves, is the
coincidence of the date of this ascent with William's earlier
journey. William Wordsworth and Robert Jones climbed the
Simplon Pass on 17 August 1790, and it was just three weeks
beyond the thirtieth anniversary of this climb that Dorothy's
party retraced William's youthful steps. This certainly seems
to play a role in the ways in which Dorothy's account shifts
between multiple perspectives – the quotation from the
Peasant is taken from *The Prelude*, while there are fragments of
William's memories among Dorothy's on-the-spot reportage.
These shifts are marked by changes in the pronouns, leading
to some peculiar effects, as Dorothy's experiencing 'me' is
subsumed entirely by William's feeling 'him', or when the
'we' of William and Dorothy's shared 'tracing of the path'

in this moment slides into 'they', referring to the younger Wordsworth and Robert Jones, seen 'dimly' across 'thirty years of life'.

When the party come to choose their onwards path with the option of the ancient mule track, or the modern military road installed by Napoleon's engineer, the decisions made by Dorothy, William and indeed Mary Wordsworth are informed by the echoes of William's earlier journey: 'Our book noted that the old road would save the foot-traveller several miles walking, & one of our party . . . chose to take it on that account, Wm. because he had travelled it before, and Mary and I from sympathy with his feeling.'[27] All three Wordsworths select this path because William has previously trodden it – they enter it because of 'sympathy' with the fifty-year-old poet, but through such decisions, Dorothy is able to experience 'sympathy' with the twenty-year-old version of her brother. Two weeks earlier, at another mountain pass in the Alps, Dorothy had noted how she had been: 'Unwilling to turn the mountain, I sate down upon a rock above the little Lake . . . Entering into my Brother's youthful feelings of sadness and disappointment when he was told unexpectedly that the Alps were crossed – the effort accomplished – I tardily descended towards the Hospital.'[28] The sensations and emotions experienced in the Alps by the younger William Wordsworth are echoed in Dorothy's later encounter with the same place, so that her response resonates with her brother's. And as the Wordsworths' party prepare to descend into Italy from near the Simplon summit, further echoes are heard, or perhaps felt, by Dorothy as she continues to retrace her brother's steps:

Soon after leaving the Spittal, our path was between precipices, still more gloomy and awful than before (what must
they have been in the time of rain and vapour when my
Brother was here before on the narrow track instead of our
broad road, that smoothes every difficulty!).[29]

Throughout the group's passage across the Alps, the
younger William always appears to be before Dorothy on the
path. Her walking, and her reflections upon that walking,
therefore become part of a conscious attempt to create, and
to reinforce, through the motion common to their bodies,
sympathetic and creative connections between herself and her
brother. As Susan Levin has observed, Dorothy's 'emphasis on
past travellers and their routes, her recurring use of the word
"trace," help establish the images of her own journal as signs
of missing presences.'[30] By reinscribing, or retracing, with
her feet the route taken by William thirty years previously,
Dorothy Wordsworth is able to bring to life in her writings
something of the twenty-year-old brother she barely knew;
because of the means of its creation through shared walks
layered in time and place, she is able to overwrite the lived
experience of their long separation.

The enabling of such bonds of imagination and sympathy
was one of the fundamental reasons why walking was so
important to Dorothy Wordsworth – it was how she understood
and manifested her relationships with those she loved – and
why her accounts of that walking should be of real importance
to later readers. Tim Ingold and Jo Lee Vergunst have argued
that walking is 'a profoundly social activity' because 'In their
timings, rhythms and inflections, the feet respond as much

as does the voice to the presence and activity of others. Social relations . . . are not enacted *in situ* but are paced out along the ground.'[31] It is hard to think of a walker to whom this applies more than Dorothy Wordsworth. Walking in company or alone, Dorothy 'paced out' a whole life of experiences, sensations and memories, all of which helped bring her into closer connection with those whom she loved wherever they were.

The virtues of such sociable pedestrianism would eventually resonate throughout the memories of a life made rich by walking. Dorothy Wordsworth made her last tour in 1828 to the Isle of Man, where Joanna Hutchinson was now living. There Dorothy walked, proudly recording one day in her journal the words of an admirer who declared of her 'That woman's so light she's made for walking'.[32] She felt joy, too, at seeing the hills of her beloved Lake District, whose ways she had trodden for thirty years, 'dimly' across the sea.[33] These memories would prove the last treasures to be added to the trove of companionable experiences stored in Dorothy's memory. The following year she was struck by a debilitating illness which prevented her from any longer leaving her home, and there were further blows to come. 'Physical fitness', as Lucy Newlyn notes, 'had always been crucial to her emotional well-being, and to her creative life with her brother', but the poor state of Dorothy's health meant that the pleasures of walking had to be obtained vicariously, or recalled in memory. Writing in her journal in 1834 after a heavy rainfall, she recollected with a mixture of melancholy and happiness the 'memory of many a moist tramp' with her brother William.[34]

Severe mental illness, possibly a form of senile dementia, eventually claimed Dorothy's mind over the next decade. The condition robbed her of her short-term memory, though it spared her earlier recollections, intensifying, as Lucy Newlyn has put it, 'her emotional attachment to the past'.[35] That attachment is evident in one of the last poems she would write, 'Thoughts on My Sick-bed', composed in the spring of 1832. Prompted by a gift of early flowers picked by her niece Dora, the poem unspools with Dorothy's memories of a life lived on foot. Transported by her recollections, she is swept up by 'a power unfelt before' that transports her from illness and pain, beyond the terrace which has been the limit of her excursions for many years, out into the hills and into a past that can be experienced anew:

> No prisoner in this lonely room,
> I saw the green Banks of the Wye,
> Recalling thy prophetic words,
> Bard, Brother, Friend from infancy!
>
> No need of motion, or of strength,
> Or even the breathing air;
> – I thought of Nature's loveliest scenes;
> And with Memory I was there.[36]

Dorothy's memories of walking with her brother are powerful enough to transcend both distance and time. She does not speak of 'feeling' as if she were once again in 1798 at the start of the creative partnership with her brother, but is *actually* there, inhabiting the moment again. Taken beyond the limitations of her frail and declining body by the memory of her years spent on foot, she exults that she has 'trod the

Hills again'.[37] Although she would never again wander – she died in 1855 after twenty years of confinement – Dorothy Wordsworth in this poem finds joy in what has been, as she had throughout the whole of her extraordinary walking life.

IN THE SPRING OF 2008 I walked up Dunmail Raise from the Grasmere side with my friend Tim and his son Anousheh. We were intent upon reaching the top of Helvellyn before descending the mountain by the thrilling Striding Edge to Patterdale, but our conversation the day before had been about the Wordsworths and their melancholy farewelling at the head of the pass. When we got to the crossroads at the top of the Raise, still sweating from the exertion of the rough climb up a boulder-choked stream bed, I tried to imagine where the siblings had said their final goodbyes. It was difficult to believe the place could have looked altogether different; with the exception of the National Trust paths heading up the fells, the rough moor grasses and stony fell sides must have been, I thought, largely the same. It was an overcast day, cool and cheerless, despite it being early May, and the dourness of the weather lent a gloom to the landscape which was sympathetic to our contemplative mood as we stood by the tarn. We saw no ghosts that day but our walk was nonetheless haunted by the memory of what had passed in that place, and our remembrance of Dorothy's grief.

It is perhaps fitting that this walk too has become a memory, and that my experiences that day have blended with other walks taken with different companions in the years since. Rather than being haunted, my Lakeland walking is peopled by memories of relationships and experiences lived on these paths, much as Dorothy Wordsworth's walks were. It is in this way, I think, that I have managed to come closest to her.

THREE

Ellen Weeton

I saw a gentleman descending with his guide, at a short
distance. They espied me. I had already left the regular
path a little, merely to quench my thirst; and now deviated
a little more, purposely that they might not distinguish
my dress or features, lest, seeing me at any other time,
they should know where they had seen me; and I should
dread the being pointed at in the road or the street as –
'That is the lady I saw ascending Snowdon, alone!'

Ellen Weeton, *Journal of a Governess*

On a sunny day in the middle of June 1825, Ellen Weeton,
a 48-year-old Lancashire governess travelling through
Wales, set off up Snowdon alone. She was confident and
strong, a capable walker who had ascended some of the highest
peaks in the Lake District, but none was as high as Snowdon,
which stands at 3,560 feet. Born in Up Holland near Wigan
around 1777 (the exact date is unknown), Weeton would have
been able to see the mountains of Wales as she grew up: Up
Holland sits on an elevated plateau above the Mersey valley,
and Snowdonia can be seen rising in the south. Weeton was

certainly not the first woman to climb a mountain – Dorothy Wordsworth's ascent of Scafell Pike in 1818 is just one example of other women who had, by this time, set off in pursuit of similar thrills – but female mountaineers of her social status were uncommon. Walking for pleasure was still the preserve of those with enough money to have leisure time.

It was also uncommon for women to be seen climbing mountains alone, though it was not necessarily for the reasons typically assumed – fear of sexual assault, or the demands of propriety. Rather, mountain ascents were often completed with the help of a guide. What made Weeton eccentric in her desire to climb Snowdon was not so much her sex as her intrepidity. Having been 'espied' by the men on their descent, Weeton sought to avoid them not only because she had no desire to be publicly labelled peculiar, but because she wished to pursue her walk independently:

> The guide, seeing I was out of the path (only because he was in it, if he had but known), called out to me, but I was *quite* deaf. He continued shouting, and I was *forced* to hear; he was telling me to keep in the copper path, &c. I knew the way perfectly well, for my Map and my Guide had been well studied at home. I could find from what the gentleman said, that he imagined I had called for the guide at his dwelling, and finding him engaged upon the mountain, had gone so far to meet him; for he intreated the man to leave him . . . I never turned my face towards them, but walked as fast as I could . . . the Guide again giving me some directions – with the best intentions, I am sure.[1]

The guide's officiousness was no match for Weeton's determination, and he was left to walk down the mountain alone.
She imagined him descending the hillside 'vexed . . . that it
should be seen that any body could ascend without him, – and
a woman, too!',[2] making the matter one of professional pride,
and only partly about her sex.

Free at last of importunities, Weeton continued her planned
walk, which was to 'ascend on the Bettws side, to cross over
the summit if practicable, and descend at Llanberris'.[3] Such
a route added considerably to the difficulty, as Weeton was
well aware, but she 'wished to have an entire range and view
down every side'.[4]

As she climbed, she discovered a glorious sense of isolation:
'Here I stood, perched on a ridge like a crow on the point of a
pinnacle; not a human creature could I see anywhere; for aught
I knew, I had the whole mountain to myself.'[5] It is a curious
description, one where the recognizable delight at being alone
on the mountain is tempered with something more essential.
Crows are often to be found on mountain sides in Britain,
sporting in the winds that eddy and whirl along their sides, or
hovering apparently motionless above mountain tops, at ease
both with the movement and the stillness of the place. In this
moment, alone on the ridge, Weeton's kinship is with these
wild creatures, not the humans who in their brief traverses of
the mountain know nothing of what it is to exist there, to fully
inhabit the mountain or to be part of its ecology. Weeton's
prose possesses a twitchy energy: aligned imaginatively with
the crow, she could, at any moment, take off from the pinnacle
to soar overhead. On the mountain side, Weeton's humanity
seems to dissolve until she appears more bird than biped.

Weeton cannot, however, take flight either imaginatively or physically, but is instead compelled to return to the realm of the earthbound by anxiety. Atop one of Snowdon's many ridges, the exposure causes something approaching vertigo, which rises to a panic that threatens to overwhelm her:

> Not far before me, the path wound along a most aweful precipice. Now I *was* startled! for the first time. This was wholly unexpected . . . I hesitated some time; there was no crossing lower down. I must either return home as I had come, or climb the only way there was . . . I had taken the precaution, on coming to Carnarvon, to write my address on a card, both to my lodgings there and my dwelling at Prescot, and wore it in my pocket, so that if any accident should befal me, whoever found me would discover where to apply . . . Strange feelings and ideas mingle! the next moment I raised a thought aloft to Him who is the Highest.[6]

Faced with an appalling drop on either side of the ridge, a 'road' which goes unmentioned in either of the guides Weeton had read before her ascent, her mind wanders to consider what might become of her body should she fall.[7] That she had contemplated the possibility of dying on the mountain before she undertook the climb indicates an impressive matter-of-factness about the realities of hill-walking, but such thoughts do little to help. Combining bravery with foolhardiness, Weeton presses forward onto the ridge, though details fall victim to adrenaline:

Whilst crossing the ridge, perhaps 100 yds, perhaps 200, or even more, for I was too terrified to ascertain – the precipice on my right and left both, was too much for my head to bear; on my right, if I slipped ever so little, nothing could save me, and Oh! it looked like an eternity of falling; it seemed to my giddy head, half a mile down.[8]

Apparently on the cusp of becoming crag-fast – too afraid to proceed or withdraw (a condition known all too well by Samuel Taylor Coleridge, whose adventures on Broad Stand on Scafell left him stuck on a precipitous ledge) – Weeton adopts a novel solution (one most unlikely to have been available to Coleridge, and an example of women's clothing proving helpful to a walker), to draw her 'bonnet close over my right cheek, to hoodwink me on that side'.[9] It makes for a sad contrast with Weeton's earlier freedom, though: the blinkers Weeton places upon herself are more suggestive of a fretful carthorse than the freewheeling crow.

For all the physical and psychological difficulties Weeton experienced ascending Snowdon, she still manages to take enormous pleasure from the experience: with 12 miles still to walk in the early evening, she 'could not help playing truant' from her intended route, choosing instead to follow her nose into the mountain's many nooks and crannies.[10] This return to her more usual behaviour on walks brought Weeton back to herself, so that she 'was very little fatigued' and even 'forgot to be frightened, I was so much pleased with the various views, and with the vale and lakes of Llanberis'.[11] Looking back up at Snowdon's heights, Weeton declared herself the 'soaring Queen of the Mountains', and arrived at last 'amongst my own species again, and on a level with my fellow creatures'.[12] As before, when Weeton imagined herself to be like a crow, here too there are hints that some kind of transmigration has occurred: walking opens up for Weeton access to non-human perspectives that both empower and destabilize the self.

Walking was for Ellen Weeton a source of comfort, pride, profound joy and immense satisfaction in a life otherwise often shot through with frustration, unhappiness, violence and fear. Walking lay at the heart of Weeton's perception of herself in the wider world, but it was also an escape from what was at times a life of drudgery and, later, intense sadness. Walking was a mode of travel that took her into ways of thinking and being that were independent of others, and that were totally her own. Walking, for Ellen Weeton, was both the source of and a path to freedom.

Her life was mostly lived in obscurity as a provincial governess, one of the few respectable occupations available to a woman during this period. Although a garrulous correspondent and ardent journal-keeper, she published nothing during her lifetime. What survives of Weeton's writings – four volumes of her correspondence and some journals – were gathered in 1936 and 1939 before being edited by J. J. Bagley in 1969 as *Miss Weeton's Journal of a Governess* in two volumes, covering 1807–11 and 1811–25, respectively. Encompassing autobiographical sketches, sporadic diary entries and letters written to friends and family, Weeton's work was not intended for a general readership, only 'for the perusal of a few, and of my own child in particular'.[13] Dorothy Wordsworth, too, wrote journals that were meant to be shared solely with friends and family, and such decisions implied no lack of literary skill in either Wordsworth or Weeton. As Morris Marples observes in *Shanks's Pony* – one of only two texts before this book to discuss Weeton as a walker-writer, 'there was a wild romantic strain in her which drove her off the beaten track, and it was the pleasure of walking, perhaps the psychological urge to walk . . . which kept her walking on and on.'[14] That sense of a 'wild romantic strain' comes through sharply in Weeton's vivid and enjoyably direct prose, which not only communicates her elation at shimmying up crags, of running up steeps very much as a mountain sheep might, but the deeply felt satisfaction of having freedom to roam.

Weeton's opportunities for walking were shaped by several external factors, including her employment as a governess and female companion and – later – her roles as a wife and mother. Working for a time in the Lake District, Weeton would steal out for walks in her employers' absence. But Weeton's pedestrianism was also conditioned by her gender, both in terms of how others perceived her (or how Weeton imagined they might perceive her – several of her letters record anxiety about the possibility of meeting with 'insult' from men especially) and Weeton's awareness of herself as a walking woman. These ideas played a role in where, when and even how she walked, in some instances limiting her walking to a regrettable degree. Writing to her friend Mrs Whitehead, she outlined how,

> A little while ago I had a very wild scheme in agitation, which was, to traverse Wales on foot; a mode of travel-ling I should prefer, were I ever so wealthy – but when I reflect on the many insults a female is liable to, if alone,

I find it impracticable. My ignorance of the language too, is another obstacle. My plan was, to get acquainted with some decent Welsh farmer's family and by their means to get acquainted with another; and so on, as long as the chain would last; and board with each family as long as I staid, and to dress in the plainest garments I had, that I might attract less notice. I must not think of putting such a scheme in practise. If I was but a man, now! I could soon do it.[15]

Weeton's walking ambitions were on a par with more celebrated male walker-writers – had she succeeded in implementing her plan to walk the whole of Wales, she might have followed – perhaps literally – in the footsteps of Wordsworth on his youthful tour of the country in 1790. Unfortunately, as a young woman, Weeton found herself frustrated in her ambitions by anxieties about the social propriety of being a solitary woman on the road; decorum did not allow for young women pitching up at farmers' doorways at night looking for a bed.

Although bound to some extent by social and practical restrictions, Weeton nonetheless sought and found satisfaction through walking – during holidays, with friends and, later, through an increasing confidence that came to override her trepidation about 'insults' – alone. Weeton remained anxious about what people would make of a solitary woman walker, but less and less frequently was her walking conditioned by the effects of the expectations of others: pedestrianism opened up prospects of all kinds. As she wrote to her friend Ann of a holiday spent walking the Isle of Man, 'The hours

I have spent here, have been hours of luxury indeed! Here, totally alone, my thoughts expanded with the prospect; and, free and unrestrained as the air I breathed, I was happy as mortal could be.'[16] The liberty accorded by the act of walking worked on both the body and the mind; the thoughts that Weeton was able to think came to be as large as the horizon; in her description, her very person dissolves, becoming as insubstantial, and as uncontainable, as the breeze.

This dissolution of the self was one means by which Weeton understood her experiences as a walker, but in other journal entries and letters, her descriptions focus on how walking embodied the self, an experience which brought different, but equally significant, joys and freedoms. On 8 July 1810, she wrote to her friend Miss Winkley of a walk she had recently enjoyed in the Lake District,

> Since Miss Rhodes came, a party was made up to go on the top of Fairfield, a high mountain a few miles from here. I made one; we were fifteen in number, besides four men who attended and carried provisions, &c. Mrs Pedder, Miss Rhodes, Miss Barton, and myself, left home soon after five o'clock in the morning, in a cart, Mr. Pedder on a poney, and the footman on an ass. We stopped to breakfast at a Mr. Scambler's, in Ambleside, two miles from here, where the rest of the party joined us. Soon after six, we proceeded, the ladies in carts, the gentlemen on foot – Mr. Pedder and Mr. Partridge, senior, excepted. We travelled up a very steep, and a very rocky, rugged road, for five or six miles . . . Fearless as I in general am, I could not divest myself of some anxiety, until we arrived at the place where we should each

be obliged to trust to our own feet alone. The other ladies
screamed several times, expecting to be either overturned,
or precipitated backwards . . .

After labouring up the steep for an hour or two, over
moss and rocks, we at length reached the summit . . . we all
sat down upon the ground, and enjoyed a hearty meal of
veal, ham, chicken, gooseberry pies, bread, cheese, butter,
hung leg of mutton, wine, porter, rum, brandy and bitters.
When our hunger was appeased, we began to stroll about
and enjoy the extensive prospect. We had several prospect
glasses, and the air was very clear. I was much pleased,
though awed, by the tremendous rocks and precipices in
various directions. I crept to the edge of several of them;
but of one in particular, when I found myself seated upon
its projecting point, and a direct perpendicular descent on
every side but one, of many hundred yards . . .

The mountain is shaped very like a horse shoe; we
ascended at one end, and descended at the other, making
a circuit of eight or ten miles at least; some say, twelve.

In descending, one or two of the party who had not provided nails in the soles of their shoes to make their footing
firm, were obliged to sit down frequently, and descend by
sliding; the mountain heath and moss glaze the shoes in
such a manner when without nails, it is impossible to stand,
much less to walk with safety where the ground is not
perfectly level . . .

I have never in my life enjoyed a more agreeable excursion; such a scramble exactly suited me. To me, there is
little pleasure in a straight forward walk on level ground.
A fine, noble, lofty, rugged mountain, has far more charms

for me than a fine, formal, artificial walk in a garden or pleasure-ground.[17]

Weeton's pleasure is joyfully evident in her sensual, highly corporeal, descriptions of the various appetites – intellectual, aesthetic and physical – that are elevated, and then satisfied, by the climb of Fairfield. Most striking is the almost indecently long list of food and drink carried to the summit, and the unabashed relish with which she details the consumption – perhaps destruction is a better word – of the feast. Also of interest, though, is the pleasure taken by Weeton in scrambling as a means of travelling on a mountainside despite what might be imagined to be the difficulties of moving through such terrain in the womanly clothing of the time. Somewhere between walking and climbing, scrambling involves using the whole body to facilitate what is sometimes uncertain or shuffling progress through challengingly steep mountainous terrain, taking advantage not only of the dextrousness of hands and the additional stabilizing strength of arms, but the safety offered by other potential points of contact with the rock that might be essential once the feet are no longer all: elbows, knees, shoulders and even backside. Such routes on the mountains are frequently more mentally involving and more physically demanding than most walkers' paths, and sometimes more dangerous. But they are also more intimate: Weeton would not have felt the mountain through her feet – so distant from the brain – but would have held it, grasped it, depended on it, in ways that would have brought her whole body into close contact with the rock. Where some of the party were forced to descend, ignominiously, on their behinds because of their poor preparations for the excursion, Weeton was not one of them: instead, she appears knowledgeable, prepared and confident, a capable walker who is not only comfortable in this tricky terrain, but takes life-enhancing pleasure in it.

Weeton's eagerness for the liberation offered by scrambling is evident in a letter written four months later to her brother. While the couple who employed Weeton as a governess, Mr and Mrs Pedder, were away from home, Weeton went wandering in the Lakes with her friend, Miss Robinson – the sister of Mrs 'P':

> I spent two days at Holm-Head, the farm where Mrs. P's father lives upon. It is 4 miles from here. The first day, Miss Robinson took me to Coniston, to shew me the lake; going and returning was 12 miles. We returned to dinner after a most agreeable walk. The next morning we set out at 8 o'clock intending to ramble 3 or 4 miles; but one object and then another drew me on, until at length I and my companion had arrived at the foot of Langdale Pikes, two lofty heads of a mountain . . . I could not think of returning without mounting to the top, which, after a long scramble, we at length accomplished, and I thought myself well repaid for the trouble; indeed, the ruggedness and steepness of the ascent and descent were to me one half the inducement, for I dearly love a scramble . . . We got back to Holms head to a 5 o'clock dinner, and having eaten nothing for 9 hours, you may imagine how abstinence and the keen mountain air had sharpened our appetites. I really thought I should never have had enough.[18]

Weeton takes here a slant view of climbing the enticing peaks of Pike of Stickle and Harrison Stickle. While reaching summits was of interest and importance for her, getting to the top is accorded the same significance as the feat of arriving. There is an uncompromising decisiveness in Weeton's description of tackling the climb *because* it was rugged and steep, *because* it was difficult, and there is a vivaciousness in the way in which Weeton seizes the opportunity to undertake this ascent simply because she can. The impression of vitality is furthered by the partnering, again, of Weeton's relish for difficulty and the physical appetites her activity engenders – her body's heightened longing for nourishment becomes representative of the numerous corporeal desires excited and embodied by her walking. Indeed, the slightly breathless assessment that 'I really thought I should never have had enough' seems to go far beyond its apparent reference to Weeton's wish for sustenance, encompassing in addition her desire to be in the mountains, her delight in scrambling, her joy in being able to indulge the 'wild romantic strain' that pushed her to follow her wandering inclinations, however circuitous the route, and whatever the terrain.[19]

Weeton undertook a number of solo walks over the course of her life, but the first substantial walking tour was round the Isle of Man in the summer of 1812:

The first long walk I took, was on the 28th, after my arrival. When I had been on Douglas-Head one day, I had seen some mountains at a distance, and this day I set out with the intention of ascending the highest, if it were not too far. By paying strict attention to a map which I purchased, I have had very little occasion to ask any questions respecting roads, distances, or places. I took my guide in my hand, and wanted no other. In this, and in all my walks, I have ever been without a companion; I prefer being alone; I can then stop, go on, sit down, proceed, turn to the right or to the left, as my fancy may prompt, without restraint; and, even were it probable I could find a *proper* companion who would with pleasure accompany me 12, 15, 20, or 30 miles a day, still, her taste would not perhaps assimilate in most respects with my own, and we should teaze each other – I, in listening to conversation which did not interest me, and she, in attending to observations to which she was indifferent. But, as it is extremely unlikely I should find one who would take such long walks, and give way to my taste, wishes, and curiosity in every thing, I choose to go alone, in places unfrequented by those of my own species, that my thoughts, as well as my feet, may ramble without restraint; when I enter towns, and crouds [*sic*], I do then like to have a companion; but when the wonders of nature alone occupy me, when my soul is filled with admiration and rapture at scenes of rural beauty, or mountainous grandeur, I never wish for the company of one earthly being, save that of my brother.[20]

This account is typical of Weeton: the ambition, the desire to climb as high as possible, the preparedness and the hunger for independence. Weeton makes explicit here that the full exercise of the mind is contingent on physical and social liberty, in a way that echoes Jean-Jacques Rousseau's declaration, in the appropriately named *Confessions of a Solitary Wanderer* that 'when I stop I cease to think; my mind only works with my legs'.[21] Only when the body is freed from constraint – practical, physical, social – can this be the case for walker-writers such as Weeton.

She found something of this freedom on the Isle of Man, where the unexpected friendliness of the people she encountered had a transformational and long-lasting effect. Of an early excursion during that tour, she writes,

> I returned home, highly pleased with my walk, which was about 13 miles; the few people I had met with, either took no notice of me, or spoke civilly; which gave me more confidence, as I confess my first walks were not without considerable apprehensions, lest I should meet with insult, as I was so totally unaccompanied.[22]

Over the course of her stay on the Isle of Man, Weeton's confidence as a woman walking alone grew considerably and increased in tandem with her physical abilities. Writing in the same letter to Ann Winkley, she noted how she tended to spontaneously lengthen the walks she undertook, so that one, which 'was only in a direct road, going and returning, 12 miles' was 'stretched into 16'.[23] As a result of feeling so 'Encouraged by the little fatigue I felt after these walks', Weeton began to contemplate 'others of greater length'.[24] Her growing strength as a walker so emboldened Weeton that on one of these longer solitary walks, she willingly engaged in conversation with a man she encountered. 'He was old,' Weeton notes, 'and rather infirm, and I was confident I could overpower him, should he attempt to rob me.'[25] Not all her anxieties had been eliminated, but rendering those anxieties inconsequential was

Weeton's physical strength: 'at any rate, I can run five times as fast, thought I.'[26] Walking, and the fortification of body and mind that it had enabled, freed her from the limiting influence of the 'social mores subscribed to by both men and women, the threat implicit in sexual harassment', which emphasize women's vulnerability when walking alone.[27] Weeton instead gained, through the superior capabilities of her body, the right to access a larger world, one where 'the individual' comes to seem 'small and solitary, . . . reliant on the strength of body and will'.[28] This, for Weeton, was true freedom.

It was a freedom that Weeton continued to foster, and to cherish, during her extensive explorations of the Isle of Man. Fixed upon an ascent of Greeba mountain (spelt by Weeton as Greeva – a rather petite mountain at 1,385 feet high), Weeton asked directions from a young girl. Having been shown through the girl's garden, Weeton 'began directly to ascend the rocks, which were very steep', noting that she 'might have ascended a much less difficult way, but this was nearer'. Clinching the case for scrambling this difficult route was Weeton's confidence that 'walls, and rocks, are slight impediments to me'.[29]

This sort of assurance perhaps lay behind her experiences days later when she undertook, almost by accident, a walk of such length that it would likely have taxed even Dorothy Wordsworth's endurance:

> You will scarcely credit me when I tell you that on the 5th of June, I walked 35 miles. I left home at half past nine, with an intention to go to Castletown, and as much farther as I found I could walk. So as to get well home, I put my map,

memorandum book, 3 boiled eggs, and a crust of bread into
a work-bag; and, thus prepared, sallied forth. I met with
nothing worth observation until I arrived near Castletown
. . . I walked 2 or 3 miles beyond Castletown, to a rising
ground that commanded an extensive view; and, springing
upon a high copse by the road side, where I seated myself,
I had the double pleasure of satisfying my appetite, and
feasting my eyes. Then, retracing a part of the road, I turned
towards Peel, thinking I would only go a little way, just to
have a more extended view . . .

'I will only go a little further, and a little further, just
to that pretty house, or to the top of that high road,' I
frequently repeated to myself, until I had got full 5 miles
beyond Castletown. To return, or go through Peel, would be
equally 15 or 16 miles. I stood hesitating for some time what
to do. I looked at my watch, and found that it was half past
4 o'clock! I confess I was a little alarmed, but as there was no
time for delay, I turned towards Peel, over a mountain road
the old woman had shewn me; preferring that to the high-
road, because it was in fact a much *lower* one; and I wanted
scenery and prospect, not caring for the additional fatigue.
Often and often, as I went on, did I turn to feast my eyes on
the beauties spread out at my feet. The air was serenely clear;
England, Ireland, Scotland, and Wales were all perfectly
distinct; some Irish mountains appeared so near, I fancied
I could row myself to them in an open boat; they were of
a deep purple, tinged with the declining sun, and did look
most beautifully! I could distinctly mark the mountains
in Cumberland and Westmoreland; Skiddaw, Saddleback,
Helvellyn, Coniston, and several others. I felt a pleasure in

looking at them, for *there* had *my* feet trodden, and some
of my happiest days been spent! To stand as I did, upon
an island, and in one half hour see three kingdoms and a
principality, is no common view.[30]

Weeton's hunger – for walking, for food, for life – is again
evident, with her enjoyment at being able to 'satisfy her appetite'
for nourishment 'doubled' by the ability to simultaneously
'feast' on the view with her 'eyes': while walking she provides
both her body and mind with the sustenance that they need.
Weeton on this walk found herself further than she had
perhaps intended. But even here, in a situation which would
make most walkers feel anxious about their ability to get
back to their starting point, she has confidence in her body:
at half past four in the afternoon and 15 miles from home,
she once again selects the more difficult route, preferring
challenge and scenery to safety. The rewards for her bravery
were great: in front of her opens up a vista which, through a
trick of the evening light, becomes an almost tangible record
not only of earlier physical exploits, but of some of Weeton's
happiest times. Optics and memory combine to bring past
pleasures into immediate contact with the present, and it
is through Weeton's feet that these parallel time frames are
brought together: there (and then) her 'feet' had 'trodden',
while here (and now) she stands, paused in the act of once
again inscribing memories and feelings into the landscape
through the act of walking. Afterwards, she walked, joyously,

into Peel at 6 o'clock, having in my way down the mountains,
and along the vales, seen many a lovely little cultivated patch

of earth, and romantic lonely little hut on the sides of the hills, the streamlets running wildly at the bottom, over their rocky beds. There is a simple grandeur and beauty in such scenes, that infuses a greater portion of enthusiasm within me, than I can express. I admire! I wonder! I adore! Oh Ann! if you knew the pleasure I feel in running wild among such scenery, you would not wonder at my temerity, or at my undergoing so much fatigue to obtain the gratification.[31]

Ellen Weeton took considerable pleasure in finding herself enlarged in mind and body through walking. There is immense pride in her accounts of her physical prowess, of her ability to rely so totally on 'the strength of body and will'. But walking was also release, remedy and restoration, sanctuary and solace, especially in her later years. Just two years after the exhilarating experiences on the Isle of Man, Weeton married Aaron Stock, a widowed cotton-spinner from Wigan. Not long after their wedding, she was describing him as 'my terror, my misery!'[32] A daughter, Mary, was born in 1815, but Stock's violence was so extreme that Weeton feared she would 'never live to educate Mary, unless I quit this place'.[33] In 1821 Stock appeared in court for an assault on his wife; Weeton's journal from this period describes being 'beaten almost to death', and being found 'With my bruises thick upon me'.[34] Shortly afterwards Weeton applied for a separation from her husband, and in doing so surrendered custody of her daughter. She would not see Mary again for seven years.

Walking was one of Weeton's comforts during this period, and served as a source of pride and emotional strength. Writing in 1825 as she approached her fiftieth year, she declared,

As thin as I am, and as skinny and bony, yet my bones cannot be dry bones, but must be 'full of marrow and fatness,' or I could never be able to endure such long walks, and be so little fatigued; my feet swell sometimes, but I can skip like a lamb amongst the rocks, and enjoy the sport, after a 10 or 12 miles walk.[35]

It is an unflattering picture in some ways – Weeton's surface appearance, certainly, is given short shrift. But under the unpromising flesh lies considerable strength of a kind that cannot be seen, only felt. It is perhaps a fitting image for a woman whose ability to keep walking largely depended not only on physical but mental strength, on emotional resilience and bravery, and for whom walking and life were so wholly entwined.

⁂

UNLIKE ELLEN WEETON, I usually walk in company, but since the birth of my son, I have found it difficult to cover any meaningful distance; my pelvis had not recovered from the induced labour, and my coccyx had been bent backwards by the baby. After just a mile or so, it felt as if my bones were grinding together, and the ache would last for days afterwards. Walk after walk had to be cut short because I had not learned to manage my new, post-birth body, and I was becoming increasingly anxious about letting down people who had made the effort to come and hike with me.

One solution was to test my body alone. I had felt for days the itch to walk up the Minchmoor Road from Yarrowford, a route I know well. Setting off from a small village in the

Yarrow valley, I followed in the footsteps of kings and drovers, bandits and thieves, as I climbed steadily along an ancient road which contours under a hill. The ascent never relented, but it was steady and without real steepness, and the wildness of the hills above drew me onwards. I reached the high point of the walk feeling a little chilly in the breeze, so lunch, sat looking over much of the Scottish border with England, was brief. While I ate, I tried to pick out the rest of the route, and found myself daunted: by the distance, by the weather, by the fact that I had just my coat to keep me warm. I panicked, fretting that I simply no longer had a body capable of walking this distance, and I wondered how I could get off the hill safely if I had to. I decided not to worry about the distance, but to make some intermediate goals, and I identified an escape route. With my panic better managed, my mind was able to take more pleasure from the day, and it was not long before I felt something of the old soul-stirring joy at being high above the world. I ignored the short cut I had identified, and instead continued round along the ridge that runs between the Yarrow and Tweed valleys. I was still relieved, though, to find the finger post for Yarrowford, and to feel certain that I would make it to the end of the walk.

The descent brought me steeply down into a beautiful birch woodland where pheasants roamed the undergrowth; my approach sent them skittering through leaf litter into even darker corners. Back in the valley, just 1 mile of flat walking from the start, I felt a surge of exhilaration at having made it, of having spent a day alone in the hills, of having 'run wild' again.

FOUR

Sarah Stoddart Hazlitt

They seemed to have a great deal of curiosity, the
Highlanders in particular: and their questions were
generally prefaced with. 'It's vara waarm the day.' 'O very
warm,' 'If you please, how far are ye come the day?' 'From
Crieff &c &c' 'O, aye! ye'll be vera tired.' 'An whar ar
ye gaun?' 'To Stirling.' 'Ou, its a sair way: ye'll ne'er get
there the night.' 'O yes I'm a very good walker. I walked
a hundred an seventy miles three weeks ago.' 'Gude sauf
us! Ye're no a Crieff woman?'

Sarah Stoddart Hazlitt, diary entry for 1 June 1822

Arriving in Edinburgh on 21 April 1822 aboard the Leith
Smack *Superb*, Sarah Stoddart Hazlitt stepped onto the
docks towards a most uncertain future. She had journeyed
for seven days up the British east coast from the Thames in
order to be divorced by her husband of fourteen years, the
essayist William Hazlitt, who had become infatuated with
the teenage daughter of the landlady of his lodging house in
London. Lacking the financial resources or the social influence
to obtain a divorce by Act of Parliament, Hazlitt hatched a

plan to be 'caught' by his wife in the arms of a prostitute in Edinburgh, where their marriage might be dissolved under Scottish law much more quickly, and more affordably, than in England. Over the next three months while she lived in Edinburgh, Sarah would be bullied by her husband's friends, commit perjury and become ill by guilt and anxiety at her complicity in his degrading schemes. She managed the complex emotions that swirled during this period by keeping a terse diary in which she documented both the circumstances of her divorce and the miles and miles of walking she undertook when she had the chance to steal away. On foot, she was able to enjoy something approaching freedom as she rambled across Edinburgh and its surrounds, in contrast to the suffocation of lawyers' offices and the distressing prospect of an anxious future as a single woman. Walking was to prove an important antidote to the debilitating emotional and physical effects of her husband's coercive behaviour.

During her first few weeks in Edinburgh, Sarah's time was split between legal matters and exploring the city. Communication with William was via her solicitor or a go-between, the better to preserve the entirely false appearance that their simultaneous presence in Edinburgh was coincidental. The terms of their arrangement were that Hazlitt would cover his wife's costs during her stay in Edinburgh, and in return she would swear – falsely – an oath of calumny asserting that she had no prior knowledge of his activities, thereby enabling the divorce to proceed. During the many delays in obtaining solicitors or legal documents, or just getting a straight answer to a simple question, Sarah walked across Edinburgh and some distance beyond, exploring well-known tourist haunts (Calton Hill, Arthur's Seat) and out-of-the-way places (Lasswade, Rosslyn Glen) with equal enthusiasm. On these excursions, she usually walked alone, typically for hours and miles at a time.

In the middle of May, William left Edinburgh for a short while, first to lecture at Anderson's College in Glasgow, then to walk in the southern Highlands. His absence, and the consequent pause in the legal proceedings, enabled his wife also to take her leave of Edinburgh for a while: on 14 May she returned to Leith to board another ship, this time heading north and west along the Forth to Stirling. With little money in her pocket, and without remark in her journal, Sarah was about to embark on an extraordinary adventure.

By the 1820s it was reasonably common for tourists to be found travelling through the southernmost Highlands, especially following the publication of the numerous works by Sir Walter Scott set in the area: the popularity of his writing drew people in increasingly significant numbers to the lochs and hills he so lovingly described. It was almost unheard of, though, for a foreign woman to be found walking alone, yet that's what Sarah did. Without a companion and only occasionally with a guide, she set off from Stirling on a week's tour of the southern Highlands that took in many of the famous sights (the Falls of Leny, Loch Katrine, the Falls of Clyde), but which veered considerably at times from the standard tourist routes. During this period she covered distances of between 20 and 30 miles each day and endured at various points considerable physical danger, typically with courage and good cheer. In the course of her tour, she walked 180 miles back to Edinburgh. She relished the chance encounters and happenstances that occurred along the way, and found, after the hardship of walking, significant physical pleasure in the simplest acts – eating, washing, sleeping.

On Monday 13 May, with no preamble at all in the journal to indicate she was planning a voyage of any length, Sarah abruptly records that she sailed, entirely alone, from Newhaven port for Stirling, several miles up the Forth. From there, she set off on foot, and two days into her journey she had walked as far as Loch Katrine in the Trossachs hills, made famous by Scott's 1810 poem *The Lady of the Lake*. Nestled in a bowl below the grand hills of Ben Ledi and Ben Lomond, the loch's singular situation enchanted the solitary walker, who hired a boatman to take her all along its 'different and beautiful windings'. Her tour of the loch's sinuous banks complete, she disembarked and set off on foot for the pass between Loch Katrine and Loch Lomond that would take her south towards her night's accommodation in Luss, on the western bank of Loch Lomond. The land between the lochs, though, was at this time remote and infrequently travelled, and with the weather closing in, she found herself in some danger. In her journal for that day, Thursday 16 May 1822, she recorded that 'in crossing the most dreary, swampy and pathless part' of the moorland beyond Loch Katrine, 'A heavy storm came on, there was not the least shelter, and the heat in climbing such an ascent, together, with the fear of losing myself in such a lonely place almost overcame me.' Sarah would have had no map or compass to help her, but despite this, she writes,

> I guided myself by the direction of the Loch as well as I
> could, and at last, to my great joy, regained a track, but the

road now was stony and difficult, over a wide and dreary
moor, full of bogs, till you arrive at Inversnaid Garrison
[. . . I was directed] to the ferry over Loch Lomond, after
crossing which, I had a most delightful walk on its banks.

What could have been a fatal disaster became in the end a
grand adventure that thrilled Sarah. She exulted in her diary,
upon her arrival in Luss 'about ten o'clock at night', at how
she had been 'quite enraptured with my walk, and the great
variety of uncommonly beautiful scenery I had passed through
in the course of the day'.

Once at Luss, Sarah picked up again the popular tourist
route between Glasgow and the Trossachs, though it is unlikely
that many tourists would have endured the physical hardships
that she experienced over the remaining days of her expedition.
Nor is it likely that many tourists would have responded to
those hardships as she did, with acceptance, perhaps even
relish. The morning after her journey across the boggy flanks
of Ben Lomond, Sarah walked to Dumbarton, 15 miles away.
On the boat from there to Glasgow, she complained of having
'Now such a violent cold in my head, that I could hardly
breathe or look up, and my limbs ached dreadfully, particularly
about my right knee, which I had wrenched in getting out of
the boat, at Inversnaid ferry.'[1] However, this did not stop her
from exploring Dumbarton the next day, nor from walking
the 17 miles from Lanark to West Calder the day after that.

At Lanark, Sarah enjoyed the beauties of the Falls of
Clyde, a series of cascades sought out by tourists from Dorothy
Wordsworth to John Constable. She also took in the curiosities
of Robert Owens's New Lanark, a model settlement established

alongside the banks of the Clyde, where its innovative owner experimented with welfare programmes for his workers. From the steep-sided gorge of the Clyde, Sarah set off on her most gruelling day's walking:

> After leaving all these beautiful scenes, I had one of the most desolate and forlorn walks that can be imagined. Immediately on quitting Lanark I entered on a wide, black boggy moor, which lasted seventeen miles, with a broiling sun, and not a tree, or the least shade all the way. I sat down several times on the ground from mere inability to proceed, but was afraid to rest many minutes at a time, as I was so stiff I could scarcely move afterwards.[2]

The fragility of her position is evident here, as it was in her account of losing her way from Loch Katrine; as a lone walker Sarah is more vulnerable to danger, with no one to aid her or, it would seem, anyone to raise the alarm should she not return. But the anxiety expressed in this entry does not arise from the sources typically attributed to women's walking – sexual harassment, or assault – but from dangers familiar to any solitary walker of either gender, then or now. There is no evidence of Sarah being aware that her walking might place her in an unusually vulnerable position, or that it might make her seem singular. Instead, what is apparent is a keen awareness of the physical realities, and necessities, of accomplishing a punishing walk like this. While her experience is not a pleasant one – she describes herself as being that evening so 'utterly exhausted with heat and fatigue', and her feet 'so swollen, and painful, that it was many hours after

I got to bed, before I could sleep' – she has actively chosen to suffer, rather than had suffering inflicted upon her.[3] Through her walking, Sarah was able to exercise the freedom to choose not only what to feel, but where and how.

The difficulty of the walks mattered to Sarah. At the end of her journey around the Forth and Clyde valleys, she summed up the distance covered in a meticulously neat table:[4]

Number of miles each day

Monday 13th May	———————	4
Tuesday 14	———————	20
Wednesday 15th	———————	32
Thursday 16th	———————	27
Friday 17th	———————	21
Saturday 18	———————	21
Sunday – 19	———————	28
Monday 20th	———————	17
		170

This reckoning includes 17 miles travelled from West Calder to Edinburgh on the morning of the 20th itself, a walk embarked upon the day after she had been unable to sleep because of the pain and swelling in her feet. She notes that 'it was with some pain and difficulty that I finished my jaunt', but the signifi-cance of the walk is measured in miles: miles over bleak and difficult terrain; miles of thirst and heat and danger; and miles walked out because she wanted to walk them, and because she physically could.[5] Hardship during her walks was, for Sarah, cathartic and refreshing, and empowering too: for the most part, she could retain control over how much pain she suffered, and when she relieved it – in contrast to the limitless distress of her divorce proceedings.

The return to business in Edinburgh was abrupt. Within days, the feelings of elation and well-being had dissipated in the confusion of the legal proceedings, and Sarah's body reacted quickly and painfully. 'Very nervous and poorly to-day,' she noted just four days after her exultant return.[6] Her decision a week later, on 31 May 1822, to embark on a second walking tour, must therefore have been a profound relief to body and mind. This time, she was intent on exploring further east in the Highlands, and on setting off over, rather than along, the Forth, towards Perth. From there, she walked to Dunkeld, to Crieff and eventually to Stirling.

Sarah's second journey began inauspiciously when she boarded the wrong boat, ending up on Burntisland in Fife on the other side of the Forth to Edinburgh, instead of on her way to Perth by boat around the coast of Fife and up the Tay. Eschewing the coach that would have taken her from Burntisland to Perth, she instead opted to walk, with an insouciance about the considerable and unanticipated physical demands of this journey:

> From Brantisland I walked to Kinross, fourteen miles; the road very fine and well wooded in some parts; in others bare and dreary. proceeding on, I came in sight of Loch Leven, and the Castle on it where Queen Mary was confined; the view of the Loch accompanies you for some miles. After passing the Toll-gate at Dam Head, the road becomes exceedingly stony and hilly for about four miles, and after-wards very good, between an avenue of trees, till you come

to the beautiful village of Brig in Ayrne twelve miles from
Kinross; Here I found a very comfortable Inn with civil and
obliging people.[7]

'Brig in Ayrne', or Bridge of Earn, is a small town
around 5 or so miles to the south of Perth, and 26 miles
from Burntisland – a distance covered by Sarah in one day's
walking. The exertion involved is passed over entirely by the
breezy 'proceeding on' – the description of this part of the
walk offers the reader just one word per mile with one for luck
– before Sarah's feet, and the reader, are off again, almost all
the way to Perth.

Her determination to walk, regardless of the circumstances,
is confirmed by the next day's journal entry. Here she describes
her journey north from Perth to the small town of Dunkeld,
a distance which Sarah notes 'is called fifteen miles and an
half, but I do not think it so little as twenty English miles'.[8]
With little fuss, she observes that 'Unluckily I had sprained my
ancle over a loose stone, and walked with pain and difficulty';
and it seems likely that she walked a considerable part of
the fifteen Scottish miles carrying the sprain.[9] In contrast to
the Edinburgh entries, which record how quickly her body
broke down under the emotional strain of her legal business,
Sarah's body rallied on this occasion under physical labour:
all that was necessary to allow her to move again with ease
was a good night's sleep and some fine Scottish whisky, with
which she 'rubbed my ancle and knee . . . which did it a great
deal of good'.[10] While this is not, alas, now a recommended
treatment for walking-related ailments, Sarah's matter-of-fact
remedy reinforces the sense of understated determination

that runs throughout her journal. Had it been written for a public audience, it might be tempting to question whether her description was mere bravado, but such incidents are so common in her journal, and are so little embellished, that I am inclined to believe she really was this brave: when walking, she was able to bend her body to her will.

The journey from Perth to Dunkeld took Sarah over the Highland Boundary Fault, a geological schism which marks the transition between lowland and upland Scotland. It slices across the country from the Isle of Arran to the southwest of Glasgow in a diagonal slash northeast to Stonehaven, near Aberdeen. Heading north from Perth, Sarah would have found the change from the soft lowlands of the Almond valley, with their rolling green hills and fertile plains, to the rougher and craggier Highlands quite abrupt, even at walking pace. At the top of a rise, with the lowlands spreading out behind her, she headed downhill into the Tay valley, with rocky cliffs and wood-clad promontories all around. There is no mistaking the point at which the rock beneath you changes from the sedimentary sandstone of the Central Belt to the fire-formed metamorphic rock of the Highlands, and this was marked for Sarah not just by a change in landscape but in the people. She records how her walking on this day brought her into contact with Highlanders in an encounter shaped by her status as an unaccompanied female. In the midst of a 25-mile day from Crieff to Stirling, she enjoyed a memorable conversation with the local people. 'It's vara waarm the day,' one of them remarked. 'O very warm,' Stoddart Hazlitt responds pleasantly.

If you please, how far are ye come the day? From Crieff
&c &c O, aye! ye'll be vera tired. An whar ar ye gaun? To
Stirling. Ou, its a sair way: ye'll ne'er get there the night.
O yes I'm a very good walker. I walked a hundred an
seventy miles three weeks ago. Gude sauf us! Ye're no
a Crieff woman?[11]

What prodigious feats of pedestrianism the Crieff women of
this period habitually performed is yet a mystery, but Sarah
was certainly pleased by the compliment that was evidently
intended by the remark.

At times, Sarah attracted attention as a solitary woman on
foot in the Highlands, but it was always kindly and solicitous –
she writes that the she was able to 'walk all through the country
without molestation or insult' among people 'universally civil
and obliging'.[12] Walking alone was when she experienced the
greatest pleasure, and when her walking held most meaning.
Having spent a day exploring a considerable area around
Dunkeld, she headed west, following the River Braan (or
'Brann', as she spells it) upstream before crossing over the
desolate pass between Glen Braan and Glen Almond. Alone
deep among the hills, Sarah found herself confronted by a
'most appalling and dreary eminence' which 'Accorded much
more with my previous idea of the Highlands than any thing I
had before met with, being an interminable labyrinth of bare
and desolate hills of an immense height.'[13] Her description
of 'desolation' among 'drear' and 'appalling' places accords
with contemporary ideas of the sublime, and as such, her
descriptions are not necessarily surprising or original. What
sets apart Sarah's account is the importance of the relationship

between the landscape and her means of travel through it. Leaving behind the Almond for River Earn,

> I had still other mountains to climb in succession; a most laborious road, and I should have been utterly exhausted with fatigue and heat, had I not found some mountain springs in my way; and lay down and bathed my face, and drank to allay the parching thirst. I was but clumsy at it at first, but I soon managed so as to drink very well, and was refreshed, and was thankful that God had provided water in the stony rock. These walks always make me more religious and more happy, more sensibly alive to the benevolence and love of the Creator than any books or church. His care and kindness seems shown in all his works. Nothing here seems contradictory.[14]

She again writes of significant physical discomfort, but in this entry, her suffering is elevated into an experience of profound personal, even spiritual, meaning. The parallels with old-fashioned religious trials by ordeal are perhaps not coincidental – it is the pain of climbing over mountain pass after mountain pass that, in the end, brings Sarah into some sort of communion with her 'Creator'. It is significant that the apprehension of the divine is understood physically and instinctively – it is the act of walking itself, of pacing out mile after mile for day after day, that *makes* Sarah 'more religious and more happy'. Indeed, walking becomes here the medium of creation itself – Sarah is *made* by her walking 'more religious', not by being compelled or forced, but in the sense of being shaped, formed, created. She does not *feel* more religious, but *is* more religious because she exists as a walker: pedestrianism for Sarah Stoddart Hazlitt is fundamental to her experience of self and her understanding of her place in the world.

The mileage for this second tour was no less impressive than that of her first:

Walked first day 28 miles – 31st May – Friday
second day 25 D° – 1st June – Saturday
third day 15 D° – 2nd June – Sunday
fourth day 21 D° – 3rd June – Monday
fifth day 23 D° – 4th June – Tuesday

That is, one hundred and twelve miles in five days.[15]

Recorded also were her physical and emotional responses to her walking excursion. On her return to Edinburgh from Stirling, Sarah noted how she did not 'feel the least fatigued or foot sore; but much pleased with my excursion', a journey on which she had walked 'all through the country without molestation or insult'.[16]

For Sarah Stoddart Hazlitt, walking underpinned a feeling of wholeness, of completeness – of belonging in the world. In her journals, she demonstrates how it enabled a profound feeling of connectedness with God, with the landscape, with the earth and with wider creation; being on foot facilitated exchanges of real significance with those she met on the road, particularly women. Walking for her was also an act imbued with a range of intellectual, emotional and creative meanings. In some ways, it was an act of defiance – against the restrictions imposed by the dismal divorce, against the husband who had compelled her presence, against the powerlessness of being forced to act against her will. But walking was also about self-assertion and self-knowledge: there is no situation, whether an absence of a bed after an exhausting day on the road, or a shortage of food, that cannot be remedied by walking a little further.

Sarah Stoddart Hazlitt undertook no further pedestrian tours after her return to Edinburgh on 5 June 1822, though she continued to enjoy city walks most days for the remainder of her residence in the city. A month later and the divorce was concluded, though the official decree was not issued until 2 August. At the conclusion of the sorry affair, Sarah prepared to return to London. 'I was now Miss Stoddart,' she wrote in the final entry of her diary, 'and was not I glad of that . . . that my situation in my own opinion, was pretty much the same as it had long been.'[17] She was as brave in the face of an uncertain and unknowable future as she had been on the dangerous pass between Lochs Katrine and Lomond. Sarah Stoddart Hazlitt might well have 'wor[n] out all her shoes' as a result of walking the 'hundreds of miles' recorded in her journals, and she may have been coerced to consent to a divorce that left her more vulnerable than she had ever been in all her miles as a solitary woman walker, but she never exhausted her body's capacity to endure, nor her mind's ability to find strength in walking.

I THINK OFTEN about Sarah when I'm walking. When I'm in Edinburgh, wandering through the winding streets of the Old Town, I think about whether Sarah's feet passed this way. I've stood above Dunkeld, where the lush Tay valley meets much wilder moorland, and imagined her striding off, alone, into the hills. Perhaps, though, it was on Ben Lomond that I found myself closest to her, and the spirit that she brought to her walking. Ben Lomond's summit grants spectacular views over Loch Katrine, but what is most apparent is the complexity of the moorland from which the mountain seems to erupt, and which clothes its flanks. It is a place that seems to be made as much from water as earth. Standing at the summit cairn, I gazed down to where I imagined Sarah might have passed that day in 1822. I climbed Ben Lomond on a track blazed so wide by walkers that it would be impossible to miss except on the darkest of nights, but Sarah had traversed the pathless land below without anything to help, beyond her own strength and courage. Rather than take the 'tourist' route down, I opted instead for the Ptarmigan Ridge – rougher, wilder, more challenging and a little beyond what I was comfortable doing as a woman walking alone. It was nothing to the bravery shown by Sarah Stoddart Hazlitt when she walked in Scotland, but it was something.

FIVE

Harriet Martineau

For the first time in my life I am free to live as I please;
& I please to live here. My life is now (in this season)
one of wild roving, after my years of helpless sickness. I
ride like a Borderer, – walk like a pedlar, – climb like a
Mountaineer, – sometimes on excursions with kind &
merry neighbours, – sometimes all alone for the day on
the mountain.

Harriet Martineau to Ralph Waldo Emerson,
2 July 1845

Harriet Martineau was born in Norfolk, the sixth of eight children of a Unitarian minister – the descendant of Huguenot refugees from France – and his wife. Over the course of a fifty-year literary and intellectual career, Martineau built an international reputation as a sociologist, abolitionist, novelist and campaigner for women and the poor. She was also a professional journalist and travel writer whose accounts of her journeys to America and to Egypt and the Middle East were enormously popular, and she consulted with government about legal reforms and social policy in Britain. The range of her intellectual interests is intimidating, and the energy with which she pursued them exhausting; by the end of her life, she had published 35 books on topics from political economy to the methodology of sociology, to guided walks in the Lake District. Harriet Martineau was in her early forties when she wrote to her dear friend – the American essayist Ralph Waldo Emerson – in the summer of 1845, but in some ways, she had been alive for just a few months. For half a decade until the previous autumn, she had been confined to her bed in Tynemouth, a village on the coast near Newcastle, by a dangerous and persistent sickness that resisted all medical interventions. Although her literary career continued during her confinement, and although the provision of a telescope in her seaside bedroom enabled some connection with the outside world, she ached for the feel of sunshine on her body and to see once again the living green of trees: none were visible from her vantage point. At the beginning of her illness, Harriet had considered herself resigned and content with her state, though a desire to comfort distraught friends (of whom she had many) may have lain behind some of the surprisingly cheery letters written during this time. To her mentor William Johnson Fox she wrote,

> My complaint is internal, & of long standing, though not fully recognized till I was at Venice, last summer. It is likely to be of long duration, – perhaps a year or two yet, – & it is of very serious consequence. The probabilities seem to be in favour of my recovery; &, if I recover, it will be completely: but there is enough of peril in the case to prevent my reckoning on the future with any confidence. Meantime, I am most thoroughly enjoying a quiet domestic life in my

sister's house, – reading much, working & talking much, & writing a little, when able.[1]

Various diagnoses have been suggested for this 'internal complaint' but at a distance of more than a century and a half, it is impossible to be sure of the exact nature of the illness that laid her so low at the height of her literary fame and powers. Perplexed by the case, medical doctors were unable to do more than treat Harriet's considerable physical pain with quantities of opium, on which she became increasingly dependent. All hopes of a cure were eventually given up, and Harriet's life was lived for several years between her bed and her sofa, and within the one room.

On 22 June 1844 Harriet began experimenting with a new technique – mesmerism. The practice involved magnets, sweeping hand gestures and no small amount of showmanship to bring subjects into a 'trance', and had gained popularity in Britain in the 1830s. Although mesmerism's reputation frequently stuttered in medical and scientific circles, it saw a sustained revival during the 1840s and proved popular with all levels of society over the next several decades. With medical science still evolving, a range of methods and techniques were thought to be acceptable treatments, including mesmerism.[2] Regardless of its scientific status, Harriet experienced immediate effects; having occupied a world of a few square feet for nearly half a decade, within three months of her first trance, Harriet reported that she was 'Now merely infirm – not at all ill – I have left off all medicine, have lost all pain and distress – walk a mile every fine day, and bask on the headlands, like the youngest and strongest – whether the case will go on to a cure, time must show.'[3]

There are grounds to believe that Harriet's health would have recovered eventually (she herself thought, at the beginning of her illness, that this would be the case), or to consider her the beneficiary of a powerful placebo effect, but as far as Harriet was concerned, the apparently miraculous recovery was entirely owing to the powers of mesmerism. So persuaded was she of its efficacy that she became a practitioner and champion of mesmerism, to the detriment of more than one familial relationship, for the rest of her life. This rapid recovery, whatever its cause, was to prove 'life-altering', marking an utter transformation in her existence from bed-ridden invalid to a period characterized 'by physical vigour and spiritual well-being' that would last for a decade.[4] In the first flush of excitement, Harriet also decided to radically alter her circumstances: she moved permanently from Newcastle to the Lake District to establish her own home among the fells, where she would be better able to walk where she wished.

As her health improved, walking became not only the measure by which Martineau gauged her returning vigour, but the means by which she celebrated all that had been returned to her in the restoration of her body to strength: walking was, for Harriet, something wondrous. Writing ten years later in her *Autobiography* of her first weeks in the Lake District as a guest in a friend's house, she recalled how

One wintry morning, while walking to Waterhead with my host, we said 'what wonderful things do come to pass!' We looked back to that day twelve months, when I was lying, sick and suffering for my life, as every body supposed, on my couch at Tynemouth; and we wondered what I should have said if any prophet had told me that that day twelve months I should be walking in a snow storm, with a host whom I had then never seen, looking for lodgings to undergo my transformation into a Laker![5]

Through walking, Harriet completed her metamorphosis from invalid to outdoorswoman who took, in contrast to the sickly steps across her bedroom, 'firm and almost manly strides'. Her body, bronzed by the sun in which she now basked, and her face, with its 'brown hue of health', were public evidence of the efficacy of her walking cure.[6]

Walking had been integral to Harriet's life from her teenage years. Her earliest letters show that walking had long been a habit, and a much valued means through which she conducted her relationships with her siblings. Harriet's intellectual development also occurred, at least in part, on the move. Writing to her sister-in-law Helen, Harriet recounted how she enjoyed walking with her younger brother and his friend. 'You cannot think', she wrote, how 'I enjoy the long walks we have together and I think you would be amused if you could hear the long and deep arguments which we sometimes have.'[7] In 1824 the siblings had ample opportunity for discussion as they undertook a walking tour of Scotland during which they covered more than 500 miles in a month. Harriet's letter to Helen captured something, but not all, of the ambition and scale of the trip:

When we meet we will talk about these things, but writing is not like talking, and till we meet I will leave all details of our beautiful trip. Few people have seen Scotland to so much advantage as we did, for few have passed through its finest parts on foot. We were able to stop when we pleased to gaze as long as we pleased; we had nothing to attend to but our own and each other's pleasures; to be sure, we had our fill of it. I am serious, Helen, when I say that I never expect to have such another month of enjoyment and I cannot be far wrong when I say that the remembrance of it can never become tasteless or less inspired than it is now. I most of all enjoyed Loch Katrine, but neither here nor elsewhere will I attempt to describe my sense of its indescribable, unimaginable beauty . . . Next to this I especially enjoyed Killiecrankie, Shenmore, Glen Ogle, Trivardy, Glen Capel, the mountains at Loch Awe, Loch Long, the whole walk down the western banks of Loch Lomond, and oh the beautiful voyage from Glasgow to Inverary, past Arran and Bute, and up Loch Fine Tweeddale as beautiful as the noble falls of Clyde, exquisite Reekies, Melrose and Kerloch. What a Tour it was. Our delightful excursion to Roslin and Hawthorneden must not be forgotten.[8]

During their walk, the siblings covered huge swathes of Highland Perthshire and Stirlingshire, in addition to considerable portions of the lowlands, but it was James who recorded just how far they had walked. Writing in a notebook, he observed that their tour ranged

As far North as the Bruar falls and West as Loch Awe. Taking the steamer from London to Edinburgh, and the coach to Perth, we there assumed our knapsack and hand basket; and never stopped till, at the average rate of 15¼ miles per day, we had walked 530 miles.[9]

Where most tourists to the Highlands, even William and Dorothy Wordsworth, used horse-drawn vehicles at some points in their journeys, the Martineaus covered the whole distance on foot, only using boats at the beginning and end of their circuit. It was an extraordinary feat, and Harriet's letter to her sister-in-law indicates that the experience left a permanent, rapturous impression upon the young writer; this month, such a 'month of enjoyment', was so extraordinary that, at just 22, Harriet expected it never to be surpassed in her lifetime.

Yet even during this magical month of touring Scotland on foot, there was a concern that walking might, in fact, be dangerous in some way. Writing two months earlier to Helen, shortly after her and her brother's arrival in Scotland, Harriet described the 'delightful excursion' of a day spent south of Edinburgh:

We have walked a great deal about the neighbourhood, and yesterday James and I enjoyed a delicious day at Roslin & Hawthornden. We walked to Roslin after an early break-fast, spent a few hours in wandering about certainly the most beautiful scenery I ever saw, admired the exquisite chapel, and had a delightful conversation during our walk home, which we reached by 8 o'clock, perfectly untired, after having accomplished 17 miles. . . . We go to Kinross tomorrow, see Loch Leven and proceed the next day on foot to Perth, the day after to Dundee and thence to Taymouth,

Kenmore, Skillin [Killin] &c to the Western Highlands . . .
I scarcely know what to expect, but if we have many such
days as yesterday, it is not easy to tell what will become of
us. Catherine gave me your caution about walking, and we
shall bear it in mind.[10]

That 'caution' was in relation to Harriet's health, the
decline of which she would come to attribute to this tour.
Harriet later described her tour to Scotland as an 'indulgence'
granted her and her brother by their father, and declared that
she was 'certainly of opinion now that that trip aggravated
my stomach complaint'. Her only wonder was that 'it was not
worse.'[11] Even at the time, in the letter written to her sister-
in-law, there seems some hesitation about the consequences
of walking long distance, as Harriet writes that she is not sure
'what will become of us' afterwards.

The potentially negative effects of long-distance walking
on a woman's body was a particular anxiety of Harriet's,
rather than a widely held view. Twenty years later, though,
and restored to full health, she would hear these sentiments
directed at her by others. Ironically, and sadly, it was Dorothy
Wordsworth who was held up as the unfortunate example
by her family, who longed for something to blame for the
dramatic decline of her health. In her *Autobiography*, Harriet
documented a conversation between herself and William
Wordsworth, who

Was kind enough to be very anxious lest I should overwalk
myself. Both he and Mrs. Wordsworth repeatedly bade me
take warning by his sister, who had lost first her strength,

and then her sanity by extreme imprudence in that way, and its consequences. Mrs. Wordsworth told me what I could not have believed on any less trustworthy authority, – that Miss Wordsworth had – not once, but frequently, – walked forty miles in a day. In vain I assured them that I did not meditate or perpetrate any such imprudence, and that I valued my recovered health too much to hazard it for any self-indulgence whatever. It was a fixed idea with them that I walked all day long. One afternoon Mr. Atkinson and I met them on the Rydal road. They asked where we had been; and we told them. I think it was over Loughrigg ter-race to Grasmere; which was no immoderate walk. 'There, there!' said Wordsworth, laying his hand on my companion's arm. 'Take care! take care! Don't let *her* carry you about. She is killing off half the gentlemen in the county!' I could not then, nor can I now, remember any Westmoreland gentle-man, except my host in Windermere, having taken a walk with me at all.[12]

This anecdote seems to typify William Wordsworth's response to strong women walkers: an uneasy combination of anxious caution and open admiration. Dorothy Wordsworth had been William's equal as a walker, but was now housebound, and what had once been Dorothy's strength was viewed by her family as the cause of her pitiful weakness. William seems to have been worried that something similar will befall Harriet Martineau.

Harriet, however, was living proof that this supposition was wrong: walking brought life and strength to her woman's body. Just under a year after she experienced the first signs of recovery, Harriet fired off a salvo of letters from the Lake District to male correspondents, in which she crowed about her physical abilities at the expense of two unfortunate gentlemen with whom she had been walking, men who come off progressively worse as the correspondence develops. To Richard Monckton Milnes, on 18 June 1845, Harriet wrote how 'in the mountain roads, on foot, Mr Greg & Mr H[arr]y Romilly find themselves unable to keep up with me. The point of fatigue is not ascertainable' (presumably only *Harriet's* 'point of fatigue' was a mystery), while in a letter to William Johnston Fox of the same day, she wrote to say how she was 'besought by the gentlemen not to tire them out so completely.[13] On the mountain roads, I distance them altogether'.[14] Six days later, Harriet wrote to Henry Crabb Robinson in part to inform him how 'In the mountain roads, Mr Greg & Mr Hy Romilly are obliged to beg my mercy, being wholly unable to keep up with me.'[15] Poor Mr Greg and Mr Romilly. But even while Martineau conjures an amusing image of the two men broken by her physical strength, there is a striking gender reversal here – the woman is in a position of power and control. The men 'beg' her 'mercy', and she has the physical prowess to do what she will to them – either bestow upon them her presence, or leave them in her wake. Harriet not only out-walked these men, but seems to have developed physical abilities beyond ordinary human powers in a body that had become extraordinary.

Harriet's attitudes towards walking and its role in the maintenance, or destruction, of her health, were often erratic, sometimes in the same text. Although her *Autobiography* frequently claims that walking was a source of her health troubles, the text also documents how Harriet walked herself back into the world in 1845. Of a decline in health in 1833, for example, she declared that she was 'confident that the serious illness began with the toils and anxieties, and long walks in fog and mud, of two years before', but her account of the period following her release from illness in 1845 cannot find words sufficient to express the wonder and excitement at once again being able to walk.[16] On a holiday to Lenton near Nottingham in the spring of 1845, just a few months after she began to recover her health, Harriet explored the meadows by the Trent 'where crocuses almost hide the grass for a few weeks of the year'.[17] In this lovely place, she found it 'an unspeakable pleasure . . . to move freely about blossoming gardens', but felt that 'no one but a restored invalid can conceive what it was to ramble for miles, to Clifton woods, or to Wollaton, drinking in the sunshine in the fields, and the cool shade under the green avenues.'[18] Harriet described this longing for natural scenery as a 'thirst' which could only be quenched by walking in such places, a 'thirst' too intense for ordinarily well people to comprehend.[19] In this text and in others, she writes as though her illness has made her preternaturally sensitive to the emotional, physical and intellectual powers of pedestrianism.

To muddle things even further, Harriet's earlier writing makes connections between walking, intellectual activity and mental and physical well-being. In a letter to her sister-in-law Helen, Harriet recommended a strict working-day routine in which Helen was to 'Read for an hour: make an Abstract of what you have read for the next hour: read French for a third hour and so on every morning for a month'. Helen was then exhorted to 'Work *hard* in your garden, walk a great deal: not much for the sake of seeing friends, for that is apt to degenerate into *dawdling*. Go for miles at a quick pace, till you are heartily tired, go to bed early and you will sleep sound.'[20] Harriet was evidently not a fan of idleness or chit-chat, and recommended here a strict schedule that made rigorous demands of body and mind. Her own routine was perhaps a little less austere, at least when she was on visits. Staying with her brother Robert in Dudley in 1827, she wrote to Helen to tell her that

> I am very glad I came here: it is exactly the place for me. I can pursue my usual occupation when I please, & turn from it when I please to talk . . . I have been walking far and wide: from six to ten miles every day lately. I am surprized to find how very beautiful the country is; and when I once get out of the smoke, I do not know how to get back again. Jane is not a great walker just now, though very well; so I go by myself first for 6 or 8 miles, & then come in for her to walk about the Castle grounds. I do not consider it any waste of time to walk so much *just now*: it does me good & helps on my writing, which is my chief object. Nothing occupies my mind so entirely & so beneficially as writing, & I enjoy it, with the exception of letter writing.[21]

Far from being the agent of her body's destruction, walking here seems to be an important means of strengthening body and mind. There is also a clear relationship between enjoyable walking and productive writing: investing time in the one yields dividends in the other.

When Harriet recovered her health in 1845, she established a strict regime for herself based on what she felt were the stimulating properties of walking and, improving in stages, she measured her progress in the miles she was able to travel. In October 1844, she wrote to her friend Henry Crabb Robinson:

> I have not touched an opiate since Thursday noon; & no previous reducing & diluting can prevent the final relinquishment from being *very* disagreeable. A few difficult days & harassed nights are inevitable: but I have had the opiates hidden away, – so as not to be tempted . . . Every bodily function is healthy, & it is now a case of mere infirmity, – itself likely, we think, to give way. I have walked above 2 miles in one day, – spreading the exercise over some hours, & basking on the rocks between times.[22]

By the end of the month, Harriet was walking daily '3 to 5 miles without fatigue' having gone without opiates for three weeks; by January she was 'climbing hills'; and by early summer she was throwing down a note to a Miss Fenwick to say 'I am in vast haste, – being just departing on a walking trip of 3 days with Mrs Turner.'[23] Eventually she settled on a routine of an early morning walk – regardless of the weather – supplemented by daytime walks with friends and visitors whenever they chanced by. To H. G. Atkinson, she wrote in 1847 with lyrical beauty how:

> I always go out before it is quite light; and in the fine mornings I go up the hill behind the church, – the Kirkstone road, – where I reach a great height, and see from half way along Windermere to Rydal. When the little shred of moon that is left, and the morning star, hang over Wansfell,

among the amber clouds of the approaching sunrise, it is
delicious. On the positively rainy mornings, my walk is to
Pelter Bridge and back. Sometimes it is round the south end
of the valley. These early walks (I sit down to breakfast at
half-past seven) are good, among other things, in preparing
me in mind for my work. It is *very serious* work.[24]

Harriet's work, from before and after her illness and
recovery, was dependent in many ways on the ability of
walking to 'prepare' the 'mind': she was, over the course of
her career, to become, in effect, a professional walker.

In 1832, aged thirty, Harriet enjoyed her first major
literary success. That year she began publishing *Illustrations
of Political Economy*, stories intended to make understandable
for a general readership the theories of prominent political
theorists and economists, including Adam Smith and Thomas
Malthus. Here Harriet made the first of her arguments against
slavery, which for her was both a moral evil and an economical
folly: she would campaign against slavery and its degradations
for the rest of her life. For two years between 1834 and
1836, she undertook an extensive tour of the United States,
witnessing slavery for herself on the Southern plantations and
experiencing life in the former colonial states. On her return
to England, she published a work based on her observations
during this period, *Society in America* (1837). With a growing
reputation as a sociologist, Harriet followed this with a treatise
on the methodology of sociology, *How to Observe Morals and
Manners* (1838). It was in this text that Martineau laid out her
views on the proper way to conduct oneself as an observer not
only of people and society, but of nature and culture. Central

to the text was Harriet's argument that being an excellent sociologist meant being an excellent observer of humankind, something which could only properly occur if the observer took the time to walk among that which they wanted see. For Harriet, the pedestrian sociologist 'can obtain access to almost every class of persons, and learn their own views of their own affairs. His opportunities are inestimable.'[25] Walking was a means of empirical observation, a way of acquiring knowledge of the external world and of how others live. But walking, she observed in this book, also had the power to break down social or cultural barriers: on the move outside people are not, she wrote, any longer confined to rigid social strata, as they would be indoors. In her writing there is also a relationship between walking and conversation, with the pedestrian sociologist better placed than any other to get at people's 'own views of their own affairs'. Being on foot, Harriet argued, was humanity's natural habitat.

Part of the power of pedestrianism as a methodological tool for sociologists was the enormous freedom it granted. Harriet articulated at some length, and with evident personal knowledge, the intellectual, emotional and perhaps spiritual liberation experienced by those who walked:

> The pedestrian traveller is wholly free from care . . . There is no such freeman on earth as he is for the time. His amount of toil is usually within his own choice, – in any civilised region. He can go on and stop when he likes; if a fit of indolence overtakes him, he can linger for a day or a week in any spot that pleases him. He is not whirled past a beautiful view almost before he has seen it . . . He can reach almost

every point his wishes wander to. The pleasure is indescribable of saying to one's self, 'I will go there,' – 'I will rest
yonder,' – and forthwith accomplishing it. He can sit on a
rock in the midst of a rushing stream as often in a day as he
likes. He can hunt a waterfall by its sound; a sound which
the carriage-wheels prevent other travellers from hearing. He
can follow out any tempting glade in any wood. There is no
cushion of moss at the foot of an old tree that he may not sit
down on if he pleases . . . His food is welcome, be its quality
what it may, while he eats it under the alders in some recess
of a brook. He is secure of his sleep, be his chamber ever so
sordid; and when his waking eyes rest upon his knapsack, his
heart leaps with pleasure as he remembers where he is and
what a day is before him. Even the weather seems to be of
less consequence to the pedestrian than to other travellers.
A pedestrian journey presupposes abundance of time, so that
the traveller can rest in villages on rainy days, and in the shade
of a wood during the hours when the sun is too powerful.[26]

It is immediately evident that the importance of walking
goes beyond the opportunities for objective observation,
and strays into more aesthetic and impressionistic areas. All
aspects were important to the serious sociologist, for Harriet;
she snootily dismissed fashionable tourists who 'want to see
pictures'. Let them 'be satisfied with learning what they can
from the windows by the way', she adjured, because 'if they
want to see either scenery or people, let all who have strength
and courage go on foot'.[27]

In 1845, newly recovered, Martineau arrived in the
Lake District with the determination to make herself into a

'Laker', rather than being simply part of the much-maligned tourist horde.[28] She had fallen in love with the area early in her convalescence, when she arrived as a guest at Waterhead with the determination of 'Basking in the summer sunshine, and roving over hill and dale in fine weather, and reading and working beside the window overlooking the lake (Windermere) in rainy hours, when lakes have a beauty of their own.'[29] She acted quickly to purchase land near Ambleside, where, over the winter of 1845–6, she built a house, 'The Knoll'. Here she would reside, the odd trip excepted, for the rest of her life. Later, Harriet recalled how, 'If I am to give an account of my most deep-felt pleasures, I may well mention that of my sunset walks, on the few fine days [that winter], when I saw from the opposite side of the valley the progress of my house.'[30] From here she set about following her own advice to seek out 'every class of person' and to learn their 'own views of their own affairs', this time as a pedestrian intent on a new epistemological project to observe and to know the Lake District. The task she set herself was 'to become acquainted with the Lake District, in a complete and orderly manner' so as to obtain a sense of 'real command', in much the same way as she had obtained mastery in other areas of intellectual activity including language, political economy and history.[31] Such a task, though, by necessity required brain and body: the knowledge Harriet sought could only be acquired by walking, and the Lakes were to become known to her through her feet as much as through her mind. In her *Autobiography*, she recalled how she approached the project:

Now, on my recovery, I set myself to learn the Lake District, which was still a *terra incognita*, veiled in bright mists before my mind's eye: and by the close of a year from the purchase of my field, I knew every lake (I think) but two, and almost every mountain pass . . . Of these joyous labours, none has been sweeter than that of my first recovered health, when Lakeland became gradually disclosed before my exploration, till it lay before me, map-like, as if seen from a mountain top.[32]

Harriet's language is of the explorer, of the discoverer of remote lands. It is also the language of the cartographer, keen to chart and measure and quantify, scientifically and systematically. Yet it is also that of the humble student, eager to 'learn the Lake District' – not its geography, or its history – but as a subject worthy in its own right of intense study and effort. And with its closing image, of Harriet stood upon a peak looking down on a land mapped with her body and imagined into totality in her mind, she is an explorer, like 'stout Cortez' in Keats's poem 'On First Looking into Chapman's Homer'.[33]

To 'learn the Lake District' so thoroughly in just twelve months was an extraordinary physical feat. With sixteen major bodies of water, numberless tarns and lesser pools, a dozen major mountain passes and a physical area of nearly a thousand miles, Harriet's claims to have knowledge of all but two lakes and almost all passes might seem overstated, especially as they were made retrospectively. However, her letters from the period demonstrate that she undertook a huge amount of walking over a short space of time. On 6 July 1846, she wrote to her friend Hugh Seymour Tremenheere from Scale Hill Inn near Crummock Water in the northeastern corner of the Lake District, to apologize for the poor-quality letter in which she regaled him with tales of her current excursion:

> Excuse journey ink. I am on a walking trip of 5 days with a dear niece & nephew from Birmm: & when I have done this, we shall set out in a drenching rain for a walk of 12 miles to Keswick, – there being no chance here of either horses or the weather clearing. Till yesy, our weather was perfect, & we saw whole days' full of exquisite sights. Yesy, we happily had a guide in crossing Blake Fell, – from Ennerdale water to Crummock. We set out in brilliant sunshine, – saw the thunder come up from the sea, had a vast wind, first in our faces, & then suddenly in our backs (throwg me flat) & then the storm closed down upon us & round us, while we saw, far far below, the vales & lakes lying in the calmest sunshine. In 3 minutes we were wet through & through, – waterproof knapsacks & all. We are thankful to have seen such a sight, – as new to me as to the youngsters. They are full of life & spirit, & capital travellers.[34]

Showing rather more equanimity in the face of a drenching than is typical among walkers (myself included), Harriet seems to have relished the adventure of the terrible weather on the remote Blake Fell. If there is a thrill in this letter, however, Harriet seems rather less enamoured at the idea of setting out into relentless soaking rain. Neither her spirits nor her knapsack would remain dampened for long, though: four days later, she wrote again to tell Tremenheere, happily, that 'We had a pleasant walk after all, on Monday night; – walked

17 miles, without undue fatigue, & reached our dear home that night'.[35] Nor was this everything. After barely a night's rest at her new home, Harriet was off again with her (apparently indefatigable) niece and nephew, both of whom seem to have fared rather better in Harriet's company than the unfortunate Romilly and Greg. To Richard Cobden she wrote, on the cusp of walking out of her door again, that

> Now presently, I am going to shoulder my knapsack, &
> march up Kirkstone pass, on my way to Patterdale, with a
> niece & nephew from Birmingham. We walk over the whole
> country, – for days together, crowned with lightening on
> mountain tops, & astonishing the natives in the valleys.
> I need not after this say that I am well.[36]

Harriet was hardly exaggerating in her description of walking 'over the whole country': in little more than a week, she had crossed much of the Lake District from west to east – a distance of around 30 miles as the crow flies, and a great deal more as the human travails over pass, lake and weather. It is unlikely that 'the natives in the valleys' were the only ones 'astonished' at Harriet's prodigious pedestrianism.

The desire to 'know' the Lake District through walking was clearly an important part of Harriet's process of becoming a proper 'Laker': traversing its many high passes, and circumnavigating its plentiful and sizeable waters helped to connect her to her new home imaginatively and physically, as well as reinforcing the totality of her recovery. But the acquisition of such knowledge served other, more professional, purposes too. According to her *Autobiography*, it was as a direct consequence of her eagerness to know the country that she was 'complimented with the task of writing a Complete Guide to the Lakes', which represented for her 'the most satisfactory testimony on the part of my neighbours that they believed I understood their beloved District'.[37] Harriet did indeed write a *Complete Guide to the English Lakes*, which was published in 1855, but from 1850 she also published, in the American *Sartain's Union Magazine of Literature and Art*, 'A Year at Ambleside' a month at a time. The success of both works rested on the unique combination of experience Harriet possessed; not only did they make much of the knowledge acquired by Martineau through her hill-walking, but they made extensive use of the powers of detailed observation perfected over years spent as a sociological observer. Both the *Complete Guide* and 'A Year at Ambleside' were also alert to the importance of the author's own literary fame, and the literary connections of the place in which she has chosen to reside, in making the texts – and the Lake District – attractive to readers.

That the presence of the author herself was an important selling point is made explicit from the beginning of 'A Year at Ambleside', where Harriet's biography is immediately woven into the ways in which the text engages with the place:

> When I came to live here, I soon learned that if I wished for a calm, meditative walk after my morning's work, I had better go up this valley of the Brathay, where I was sure never to meet anybody. I could look from its high church-yard upon its unsurpassed view, and then go down and skirt Loughrigg, and lean upon a gate, or rest upon a heathery perch of rock, without much probability of seeing a face

for three hours together. Whereas, if I was tired of thinking, and socially inclined, I had better take my way up the
other valley – that of the Rotha, where the little town of
Ambleside nestles under the shelter of the swelling Wansfell,
and which is scattered over with dwellings throughout its
circuit. In going round this valley, a walk of about five miles
from my friend's house, it was pretty certain that we should
meet the majority of our acquaintances on any fine winter
afternoon.[38]

The reader is treated to Harriet's daily habits as a walker
and as an intellectual, and this creates a powerful sense
of intimacy between reader and writer. That intimacy is
furthered by Harriet's inclusion of the reader in these walks
through the use of pronouns such as 'we', 'our' and 'us'. They
are not simply reading about the walks taken by a famous
writer, but are being taken on those walks *by* that writer: from
the description of Harriet's individual preferences, the text
sweeps up the reader with a gentle, though insistent, 'Well,
we go down the road to the toll bar', 'we see' or 'We leave the
highway now'.[39] There is more to this than companionship,
though. As the walk around the neighbourhood progresses,
Harriet points out to her reader not just the sights, but the
people of interest, so that within the space of a page, we have
mentioned not only the hills of Loughrigg, Nab Scar and the
Fairfield horseshoe, but Fox How, which 'Everyone knows'
is 'the abode so beloved by Dr. Arnold', 'Lady Le Fleming's
large, staring, yellow mansion', 'Wordsworth's cottage' and
the 'large gray house built by the brother of Sir Humphry
Davy', in addition to a description of the location of Harriet's

home at the heart of a place populated by social, intellectual and literary luminaries.[40]

In much the same way, Harriet's accounts of her walking are linked carefully to the illustrious history of the Lake District, especially its recent literary history. In the entry for March, she takes the reader with her up Loughrigg, before turning attention to the higher mountains enclosing Grasmere and Ambleside:

The circuit of mountains shows every variety of wooded ravine, with a waterfall here and there, seen glittering in the intervals, and grassy slopes, and a few gray stone dwellings, which indicate that the scene is enjoyed by human residents. Off to the left (the north-west), Easedale opens grandly – the position of the summits telling that a solemn valley lies among them. Immediately opposite, on the level at the end of the lake, stands the old-fashioned little church of Grasmere, with the village gathered about it. A little to the right, running due north, and mounting the long ascent of Dunmail Raise, is the road (like a mere path now to our eyes) which passes by the foot of Helvellyn to Keswick. Faint and far appear the Keswick mountains – Skiddaw and Saddleback; and nearer, and swelling up boldly from the Raise, is old Helvellyn. That white house, somewhat nearer to us, is the Swan Inn, where Scott used to have his daily draught and chat with the landlord, when he was Wordsworth's guest, when both were young men; and where they and Southey met, to begin the ascent of Helvellyn.[41]

The reader is alongside Harriet on this mental tour of the nearby mountains, invited to stand with her at a very precisely described point from which all the natural and intellectual wonders of the valley can be seen. Harriet herself climbed Helvellyn on at least one occasion, along with Skiddaw and Blencathra (as Saddleback is now more commonly known), and her knowledge of this mountain, and the deep bowl of Easedale, is apparent. The consequence is not only the creation of an authoritative account of the area, but of a tangible link between the earlier generation of walker-writers of Sir Walter Scott, William Wordsworth, Robert Southey and Harriet herself: she follows in their footsteps literally, as well as imaginatively and poetically.

Harriet did not stop there, but sweeps the reader up with her to walk what becomes a kind of pedestrian pilgrimage of the valley's literary shrines:

> Then on – briskly – for it is an hour later than we supposed – on, by the winding road, past the water cure establishment of St Oswald's – on through Grasmere, under the church tower, over the bridge, rounding the lake all the time – past the cottage where Wordsworth lived with his sister before he married – up and up, passing over the Roman road, to go by a still higher, and shorter, and more beautiful cut over the promontory – past a little tarn: – down upon Rydal quarries, where we join the mail road – past Hartley Coleridge's dwelling on the brink of the lake, where he, standing in the porch, offers his peculiar salutation of a bow, almost to the ground, hat in hand – past the row of noble sycamores, where we have no time to rest now, seated on

the roots; past the foot of Rydal Mount – past Pelter Bridge again, and home . . . we have walked ten miles.[42]

Everything in this passage comes out of Harriet's repeated walking of the local area, from her understanding of which is the most 'beautiful cut' down onto Rydal, to her knowledge that to get home in time the pace needs to be significantly quicker: she is an authority on the area, and authoritative. What is on offer to the reader is privileged access to this famous place – access that can only be provided by a knowledgeable and long-standing resident. But implicit in these entries of 'A Year at Ambleside' is access to Harriet herself, whose home – frequently mentioned and described – becomes as much a literary landmark as Wordsworth's early home, or Hartley Coleridge and his bow.

Harriet would do the same when she published *Complete Guide to the English Lakes*, only this time she was writing herself into the literary landscape not as an aspirant successor to the legacy of William Wordsworth, Coleridge and Southey, but as a rival. Wordsworth's *A Guide through the District of the Lakes in the North of England* had first been published in 1810 as an essay accompanying a book of sketches of the local area, and it was reprinted several times during the next forty years, over which time it came to be known as *A Complete Guide to the Lake District*; Harriet's choice of an almost-identical title for her own work could well have been a deliberate strategy to profit from the popularity of Wordsworth's text. According to the literary critic Alexis Easley,

Wordsworth, like Martineau, seemed to view the publication of a guidebook as a self-authorizing act meant to forge a connection between a sense of place and a sense of his own career as a writer. By creating textual representations of the landscape through literary acts of self-representation, both writers hoped to locate themselves and their writing careers on the map of England.[43]

The tone of Harriet's *Guide* is one of solicitous, empathetic concern for what the inexperienced walker would most like to see, offering itineraries and hints about transportation as well as kit lists, insight into the most beautiful nooks of the area, and understanding of the physical demands of walking in the area. Early in the text, Harriet describes the climb up to Easedale Tarn near Grasmere, a long walk up the moderately steep ghyll that flows from the tarn, with the body of water invisible to the walker until the very last moment:

At last, when he is heated and breathless, the dark cool recess opens in which lies Easedale Tarn. Perhaps there is an angler standing besides the great boulder on the brink. Perhaps there is a shepherd lying amongst the ferns. But more probably the stranger finds himself perfectly alone. There is perhaps nothing in natural scenery which conveys such an impression of stillness as tarns which lie under precipices: and here the rocks sweep down to the brink almost round the entire margin. For hours together the deep shadows move only like the gnomon of the sundial; and, when movement occurs, it is not such as disturbs the sense of repose; – the dimple made by a restless fish or fly, or the gentle flow of water in or out; or the wild drake and his brood, paddling so quietly as not to break up the mirror, or the reflection of some touch of sunlight, or passing shadow.[44]

The reader is brought by Harriet to the edge of the tarn, a place of extraordinary peace and stillness. Yet while we can, sweating and breathless, follow the path described to the water's edge, it would take many more visits to be able to exist in this place as quietly and unobtrusively as Harriet herself: as a result of her repeated walks to this place, she seems to have disappeared within the grasses and tussocks that surround the water.

If readers are 'invited' to accompany Harriet on her walks, they are commanded to ascend the mountains of the Lake District. In a chapter dedicated to considering 'A Day on the Mountains', she informs the reader that before he leaves the old county of Westmorland 'He must spend a day on the Mountains: and if alone, so much the better', because 'If he knows what it is to spend a day so far above the every-day world, he is aware that it is good to be alone.'[45] He must also go equipped with a 'stout stick', a 'knapsack' for provisions (an item that Harriet herself carried on every walk), a 'map' to 'explain to him what he sees' and a 'pocket compass in case of sudden fog'.[46] And, of course, a copy of her guide, which is itself 'a necessary addition to the literary walker's kit bag' because it will 'guide and shape the traveller's experience of the natural setting'.[47] After rejecting several possible walks, including the ascent of Coniston Old Man (too long a walk 'for the day's treat') and Loughrigg ('not commanding enough'), the Fairfield horseshoe is selected as the perfect walk for the mountain-loving tourist.[48] Having offered a description of the climb, Harriet outlined what the reader–walker might expect to see higher up:

> The finest point of the whole excursion is about the middle of the *cul-de-sac*, where, on the northern sides, there are tremendous precipices, overlooking Deepdale, and other sweet recesses far below. Here, within hearing of the torrents which tumble from those precipices, the rover should rest. He will see nothing so fine as the contrast of this northern view with the long green slope on the other side, down to the source of Rydal Beck, and then down and down to Rydal Woods and Mount. He is now 2,950 feet above the sea level; and he has surely earned his meal . . .
>
> The further he goes, the more amazed he is at the extent of the walk, which looked such a trifle from below.[49]

It is a matter of opinion whether the Fairfield horseshoe ever appears a 'trifle' – it is a long day from Grasmere, with steep climbs out of the valley bottom, but Harriet certainly spoke from her own experience when delineating the great beauties of the walk, and the triumph of ascending to such a height. Her account of the descent from the ridge, though, is sad and regretful – it seems a pulling back or retreat from a special place, or perhaps a special state of being. At Nab Scar, at the end of the horseshoe, the tourist

> Must take his last complete survey; for from hence he must plunge down the steep slope, and bid farewell to all that lies behind the ridge. The day has gone like an hour. The sunshine is leaving the surface of the nearer lakes, and the

purple bloom of the evening is on the furthest mountains;
and the gushes of yellow light between the western passes
show that sunset is near. He must hasten down . . . is driven
home, and is amazed . . . to find how stiff and tired he is.
He would not, however, but have spent such a day for ten
times the fatigue.[50]

The use of the present tense creates a powerful sense
of immediacy in this passage, and underlines the urgency
of the descent from the hills with the last of the light. The
lyrical description of the mountains at the day's close does
more than this, though, by inviting the reader to experience
the region's 'geography through the lens provided by a
famous writer, whose interpretation of the landscape is more
authentic' because it is rooted in repeated walking and longer
acquaintance. In consequence, Lakeland tourists are able to
access an interpretation that is 'more real' than their own,
'unmediated experiences and impressions of place'.[51] Memories
of walks of the Fairfield horseshoe will therefore be interlaced
with Harriet's description, and the reader's experiences shaped
by hers.

The journey over the Fairfield horseshoe was just one
of the walks included by Martineau in her *Guide*. Detailed
descriptions of hikes up Skiddaw, Blencathra, the Langdale
Pikes (complete with options for descending into Easedale or
Borrowdale), 'Scawfell', the Kentmere round and Helvellyn
via the ridge of 'Catchdecam' (Catstycam) testify to Harriet's
love of high ground. This passion is also evident in the way
the text slips at times between dispassionate delineations of
routes and topography and something more personal, as in

the description of the mountain pass at Esk Hause linking Eskdale, Borrowdale, Langstrath, Langdale and Wasdale at the heart of the Lake District:

> There is also a very rough path at Langdale Head up Rosset Ghyll, answering on the left to the Stake road on the right . . . This track leads by Esk Hause and Sprinkling Tarn to the Sty Head Pass. This is truly a glorious mountain walk. From Esk Hause, there is a singular view, composed of three lines of landscape . . . When we were on Esk Hause, the spectacle of these three lines of landscape was remarkable. Towards Keswick, the atmosphere was thick, just to the degree that gave a visionary character to the long perspective . . . In the direction of Eskdale, all was bright and glittering; while from Langdale and the head of Borrowdale the white mists came tumbling out towards us, as if to stifle us; and nothing could be seen, except at intervals, when a whiff of wind disclosed long sweeps of the sides of the valleys, and stretches of the streams and fields below. It is these changes that give a singular charm to this mountain district.[52]

The 'we' that encompassed the writer and the reader earlier in the text here gives way to an unknown 'we' that does not include the reader. Excluded from the companionable 'us' observing these shifting patterns of light and colour on the hillside, the reader can only imagine in envy the beauties of the day's walking Harriet describes.

Throughout the *Guide*, Harriet's writing evidences her hard-won walking experience, whether in detailed accounts of how to navigate key mountain passes, or in her instinctive empathy for the fatigued walker – she describes Sty Head tarn as the 'little clear rippling lake, where the mountaineer throws himself down to rest on the bank, when heated by the ascent from the vales'.[53] The water is also handy, I discovered one blazing June, for those heated by a long descent of Scafell Pike via the Corridor Route. I had fantasized about swimming in the tarn since I spotted it from the mountain's summit, and when I got there, I swam across it twice, the cold water even more delicious and refreshing than I had imagined.

The publication in 1855 of *A Complete Guide to the Lakes* marked the end of Harriet's life as a walker-writer. The year before she had acknowledged that her body, now more than fifty years old, was not what it had been. In a letter to a friend sent not long before the publication of the *Guide*, she wrote,

> I was up Kirkstone Pass with some friends in Octr, & we saw a party up the mountain, – looking like mites on a pinnacle of cheese. – I thought of you then, & that tremendous scramble you must have had that Sunday. If you had died on the spot, I shd not have wondered. The mountain is practicable enough; but then, it takes time, – much more time than you had that day. –
>
> I don't climb mountains now; & I am assuming the elderly title wh will, I think, be a great convenience to me, – of 'Mrs Harriet Martineau'.[54]

Trading in her waterproof knapsack for the honorific 'Mrs' – a title then accorded out of respect to women of importance and influence regardless of marital status – Harriet's letter articulates a fundamental shift in her perspective. Instead of the imagined 'summit peak' from which she intended to have the Lake District open out before her mind's eye, or the perilous scramble up a precipitous mountain, she would once again be returned to the rather flatter view of her bedroom window. In 1855, she was diagnosed with a heart condition which she believed would prove fatal and, at 'the end of a decade of remarkable physical vigour . . . she never left her Ambleside home again'. She was 'Convinced she would die at any moment', and 'resigned herself to the invalid life'.[55] Reflecting shortly after her return to confinement in a letter to Lord Carlisle, Harriet told him,

> You would find our valley as beautiful as ever, though there are great changes among the inhabitants . . . Ten years have made a great change; but somehow, life seems the richer & the more solemn & sweet for all natural experiences, whether we call them joyous or sad. And the gradual leaving of life, with the experiences of the process, is the sweetest of all.[56]

It is a magnanimous reflection in the face of great anxiety and disappointment that could perhaps only be made by somebody who had known total immobility and who had been returned to good health and vitality. In the ten years of her remarkable recovery, Harriet covered thousands of miles of the Lake District's roads, byways and fell sides, and found in her walking pleasure and purpose, comfort and life. Recognized in her own time as a walker-writer to rival the Lake poets who put the area on the literary map, it is important we recognize that the map we carry of walking's history is incomplete without her.

I HAD NOT HEARD about Harriet Martineau when I first saw the fells of Lakeland in February 2008. I'd been walking in the Yorkshire Dales, gradually building up to more challenging outings, and I had recently climbed Whernside. I thought I knew hills, but the rounded humps of Yorkshire proved to be nothing compared to the sustained majesty I encountered as I drove through the Lakes towards Keswick. I fell in love immediately. I was there to attend a conference on the Lakeland poet Robert Southey, organized by a man I had become friendly with over the previous few months. At the end of the conference Tim invited me to climb a peak with him. Not knowing then that climbing mountains in winter is difficult and dangerous, in my ignorance, I said yes.

Our aim was to climb Great Gable. Gazing in wonder at the map the night before, I enjoyed the feel of the Cumbrian place names on my tongue, and was delighted that we would ascend by Sourmilk Gill. I was less pleased the next morning when I saw how steep the climb would be next to the beck. All romance vanished as the hard reality of climbing nearly 2,625 feet of winter mountain gradually revealed itself. I remember hours of slog, often with Tim waiting in the far distance for me to huff and puff my slow way towards him. On the boulders that make up Great Gable's summit, Tim disappeared, vanishing ahead on a pathless slope, leaving me feeling suddenly very exposed and afraid. Knowing no other way to proceed, I ambled upwards, relieved to find the top of the mountain was closer than I had feared. It was icy, though, and incredibly slippery. We had no crampons, no ice axes – and I would not have known what to do with them if we had.

The descent was even more frightening than the lonely final climb had been. I opted to slide down the ice on my backside, using my legs for brakes and my arms for emergencies. For a time, I made excellent progress, but without warning, my trousers snagged on a rock. I stood up on the next bit of safe ground to examine the damage. As I felt behind, I realized the seat of my trousers was flapping in the wind, and my underwear was on full view. No matter – we had not seen another soul all day and we were heading down a steep scree run to the mountain pass, where the wind would be calmer. We walked on, Tim leading while I tried to keep some semblance of dignity by keeping my behind behind. I managed moderately well, until the moment we dropped down onto the pass – and emerged into a large group of teenage boys on their Duke of Edinburgh expedition. It was mortifying, but my embarrassment did not last long. Next to me, Tim was pointing out the wonders that surrounded us: Great End, Scafell and Scafell Pike. Wastwater. Borrowdale. Paths arrived at the pass from all directions, their origins mysterious and tantalizing. As I stood there at the central point of the Lakeland mountains, my backside chilled and exposed, my mind raced with the thrilling thought that I could explore every path, peek into every valley. How much more wonderful would it have been to have known that I was feeling then what Harriet Martineau felt when she realized where her newly strong body could take her?

SIX

Virginia Woolf

One day walking round Tavistock Square I made up, as I sometimes make up my books, *To the Lighthouse*; in a great, apparently involuntary, rush. One thing burst into another. Blowing bubbles out of a pipe gives the feeling of the rapid crowd of ideas and scenes which blew out of my mind, so that my lips seemed syllabling of their own accord as I walked. What blew the bubbles? Why then? I have no notion.

Virginia Woolf, *Moments of Being*

Virginia Woolf, strolling around the tree-lined squares of Bloomsbury, becomes the passive instrument for a great creative force which inhabits the rhythm of her footsteps, and *To the Lighthouse* appears to emerge through some form of 'automatic writing'. The force propelling the words is not an external spirit, however, but the gentle jolting of the walking body: the ideas are given shape by the body, and map directly onto its dimensions. Woolf's footsteps elicit from Woolf's lips the syllables of her novel, so it is paced into existence.

Walking features in every type of Woolf's writing, and in many of the most important of her experiences. At various points in her life, it served as a health-giver, friendship-maker, memory and muse, and was key to the composition of a number of her most celebrated novels. It was both habitual and remarkable, an act of defiance and an act of submission. Nor did Woolf discriminate between the walks of wide-open spaces and remoteness, and the strolling of city pavements, but explores in her work the role played by all kinds of pedestrianism.

Walking was a feature of Woolf's life from her youngest days, especially during childhood holidays in St Ives, where her family rented a house for a number of years. Later, while residing in Sussex in her thirties, Woolf lived a pedestrian life that would have been quite recognizable to Dorothy Wordsworth. As Wordsworth did, Woolf gathered on these walks observations of the natural world. In a diary entry, Woolf recorded how she 'Went to post at Southease . . . Home over downs. Fair haul of mushrooms again, but in hollow.'[1] This kind of walking – domestic necessity blended with habit and desire – was at the heart of Woolf's daily routine for weeks. As the season changed from summer to autumn, the raids on local mushroom troves were replaced by earnest blackberrying. Meanwhile, the weather worsened, though the walks continued, sometimes alone, sometimes with company and frequently on long-familiar paths. On other occasions, Woolf would determine, suddenly, to try a new route, its qualities to be evaluated later in her diary. Though life did not always allow it, Woolf made for herself wherever she could an existence rooted in these daily wanderings on foot. For Woolf, walking was where she found companionship, happiness and inspiration.

Pacing – the timing of key moments throughout a text – matters to all novels, but in Woolf's case, the pacing was literal and physical: the plots of her fiction were frequently paced out by the author as she walked. The plots too were, on occasion, driven by pedestrianism, so that Mrs Dalloway's internal life, for instance, unfolds as she strolls through London. Woolf herself set out on walks in search of characters and situations, a hunter of the remarkable, running down her prey, 'those wild beasts, our fellow men', at 3 mph.[2] The habit of seeking out stories and incidents, phrases and ideas, so permeated Woolf's walking that even when there was no medium beyond letters or diary entries to record what came to her, Woolf's walking still provoked fantastical scenes and shimmering images.

It was a habit born early in Woolf, and one that would shape how she approached both walking and writing throughout her life. In Norfolk in 1906, with her beloved sister, the artist Vanessa Bell, the 24-year-old Virginia Stephen wrote how 'Nessa paints windmills in the afternoon, and I tramp the country for miles with a map, leap ditches, scale walls and desecrate churches, making out beautiful brilliant stories every step of the way.'[3] The contrast between Vanessa's quiet occupation, quietly painting peaceable windmills, and Virginia's wild roaming lies not only in Woolf's choice of language, but in the differences of their creative practices: Vanessa's windmills sit quietly and patiently by while she captures them in her brushstrokes, but Virginia's 'brilliant stories' emerge from her transgressive walking. Describing herself as a 'tramp', Woolf associates herself with vagrancy, of existing outside the ordinary bounds of settled society – with echoes of Elizabeth Carter two centuries earlier. The impression of unruliness is enhanced by her 'desecration' of churches, and her unfeminine 'leaping' and 'scaling' of obstacles man-made and natural. Woolf's creativity requires action – illicit and unlawful action at that. That there was a link between her tendency to wildness, her walking and her literary activities was acknowledged by Woolf herself. In Yorkshire earlier that year, she had written to Violet Dickinson that

> There is a Greek austerity about my life which is beautiful and might go straight into a bas relief. You can imagine that I never wash, or do my hair; but stride with gigantic strides over the wild moorside, shouting odes of Pindar, as I leap from crag to crag, and exulting in the air that buffets me, and caresses me, like a stern but affectionate parent. That is Stephen Brontëized; almost as good as the real thing.[4]

The literariness of this account is stylized, ironic and knowing, but it is nonetheless significant that the young Virginia Stephen, an aspiring writer alone on the Yorkshire moors above Giggleswick, turns to Emily Brontë and her wild tales of lovers on the rugged moorland as her pattern.

Two years later, when Woolf was composing what would become her first novel, *The Voyage Out*, published in 1915, her letters suggest a tension between the desire – and need – for the creative wildness described in her earlier correspondence, and the necessity of sitting quietly and physically writing down her ideas. To her brother-in-law, Clive Bell, she wrote,

I think a great deal of my future, and settle what book I am
to write – how I shall re-form the novel and capture multitudes of things at present fugitive, enclose the whole, and
shape infinite strange things. I take a good look at woods
in the sunset, and fix men who are breaking stones with an
intense gaze, meant to sever them from the past and the
future – all these excitements last out my walks, but tomorrow I know, I shall be sitting down to the inanimate old
phrases . . . I am going to contrive a scheme as I walk.[5]

Writing without walking was, for Woolf, inert, dead,
'inanimate'. Only by placing her body into physical animation
did she feel capable of animating her words, of giving life to
sentences. On the move, Woolf had the mental power to carve
out time, to 'sever' men from their 'past and the future', to
hold them with her 'gaze' wholly in the moment. Such exciting
possibilities compare sadly with the weary inevitability of being
compelled to 'sit down', with no power to bring life to dead
expression. The only solution, of course, was to go for a walk.

This would prove to be the case throughout Woolf's life,
though she got better at balancing the urge to walk that
enabled the creative connection between feet and brain, and
the need to write down what her body had brought into being.
There continued to be a tension between these impulses, but
it was increasingly a creative tension: 'I keep thinking', she
wrote in her diary for 3 November 1918, 'of different ways
to manage my scenes; conceiving endless possibilities; seeing
life, as I walk about the streets, an immense opaque block of
material to be conveyed by me into its equivalent of language.'[6]
Such pedestrianism also brought its dangers. Walking around

London in the evening, Woolf 'rambled down to Charing Cross in the dark, making up phrases & incidents to write about. Which is, I expect, the way one gets killed.'[7] It is easy to imagine Woolf wandering abstractedly around London composing, in an urban parallel of William Wordsworth's pacing of his poems into being along the path in his back garden at Dove Cottage.

Becoming absorbed in her work was rather more perilous for Woolf in the traffic-filled streets of London, though it was a danger she found stimulating. On 28 March 1930, she recorded how 'I walked along Oxford Street. The buses are strung on a chain. People fight and struggle. Knocking each other off the pavement. Old bareheaded men; a motor car accident; &c.'[8] It is a scene of anarchy and violence; the percussive phrases slap against the punctuation, mirroring the pugilistic behaviour Woolf witnesses. And yet, she declares, 'To walk alone in London is the greatest rest.' Being on foot both soothed and stimulated Woolf, keeping quiet the gnawing doubts about her own literary abilities that crept in when her mental health weakened and she became vulnerable to the paralysing depression that struck from time to time. If she was lucky, her boot-clad feet could outpace her distress. When anxiety began to gain upon her during the writing of *Jacob's Room* in 1920, it was through images and metaphors of walking that she tried to understand what was happening to her mind. On 25 October, she asked her diary 'why is life so tragic; so like a little strip of pavement over an abyss. I look down; I feel giddy; I wonder how I am ever to walk to the end.'[9] Woolf imagined her mental health in topographical terms: madness was the plunging, disorienting abyss, and its proximity caused the internal equivalent of vertigo. Yet control, and hope, remained: the way may have been narrow, but it could be traversed by a walker, just as a narrow mountain arête could. The topography is certainly frightening, but it is not alien – the pavement, if not the abyss, belong to the modern world, and to London; and while the head might falter and become dizzy, the feet will find a way. Certainly, this is how Woolf understood the landscape of her mind: she observed two weeks later how 'I have walked some way further along the strip of pavement without falling in.'[10] She does not mention whether this mental pavement walking was achieved on this occasion in parallel with the physical walking of London's pavements, but the link between the two – into and out of the self – is evident throughout Woolf's work.

This can be seen in two contrasting diary entries: one from August 1921, written when Woolf was recovering from another attack of mental ill health; the other written at the height of the creative burst that yielded *Mrs Dalloway*, three years later almost to the day. The earlier entry fizzes with frustrated energies, the consequence of being forbidden to work – or to walk:

> Nothing to record; only an intolerable fit of the fidgets to write away. Here I am chained to my rock: forced to do nothing: doomed to let every wrong, spite, irritation & obsession scratch & claw & come again. This is to say that I may not walk, & I must not work . . . what wouldn't I give to be coming through Firle woods, dusty & hot, with my nose turned home, every muscle tired, & the brain laid up in sweet lavender, so sane & cool, & ripe for the morrows

task. How I should notice everything – the phrase for it coming the moment after & fitting like a glove; & then on the dusty road . . . so my story would begin telling itself.[11]

Woolf appears as Prometheus, helpless and 'chained', a victim of the gods' punishment and forced into inactivity while a vulture pecks away at her mind. She is compelled to remain still, inert, unanimated: it is not just phrases and sentences that are left lifeless in the absence of walking. The contrast that Woolf draws between her inactive self and her self-on-the-move is total. The submissiveness of the first sentences, with their passive voice and agentless verbs, gives way to a scene of intense doing, replete with verbs and adverbs which bring vitality and vibrancy. This description of walking yokes the whole body to the purposes of writing and being afoot: the extreme fatigue of the muscles yields a curious harvest of 'sweet lavender' for the brain; as the body grows hot, the brain becomes cool. Walking thereby becomes an important safety mechanism, so that the body, and not the mind, is left 'dusty & hot'. As a result, it is also the means of turning physical energy into intellectual perspicuity: as the body moves, the eye sees, and the words are formed in a seamless, pauseless process. Curiously, the final result is a return to passivity, with the 'story' beginning to 'tell itself', independent of any creative agent. As with Woolf's description of composing *To the Lighthouse* on foot, this has a hint of the automatic about it. Woolf's mind when walking is highly susceptible to the motion of the feet.

This connection between the creative powers of the mind and the motion of the feet becomes clear in Woolf's description of bringing *Mrs Dalloway* to completion:

> I think I can go straight at the grand party & so end; forgetting Septimus, which is a very intense and ticklish business, & jumping Peter Walsh eating his dinner, which may be some obstacle too. But I like going from one lighted room to another, such is my brain to me; lighted rooms; & the walks in the fields are the corridors.[12]

Woolf imagines here a curious mental geography which blurs the features of a London townhouse with the rather different furniture of the countryside. The internal topography of Woolf's mind maps onto that of the external world, and vice versa, so that without a body with which to pace the routes in (and into) physical existence, the brightly lit rooms inside Woolf's brain would be left isolated, unconnected, inaccessible. On foot, Woolf walks out into the fields and into her mind. So enmeshed were walking and writing for Woolf that she came to see working on a novel *as* a form of walking. Early on in the development of *Jacob's Room*, she noted to herself how 'Directly one gets to work one is like a person walking, who has seen the country stretching out before.'[13] For Woolf, without the vocabulary of walking to shape and contain how she imagined the world, writing would have been impossible.

All of Woolf's writing – her diaries, letters and fiction – connects walking with thinking. Returning to her family's house in St Ives in 1909 after a period away, Woolf quickly settled down into a rhythm of walking, thinking, reading and imagining that would be the pattern for much of her life, where walking became the fuel that sustained and fired all her mental activities:

After dinner is a very pleasant time. One feels in the mood for phrases, as one sits by the fire, thinking how one staggered up Tress Cross in the mist this afternoon, and sat on a granite tomb on the top, and surveyed the land, with the rain dripping against one's skin. There are – as you may remember – rocks comparable to couchant camels, and granite gate posts, with a smooth turf road between them. Thinking it over is the pleasant thing . . . The life I lead is very nearly perfect . . . What with the silence, and the possibility of walking out, at any moment, over long wonderfully coloured roads to cliffs with the sea beneath, and coming back past lighted windows to one's tea and fire and book – and then one has thoughts and a conception of the world and moments like a dragonfly in air – with all this I am kept very lively in my head.[14]

Woolf's imagination brings the exotic and dazzling to a rain-soaked Cornish December day – camels and dragonflies are brought to mind as a result of Woolf's peregrinations: rocks, thoughts and time are given strange bodies to inhabit, making the familiar weird and dream-like, but also material, tangible. What gives physical presence to these things is walking. Later, Woolf's prose mirrors the sequence of movement and ideas that gives rise to such imaginings: as the walker hurries back to warmth and light and sustenance, the commas accumulate, tumbling one after the other. Then, as cognition begins, the dashes enable both writer and reader to pause for breath. The mind is fuelled by the dynamism of the body's motion.

Walking also held a visionary power: not only did it enable Woolf to give life to rocks, conjure shapes out of the air and pause time, but it granted her the ability to see into what she felt was the truth of things. At Asheham House in Sussex in 1918 – the county where she kept a country home from 1911 until her death – Woolf wandered frequently on the Downs above the house. While the winter mists may have obscured what it was possible to see with the eyes, it opened up new internal vistas:

> What I like most about Asheham is that I read books there; so divine it is, coming in from a walk to have tea by the fire & then read & read – say Othello – say anything. It doesn't seem to matter what. But one's faculties are so oddly clarified that the page detaches itself in its true meaning & lies as if illumined, before one's eyes; seen whole & truly not in jerks & spasms as so often in London. And then the trees, spare & leafless; the brown of the plough, &, yesterday, downs mountainous through a mist, which isn't palpable, for only dead detail vanishes.[15]

On the Downs, and on the page, the 'dead detail vanishes', revealing the 'true meaning' of book and land 'illumined'. In both cases, the vision comes whole, transforming what is seen, so that the Downs become mountains, and the 'truth' becomes clear.

The importance of that clarity to Woolf's novel-writing is made evident in an impressionistic portrait of the Downs entered into Woolf's diary on 7 January 1920 at Monk's House, Rodmell, which would be the Woolfs' home-from-home for more than twenty years:

Heres the sun out for example & all the upper twigs & the trees as if dipped in fire; the trunks emerald green; even bark bright tinted, & variable as the skin of a lizard. Then theres Asheham hill smoke misted; the windows of the long train spots of sun; the smoke lying back on the carriages like a rabbits lop ears. The chalk quarry glows pink; & my water meadows lush as June, until you see that the grass is short, & rough as a dogfishes back. But I could go on counting what I've noticed page after page. Every day or nearly I've walked towards a different point & come back with a string of these matchings and marvels. Five minutes from the house one is out in the open, a great pull over Asheham; &, as I say, every direction bears fruit.[16]

Walking provided Woolf with a rich harvest of moments and characters and incidents, with her diary often serving as a literary laboratory in which to experiment with language. The observations collected during Woolf's walks became the raw materials for the development of her distinctive novelistic style: while on some walks she would bring home foraged treasures, on others she collected beautiful and succinct descriptions that captured the essence of what she had seen. Walking was essential to both types of gathering.

Woolf certainly saw the phrases and ideas that came to her through walking as some sort of produce of the land: writing then became an act of harvesting the linguistic and visual bounty. Back in Sussex for the summer in 1926, she wrote,

As I am not going to milk my brains for a week, I shall here write the first pages of the greatest book in the world. This

is what the book would be that was made entirely solely &
with integrity of one's thoughts. Suppose one could catch
them before they became 'works of art.'? Catch them hot
& sudden as they rise in the mind – walking up Asheham
hill for instance. Of course one cannot; for the process of
language is slow & deluding.[17]

Work, Woolf thought, 'squeezed' her brain, or emptied
it, while walking replenished it: she imagined her mind as a
vessel or receptacle stored with the abundance collected on her
walks, which was to be offered up in its turn to be gathered
by publishers and readers. As Woolf wrote in August 1929,

Now my tugging & distressing book & articles are off my
mind my brain seems to fill & expand & grow physically
light & peaceful. I begin to feel it filling quietly after all the
wringing & squeezing it has had since we came here. And so
the unconscious part now expands; & walking I notice the
red corn, & the blue of the plain & an infinite number of
things without naming them; because I am not thinking of
any specific thing. Now & again I feel my mind take shape,
like a cloud with the sun on it, as some idea, plan or image
wells up, but they travel on, over the horizon, like clouds, &
I wait peacefully for another to form, or nothing, it matters
not which.[18]

Woolf's conceptualization of writing is firmly corporeal –
the whole process is understood through similes and metaphors
to do with the physical. Books and articles 'tug' her brain,
while she documents being able to *feel* her brain 'expand &

grow physically light': even peacefulness is understood as a physical sensation. As her eyes fix on details of light or colour, Woolf's mind transmogrifies, and she *feels* it becoming a cloud (what an extraordinary sensation that must be!). Comfortably, pleasurably, the mind then seems to change form as each new idea 'wells up' into it: thoughts in Woolf's mind behave in the same way as convection currents in air, condensing into magical shapes that flicker into perception, and out again.

At the heart of this process is walking, and knowledge of this was the source of profound happiness to Woolf throughout her life. In a diary entry for 2 October 1934, she observed,

> So the summer is ended . . . Oh the joy of walking! I've never felt it so strong in me . . . the trance like, swimming, flying through the air; the current of sensations and ideas; & the slow, but fresh change of down, of road, of colour: all this churned up into a fine thin sheet of perfect calm happiness. Its true I often painted the brightest pictures on this sheet[.][19]

Walking places Woolf in a series of altered states – she is in a 'trance', she is 'swimming', she is 'flying through the air', and the prose raises the blissful possibility that she is all of these at once. The magic of these states, blended with the powerful 'joy of walking', are the raw materials from which Woolf's mind is able to make the 'fine thin sheet' on which her translucent, cloud-like ideas are both imaginatively and literally impressed.

For most of her married life, Virginia Woolf divided her time between Sussex and London. Her writing makes clear that the very different environments provided by the two locations were equally necessary: too much London risked a kind of 'over-stimulation' that could threaten her mental equilibrium, while too much Sussex could lead to feelings of isolation. Similarly, the two places provided Woolf with contrasting, but complementary, sorts of walking, both of which she valued for the differing ways in which they opened up worlds for her mind. Woolf summarized why she loved London walking in her diary for 31 May 1927, writing that the city itself 'perpetually attracts, stimulates, gives me a play & a story & a poem, without any trouble, save that of moving my legs through the streets'.[20] In common with quite a lot of Woolf's writing about her walking, she figures herself here as passive: creativity is a gift 'given' by the city. There is something slightly alarming, though, in the size of the gift: London does not bestow a play *or* a story, but 'a play & a story & a poem'. The absence of punctuation reinforces the sense of superfluity, as each work arrives immediately after the last: there are no pauses. But what is a writer to do with all three at once? Walking in London is perhaps something to be done with caution; if walking provides the writer's harvest, city strolling is inclined to glut.

While care was required walking London's streets, it yielded to Woolf experiences and ideas that were unavailable in the country:

> London is enchanting. I step out upon a tawny coloured magic carpet, it seems, & get carried into beauty without raising a finger. The nights are amazing, with all the white porticoes & broad silent avenues. And people pop

in & out, lightly, divertingly like rabbits; & I look down Southampton Row, wet as a seal's back or red & yellow with sunshine, & watch the omnibus going & coming, & hear the old crazy organs. One of these days I will write about London, & how it takes up the private life & carries it on, without any effort. Faces passing lift up my mind; prevent it from settling, as it does in the stillness at Rodmell.[21]

No sooner has Woolf left her front door than she is transported into the land of the *Arabian Nights*, filled with enchantment, magic carpets, colours and sounds. Running through this description, though, is the importance of, and pleasure in, diversion. In Sussex, Woolf had written of the creative power of the 'slow . . . change of . . . road', but in London it is the great speed at which things – people, objects, ideas, thoughts – 'pop in & out' of sight that is stimulating. Here the inability for the 'mind' to 'settle' is of value, as the brain and senses are overwhelmed by information. For all this, the dangers of superfluity continue to lurk: how can experiences and ideas be turned into language if the mind is perpetually 'prevented' from 'settling'? And if, as Woolf's descriptions suggest, there is a symbiosis between the 'emptying' of the brain by work, and its filling up by walking, there is danger in a place that continues to fill and fill and fill.

An elegant solution seems to have been found in the keeping of Woolf's word to 'write about London'. This work took the form of an extended essay, 'Street Haunting', which was published in 1927. In it Woolf articulated the creative and imaginative possibilities made available by walking London's busy streets. While the walking that is described seems innocent enough (the speaker leaves her home in order to purchase a pencil), there are hints of transgression, as social codes are challenged and, occasionally, breached:

> The evening hour, too, gives us the irresponsibility which darkness and lamplight bestow. We are no longer quite ourselves. As we step out of the house on a fine evening between four and six, we shed the self our friends know us by and become part of that vast republican army of anonymous trampers, whose society is so agreeable after the solitude of one's own room.[22]

City walking, in Woolf's description, is a radical act through which individual responsibility, even identity, is dissolved. Indeed, the self is 'shed', sloughed off like a skin or a mask, to be replaced by another, shared, identity. No longer an individual, the narrator merges with this 'vast republican army', a faceless yet substantial group whose numbers are sufficient to challenge the existing social order. In this description, Woolf picks up on long-held views of walking not only as dangerous but legally suspect – there is little distance between a 'tramp', who might be hauled before a magistrate for vagrancy because he is walking the land, and a 'tramper' – a walker who has the power to disrupt the social order.

The true power of walking for Woolf, though, was in its ability to utterly transform the self. In a striking image, she describes how walking smashes the brittle social structures in which individuals clothe themselves. On leaving the house, and entering the community of 'trampers': 'The shell-like covering which our souls have excreted to house themselves, to make for themselves a shape distinct from others, is broken, and there is left of all these wrinkles and roughness a central oyster of perceptiveness, an enormous eye.'[23] Again, walking breaks down individual identities until all that is left is our shared ability to perceive: the 'enormous eye' could belong to anyone, and belongs to us all. No longer tethered to the self, the eye is connected only to the physically moving body as it wanders through London's night-time streets, and is therefore able to construct whatever it wants, and to be whatever it wants. Woolf asks in this essay whether the 'true self' is 'Neither this nor that, neither here nor there, but something so varied and wandering that it is only when we give rein to its wishes and let it take its way unimpeded that we are indeed ourselves.'[24] The nature of the self can only be understood through walking: it does not 'wonder', but 'wanders':

> Walking home through the desolation one could tell oneself the story of the dwarf, of the blind men, of the party in the Mayfair mansion, of the quarrel in the stationer's shop. Into each of these lives one could penetrate a little way, far enough to give oneself the illusion that one is not tethered to a single mind but can put on briefly for a few minutes the bodies and minds of others . . . what greater delight and wonder can there be to leave the straight lines of personality and deviate into those footpaths that lead beneath brambles and thick tree trunks into the heart of the forest where live those wild beasts, our fellow men?[25]

In a manner that parallels Woolf's description of how her 'walks in the fields are the corridors' to the individual, lighted rooms of her own mind, here other selves become footpaths to be walked; and just as routes on the ground are available to all, so too in Woolf's imagination are the footpaths to 'our fellow men' open and shared. Other selves become accessible as the pathways leading to them may be trodden by any who can find the way.

That walking was integral to Woolf is beyond doubt: it was through the language of walking that she came to understand the ways in which her own mind functioned, and the physical world through which she walked served as an important pattern into which her internal world could be fitted, enriching her experiences of both. During periods of mental ill health, Woolf walked herself back to well-being, finding ways as her corporeal body trod well-known paths to render the internal topography of her mind familiar again. And as a writer, Woolf saw herself as an intrepid explorer of an invisible network of routes connecting her mind with others': the charting of this complex, unsettling and thrilling psycho-geography that underpinned so much of what Woolf sought to achieve as a writer and as a human being would have been impossible without her life-long walking of the physical world.

IT'S DARK BY THE TIME I finish at the British Library, but I am looking forward to the walk back to my room in Bloomsbury. Euston Road thrums with traffic, taxis and buses jostling loudly with lorries and vans, and it is with relief that I dart into the streets beyond the Congestion Charge zone, where it is quieter. I am alone, but I do not feel vulnerable. I walk past Tavistock Square, then towards Russell Square. I linger here, enjoying the warmth of the evening. I find a bench and sit for a while, the relative dark and quiet a soothing antidote to the city's business and a day spent in the archives. Later, after I've eaten, I set off to explore. I have no destination in mind. Rather, I am walking out of curiosity. I have never been to this part of London before, and I am thrilled at the thought of wandering where Woolf walked her novels into being. I pace the streets for hours, enjoying the sensation of observing without being observed. There is something magical, and subversive, in being invisible.

SEVEN

Nan Shepherd

But in the climbing ecstasy of thought,
Ere consummation, ere the final peak,
Come hours like this. Behind, the long defile,
The steep rock-path, alongside which, from under
Snow-caves, sharp-corniced, tumble the ice-cold waters.
And now, here, at the corrie's summit, no peak,
No vision of the blue world, far, unattainable,
But this grey plateau, rock-strewn, vast, silent,
The dark loch, the toiling crags, the snow;
A mountain shut within itself, yet a world,
Immensity. So may the mind achieve,
Toiling, no vision of the infinite,
But a vast, dark and inscrutable sense
Of its own terror, its own glory and power.

Nan Shepherd, 'Summit of Coire Etchachan'

Anna, or 'Nan', Shepherd was a prolific walker and mountain writer who came to know the Cairngorms intimately over decades of what she called 'traffic'. Her intimacy with the mountains was fundamental to her writing, with her three novels, poems, essays and letters shaped by her years of walking. The hills were her neighbours – she could see them from the garden of the house near Aberdeen where she lived most of her life – and they were also her sanctuary and escape. At times she sought refuge from her employment as a lecturer in the city: an interview in 1931, given at the height of her fame, recorded how Shepherd escaped, whenever possible, to 'a crofter's house away up there on the mountainside, undeterred by Easter snows'.[1] But occasionally she also fled to the mountains to obtain respite from her writing. 'I'm going to run away from the novel yet once again before winter – end of next week – for another blessed mountain week,' she wrote to her friend and fellow writer Neil Gunn; 'Aviemore this time. Perhaps I might even make more poetry, who knows. At any rate I shall see the Cairngorms – and the precipices – and the cold cold snows.'[2] In inhospitable conditions in an often-inhospitable place, Shepherd found her home.

Despite such urges to 'run away' from her writing, Shepherd was, for a time, hugely productive; her three novels were published during a fevered five-year period from 1928 to 1933, with a volume of her poetry appearing the year after, to considerable acclaim. Then, silence – at least publicly. Only forty years later, in 1977, and towards the end of her life, was her creative work again in print: *The Living Mountain*, which had lain complete but hidden for decades, was published by Aberdeen University Press. The unsettling beauty of its 30,000 words disturbed its readers, for whom Shepherd's writing articulated long-unspoken truths. 'I'm glad you "look" on Clochnaben "*Your*" hills –' wrote the novelist Jessie Kesson, Shepherd's friend and a fellow mountain-haunter.

And I know you do *more* than look – You '*know*' the 'feel'
of it, beneath your *feet* – The 'sting' of its rain on your face,
– you 'breathe' In the hill smells – I *know* this – because I,
too, can '*merge*' my – being – into beloved places – Nor –
quite – the *same* thing – as the Once Was – but a blessing
despite –.[3]

Knowledge of the hills comes only through direct encounter
and 'attention', which, for Shepherd, is so acute that her very
'being' 'merges' with these 'beloved places'. That 'attention' is
also demonstrated through linguistic deftness, using 'precision
as a form of lyricism, attention as devotion, exactitude as
tribute, description structured by proposition'.[4]

Shortly after *The Living Mountain* was published in 1977,
her friend and fellow poet Ken Morrice wrote to Shepherd
in raptures. 'Your book is (as they say) really something,'
he declared. 'Rarely can such acute observation be matched
by a gift for poetic expression. "Gentle" it is not: powerful,
muscular, vivid, experiential . . . The experience of reading it
stays with me.'[5] Morrice's observations of the text's strengths
echoed Kesson's: both considered the physicality of the text
– and of the experiences that brought *The Living Mountain*
into being – to be key to its success. They were right. At the
heart of Shepherd's writing is a careful and subtle articulation
of the complex interactions between physical movement,
introspection and the landscape that create meaning in a
human life. There is more, though. For Shepherd, whose vital
being was bound fast to her experiences in the Cairngorms,
the mountain is *living*. Shepherd's writing does not attempt
to simply take – with all its connotations of appropriation and

one-sidedness – meaning from the landscape. Rather, running through both her poetry and prose is an intense and deeply felt certainty that both humans and mountains *are*, and can share meaning with and in each other; for Shepherd both are types of being, accessible to each through conversation, proximity and empathy. She writes of the hills of the Cairngorms as 'friends' whom she 'visits', and in whose presence her imagination lights up as if touched by 'another mind'.[6] This should not be mistaken for simple anthropomorphism, though. Rather, Shepherd offers the possibility of a transmigration, an exchange of some kind of essential matter between the human and the lithic – a vital, and vitalizing, petrification. Such a profound transformation is made possible for Shepherd by walking to, and with, the mountains:

> Walking thus, hour after hour, the senses keyed, one walks the flesh transparent. But no metaphor, *transparent*, or *light as air*, is adequate. The body is not made negligible, but paramount. Flesh is not annihilated but fulfilled. One is not bodiless, but essential body.
>
> It is therefore when the body is keyed to its highest potential and controlled to a profound harmony deepening into something that resembles trance, that I discover most nearly what it is *to be*. I have walked out of the body and into the mountain. I am a manifestation of its total life, as is the starry saxifrage or the white-winged ptarmigan.[7]

Over the course of these few sentences, the walking self undergoes a complete change, impelled by a quasi-mystic process that moves the body – literally and psychically

– from 'profound harmony' deeper into a trance state. The feet act as finely balanced pendula, with the body its own hypnotist; 'the beat of the placed and lifted foot', which has its verbal counterpart in Shepherd's iambic 'I am', becomes a chant uttered by the feet.[8] Thus entranced, the walker is sublimated from the corporeal to the ethereal. The body is left behind – though the self remains intact – and enters 'into the mountain': there is more than an echo of the Pied Piper about the disappearance of the body into the hillside. The 'I', without physical being, seems then to float free, speaking from no identifiable position as its existence blends readily with that of the 'starry saxifrage' and the 'ptarmigan' which haunt the upper slopes of the Cairngorms massif, so that there is little to indicate where the human ends, and the mountain world begins.

This sequence is suggestive of the possibility of an extraordinary intimacy between human and mountain, an intimacy that is the result of years of living with, among and within these hills and corries. Shepherd walked in the Cairngorms throughout her life, until she was 'harrowed by old age' at last.[9] She was a fit, determined and adventurous walker rendered joyously half-mad when in company with the mountains with and in whom she was in love. For Shepherd, mountain-love was 'an appetite that grows in feeding', which, 'Like drink and passion', will intensify 'life to the point of glory'.[10] Drunk on mountains, Shepherd became '*fey*', and could be found walking 'securely over dangerous places with the gay abandon that is said to be the mark of those who are doomed to death'.[11] While she acknowledged that when remembering 'the places I have run lightly over with no sense of fear', she would go 'cold to think of them', 'unmanned' by fear and 'horror', whenever she returned to the hills, 'the same leap of the spirit' would 'carry her up', leaving her '*fey* again'.[12] As an inexperienced youth at the start of her love affair with the mountains, Shepherd records how mountain-love propelled her recklessly up into high hills she barely knew:

I had driven to Derry Lodge one perfect morning in June with two gentlemen who, having arrived there, were bent on returning at once to Braemar, when a car came up with four others, obviously setting out for Ben MacDhui. In a flash I had accosted them to ask if I might share their car back to Braemar in the evening: my intention was to go up, the rag-tag and bob-tail of their company, keeping them in sight but not joining myself on to them. The request was granted and I turned back to say farewell to my former companions. When I turned again, the climbers had disappeared. I hastened after them, threading my way through the scattered pines that lie along the stream, but failing to overtake them and hurrying a little more. At last I got beyond the trees, and in all the bare glen ahead, I could see no human being . . . Prudence – I had only once before been on a Cairngorm – told me to wait; I had begun to suspect I had outdistanced my company. But I couldn't wait. The morning was cloudless and blue, it was June, I was young. Nothing could have held me back. Like a spurt of fire licking the hill, up I ran. The Etchachan tumbled out from under snow, the summit was like wine. I saw a thousand summits at once, clear and sparkling.[13]

Shepherd's desire to be on the mountain is elemental in its fierceness and simplicity, but she is lucky not to fare worse as mist descends abruptly on her at the summit: her youthful 'fire' might easily have been extinguished by the chilly moistness of the cloud enshrouding the mountain.

Yet for all the vital appeal of Shepherd's high-wire derring-do in the mountains, such excursions left Shepherd hungering for something more. That something 'lies', she discovers, 'within the mountain'. But understanding travels both ways in the Cairngorms. 'Something', Shepherd writes, 'moves between me and it' – between walker and the mountain. That 'something' is undefined, but means for Shepherd that 'Place and a mind may interpenetrate till the nature of both is altered.'[14] The medium of this 'interpenetration' remains vague; indeed, Shepherd 'cannot tell what this movement is except by recounting it'.[15] Walking, writing and comprehension, therefore, must be the same – neither walking nor writing is the means *of* comprehension but *are* themselves two aspects of understanding, and comprehension is both walking and writing. Neither body nor intellect alone is sufficient to satisfactorily articulate the nature of the relationship between human being and mountain.

Nor is striving for the mountains' summits adequate. Shepherd certainly loved a peak – she wrote rapturously of her first climb in the Cairngorms, up Ben Macdui (or 'Macdhui') – the highest peak of the massif at 4,300 feet, and the second highest peak in Britain. And she didn't stop there, but carried on over the other nearby giants: Braeriach, Cairn Toul and Sgor an Lochain Uaine, the three lowering cheek by jowl on the other side of the trench of the Lairig Ghru; and Cairngorm, itself over 4,000 feet in height, but in comparison with such elevated company, a lesser mountain. These are peaks to prize, with views from the top that might extend, with luck and a clear day, from the Lammermuirs to Glen Affric, from Ben Nevis to the Black Isle – as I can fortunately attest. But it was not climbing up that brought Shepherd to the hills, but 'clambering down'; down into their private depths, down into the hollows of their hidden waterways and hiding places, down below the sight lines of those people 'mad to recover' what Shepherd called 'the tang of height'.[16] Thus it is that *The Living Mountain* has very little to say about mountain tops or spot heights; instead, it feels keenly the power of awkward, obscure places accessible only through determined pedestrianism. One such is Loch Avon. The detail of Shepherd's account has a hint of Captain Cook or Mungo Park about it – charters of unknown waterways both – but this precision is born of enduring love rather than scientific imperative:

> This loch lies at an altitude of some 2,300 feet, but its banks soar up for another fifteen hundred. Indeed farther, for Cairn Gorm and Ben MacDhui may be said to be its banks. From the lower end of this mile and a half gash in the rock, exit is easy but very long. One may go down by the Avon itself, through ten miles as lonely and unvisited as anything in the Cairngorms, to Inchrory; or by easy enough watersheds pass into Strathnethy or Glen Derry, or under the Barns of Bynack to the Caiplich Water. But higher up the loch there is no way out, save by scrambling up one or other of the burns that tumble from the heights: except that, above the Shelter Stone, a gap opens between

the hills to Loch Etchachan, and here the scramble up
is shorter.

The inner end of this gash has been howked straight from
the granite. As one looks up from below, the agents would
appear mere splashes of water, whose force might be turned
aside by a pair of hands. Yet above the precipices we have
found in one of these burns pools deep enough to bathe in.
The water that pours over these grim bastions carries no sedi-
ment of any kind in its precipitate fall, which seems indeed
to distil and aerate the water so that the loch far below is
sparkling clear. This narrow loch has never, I believe, been
sounded. I know its depth, though not in feet.[17]

The language of geology, geography and cartography
are combined here, with descriptions of watersheds, valleys,
distillation and aeration. The relationship between places
is also carefully articulated: distances and connections are
listed exactly, so that a reader has a clear understanding of
how the various glens near Loch Avon interlink. Should they
wish to explore those glens for themselves, Shepherd's precise
descriptions of the routes through the complex terrain at the
heart of the Cairngorms make such an adventure possible. In
this way, Shepherd's prose is part route guide and part word
map, but for all its keenness, the scientific terminology is unable
to grant the reader knowledge of the place. That knowledge
can only be achieved through the physical movement of the
body across the landscape, rather than the movement of
instruments; only human feet, not the unitized variety, are
capable of taking the mountain's measure. Shepherd's detailed
knowledge has been hard won through repeated walkings in,

and out, of Loch Avon and its formidable bowl; her body is far better at measuring the distances, depths, hollows and stones than any theodolite or sounding, for it is capable of sifting meaning in the rocks and the water.

Indeed, the maps made by cartographers wielding plumb lines or sonar, lasers or GPS, would capture little of the mountains as Shepherd experienced and knew them. Concerned with surfaces, standard maps barely acknowledge the interiority of mountain landscapes. The hollows, caves, nooks and crannies of the mountains were, for Shepherd, essential to understanding the hills; a fascination with expansiveness and elevation was evidence of ignorance and inexperience, an indication of immaturity:

> I was well accustomed to hills, having run from childhood on the Deeside hills and the Monadhliaths, those flow-ing heights that flank the Spey on the other side from the Cairngorms, an ideal playground for a child; and the end of a climb meant for me always the opening of a spacious view over the world: that was the moment of glory. But to toil upwards, feel the gradient slacken and the top approach, as one does at the end of the Etchachan ascent, and then find no spaciousness for reward, but an interior – that astounded me.[18]

Going into the mountain, Shepherd goes inside herself, dis-covering as she does so that she is thrilled by being 'barricaded' within 'towering mountain walls' on 'every side'.[19]

The bravery of this should not be underestimated: Shepherd makes clear in her descriptions of Loch Avon that accessing these interior spaces could be difficult and arduous, though her account is understated about her own physical gifts. In climbing into places like the Barns of Bynack, she was often undertaking a potentially dangerous physical challenge. Lying on the eastern side of the Cairngorms above the Lairig an Laoigh, which links Aviemore in the north with Braemar in the south, Bynack More is a prominent mountain with an appealingly rocky summit. But hidden on its north face at 330 feet below the top, beyond a small lip, are its Barns. The largest is a giant erratic, an 'enormous black cube of rock that lies like a Queen Anne mansion', though for all its size, it is invisible from the mountain summit not half a mile away. Shepherd writes that 'One can walk up a sort of staircase within and look out by a cleft as though from a window,' rendering them homely with the familiar presence of stairs and windows – and making entering into them seem no harder than climbing to the first floor of a house.[20] But entering into the Barns is no small thing, and quite unlike climbing any domestic staircase I have encountered.

In exploring with such ardour the interior, private spaces of the mountain, Shepherd's writing teems with observations about place and self not often found in walking literature. These observations were borne out of a deep knowledge of the Cairngorms massif accumulated over many years of walking through and across its many passes, into its complex corrie systems, and along the burns, rivers and lochs. The waterways of the Cairngorms held a particular power for Shepherd, perhaps because they often emerged from the dark and secret places that she so enjoyed exploring, but perhaps also because she lived for almost all her life alongside the Dee, the mightiest river to which the mountains give birth high on the plateau between Cairn Toul and Braeriach. The village of Cults at the eastern edge of Royal Deeside, just outside Aberdeen and the flat land of the river's estuary, is many miles from the windswept, rain-scoured mountainside 4,000 feet up from which the Dee first emerges, but for Shepherd, there was an integral affinity between the two, a recognizable and tangible kinship. With her home on the river, Shepherd had a visible link to the high places to which she loved to go – the waters that ran past her house had emerged, however many weeks or months or years earlier, from the falls or pools at the heart of the massif.

Yet for all the time spent as near neighbour to the Dee, for Shepherd, real understanding of the waters of the Cairngorms could only come by seeing 'them at their sources', by tracing them back to their beginnings. Such attempts were not without risk, however, beyond the danger of being in high places. Writing at the beginning of *The Living Mountain*, Shepherd cautioned that 'This journey to the sources is not to be undertaken lightly. One walks among elementals, and elementals are not governable. There are awakened also in oneself by the contact elementals that are as unpredictable as wind or snow.'[21] The walking of the rivers and burns of the Cairngorms ran the risk of encountering not only the changeable, and potentially dangerous, weather of the mountains, but an equally changeable, perhaps equally dangerous, internal 'weather' from which it is impossible to protect oneself. Walking the plateau below Braeriach's broad summit dome, Shepherd recounts a meeting with the infant Dee, an event that brings the continuous, relentless life of

the mountain into direct contact with the flitting, fleeting
existence of the human walker:

> As I stand there in the silence, I become aware that the
> silence is not complete. Water is speaking. I go towards
> it, and almost at once the view is lost: for the plateau has
> its own hollows, and this one slopes widely down to one
> of the great inward fissures, the Garbh Coire. It lies like a
> broad leaf veined with watercourses, that converge on the
> lip of the precipice to drop down in a cataract for 500 feet.
> This is the River Dee. Astonishingly, up here at 4000 feet,
> it is already a considerable stream. The immense leaf that it
> drains is bare, surfaced with stones, gravel, sometimes sand,
> and in places moss and grass grow on it. Here and there in
> the moss a few white stones have been piled together. I go
> to them, and water is welling up, strong and copious, pure
> cold water that flows away in rivulets and drops over the
> rock. These are the Wells of Dee. This is the river. Water,
> that strong white stuff, one of the four elemental mysteries,
> can here be seen at its origins. Like all profound mysteries,
> it is so simple that it frightens me. It wells from the rock,
> and flows away. For unnumbered years it has welled from
> the rock, and flowed away. It does nothing, absolutely
> nothing, but be itself.[22]

Shepherd's switch here to the present tense enhances the
impression of the river having perpetually existed: a human
life is a mayfly's in comparison. This is an unsettling place,
a locus for primal 'mysteries'. It is also, evidently, a place of
considerable power. Here Shepherd seems to name the river

into being, her brusque phrases identifying it in the same sort of way, perhaps, that Adam did the animals in Genesis.[23] 'This is the River Dee,' she says; 'These are the Wells of Dee. This is the river.' And so it is. But where Adam, and the many namers of things in mythology and folklore since, gained power over the things they named, Shepherd does not; in the face of the deep time embodied by the river's unceasing 'welling', human endeavours are nullified. Indeed, it is in the acknowledgement of her powerlessness that Shepherd gains knowledge of herself in relation to the mountain. Incapable of understanding 'that sure and unremitting surge of water', unable to 'fathom its power', aware that any attempt to hold back the water is an 'Absurd and futile gesture', Shepherd manages to live – metaphorically and literally – with its mysteries.[24] It is enough simply to know that 'man can't live without it', and that 'moving water is as integral to the mountain as pollen to the flower.'[25]

Travelling the waterways of the Cairngorms, physically and imaginatively, was 'integral' to Shepherd's understanding of the hills, and she attempted to explore the rivers and rills not only on foot, but through poetry. Poetry was, for Shepherd, a form reserved for very particular uses, and writing it could be a physical torment: in a letter to Neil Gunn, she explained her reluctance to compose poetry because of a tendency to 'shrink too from the subsequent exhaustion. Not being physically very strong, I grudge the way that it eats up my vitality. And that is cowardice.'[26] It is hard to imagine Shepherd being rendered physically weak; her walking body was lithe and powerful, but she was also very slight – in 1948 she weighed just 44 kg (98 lb).[27] Poetry, it seems, required resources that her body was not always able to supply; poetry consumed something of her spirit. Despite the unsettling idea that Shepherd felt her poetry to be 'eating' her, it remained an extremely important way of understanding herself and the essence of the world she inhabited:

> Poetry means too much to me – it seems to me to hold in intensest being the very heart of all experience; and though I have now and then glimpsed something of that burning heart of life – have intimations and hauntings of its beauty and strangeness and awe – always when I try to put these things into words they elude me. The result is slight and small.[28]

It was with poetry that Shepherd first attempted to capture the 'burning heart of life' of the rivers in the Cairngorms, to express something of the nature of the incomprehensible, and uncomprehending, elemental forces that were at work in the mountains.

Published in 1934 in *In the Cairngorms*, 'The Hill Burns' takes the reader on an extraordinary and unsettling journey into the deep time that still holds in the high places:

> So without sediment
> Run the clear burns of my country,
> Fiercely pure,
> Transparent as light
> Gathered into its own unity,
> Lucent and without colour;
> Or green,

Like clear deeps of air,
Light massed upon itself,
Like the green pinions,
Cleaving the trouble of approaching night,
Shining in their own lucency,
Of the great angels that guard the Mountain;
Or amber so clear
It might have oozed from the crystal trunk
Of the tree Paradisal,
Symbol of life,
That grows in the presence of God eternally.
And these pure waters
Leap from the adamantine rocks,
The granites and schists
Of my dark and stubborn country.
From gaunt heights they tumble,
Harsh and desolate lands,
The plateau of Braeriach
Where even in July
The cataracts of wind
Crash in the corries with the boom of seas
    in anger;
And Corrie Etchachan
Down whose precipitous
Narrow defile
Thunder the fragments of rock
Broken by winter storms
From their aboriginal place;
And Muich Dhui's summit,
Rock defiant against frost and the old grinding of ice,

Wet with the cold fury of blinding cloud,
Through which the snow-fields loom up, like ghosts
   from a world of eternal annihilation,
And far below, where the dark waters of Etchachan
  are wont to glint,
An unfathomable void.
Out of these mountains,
Out of the defiant torment of Plutonic rock,
Out of fire, terror, blackness and upheaval,
Leap the clear burns,
Living water,
Like some pure essence of being,
Invisible in itself,
Seen only by its movement.[29]

The poem is poised between worlds. The first is one of purity and light, an Edenic world ruled by the Christian God and overseen by his angelic train. This world is young: biblical time spans just 6,000 years, at least according to the calculations of Bishop Ussher, and the clarity of the water is suggestive of a world as yet untainted by the original sin of Adam and Eve. The second world, though, is ancient, and is characterized and created by violence and 'upheaval'. This world is Hadean, and perhaps Satanic: the rocks of the mountains are enduring 'torment' as a human soul might in penance, and the land has been forged by 'fire'. The hill burns are brought into being by both these worlds. They emerge here from the 'gaunt heights' and the 'harsh and desolate lands' of Braeriach's plateau to flow as the 'essence' of life which bears no taint of its origins. The burns are therefore both ancient and new, but what might have been a contradiction is resolved in the poem by Shepherd's description of them 'being': the continuous tense is able to contain both past and present within it.

Nor was Shepherd any less awed by what happens to the mountains' waters when they grew still in the winter freeze. With so much ground over 4,000 feet in height, the Cairngorms experience a climate more typically seen in the high northern latitudes, one of 'rasping' winds and 'scouring' avalanches.[30] Its passes were once giant roads for ice, and the slopes of its high mountains and many eastern-facing corries can hold snow the year round. As a walker, Shepherd found the 'elementals' of water and ice, and their effects on the landscape, intriguing but unsettling; as a result, her writing never romanticizes their power, even as she expresses a profound love for the ways in which they have sculpted the mountainside. And Shepherd knew directly what snow and ice could do to frail human bodies. In the time of her youthful acquaintance with the mountain, four people 'were lost in a blizzard', while another slipped to his death on a patch of snow, 'in May'.[31] Looking back thirty years later, in preparation for the publication of *The Living Mountain* in 1977, Shepherd had an even sorrier litany to recount. During that time – which 'in the life of a mountain is nothing', but was, to some of the human existences she recalled, everything – many tragic things had occurred in the snows of the mountains:

> A man and a girl are found, months too late, far out of their path, the girl on abraded hands and knees as she clawed her way through drift. I see her living face still (she was one of

my students), a sane, eager, happy face. She should have
lived to be old. Seventy men, with dogs and a helicopter, go
out after a lone skier who has failed to return, and who is
found dead. And a group of schoolchildren, belated, fail to
find the hut where they should have spent the night. They
shelter against a wall of snow, but in the morning, in spite
of the heroic efforts of their instructress, only she and one
boy are alive.[32]

Shepherd's sadness at the fate of her former pupil, in
particular, is evident, with the use of the present tense bringing
these tragedies, spread over half a human lifetime, hauntingly
back into the present. But such emotion was balanced elsewhere
with a cold rationality about the risks of mountain walking.
Declining to pass judgement on the decisions that brought so
many people to such bleak ends, Shepherd instead saw such
choices as part and parcel of an important quest to know the
mountains. Such danger 'is the risk we must all take when we
accept individual responsibility for ourselves on the mountain',
she wrote, 'and until we have done that, we do not begin to
know it.'[33]

Shepherd accepted that 'individual responsibility'.
Eschewing any grander aim, she spent one 'whole midwinter
day wandering from one burn to another', simply watching the
'fluctuation between the motion in water and the immobility
of frost'.[34] Elsewhere, though, the constant shifting of the
snow meant that any understanding of the mountain was
temporary, a boon granted for a moment but easily withdrawn
by a change in the wind. While 'Loose snow blown in the
sun looks like the ripples running through corn,' it could also

'blow past in a cloud, visible as it approaches, but formed of minute ice particles, so fine that the eye cannot distinguish them individually as they pass'.[35] Shepherd captured the shifting patterns of her mountain-knowing best in poetry; the simplicity of the title, 'Snow', understating the complexity of the natural and human agents at work in the poem:

> I did not know. How could I understand,
> I, who had scorned the very name of love?
> Clear were my eyes and heaven was clear above;
> Clarity held the long lines of the land;
> Hill after hill raced proud at my demand.
> Too careless to be triumphant, O enough
> Of triumph had I who knew the transience of
> Clear cloud and wind: clear colour; earth blown
>   and tanned.
>
> And now – and now – I am mazed to find my world
> Sore altered in the passing of a night
> (And never a dream all night had round me curled)
> No sound, no proclamation, no delight
> Of haunting prophecy came, no hurricane swirled.
> But at morn the earth was strange, a blur, white.[36]

Shepherd's poem holds in tension knowing and not-knowing, though the distinction between the two, like the outlines of the land, is 'blurred' by the snow. The speaker is an experienced frequenter of the mountains who knows enough to appreciate 'the transience of / Clear cloud and wind', to know that mountain weather rarely lasts for long. Yet knowledge is also posited as an impossibility from the very beginning of the poem, from the first four words, which proclaim, simply, 'I did not know.' Knowing, then, is not the same as 'clarity', which is an idea that reverberates throughout the opening stanza, first as a quality of sight, then of weather and then of power: it is 'clarity' that holds 'the long lines of the land', and which cause the optical illusion of lines of hills 'racing proud' into the distance at the speaker's volition. But neither sight, clarity nor knowledge is sufficient to understand the appearance of the snow, which materializes in the second stanza with none of the warning signs that would have made its presence comprehensible. Nothing is the same following the snow's fall – not the land, not the view, and certainly not the speaker, who is left uncertain of everything as a result of the overwhelming surprise as the earth is rendered utterly 'strange'.

Knowing, for Shepherd, was hard-won through physical experiences that were painful and perilous: those experiences add a tang to the work. In the eastern Cairngorms, in what should have been the beginning of spring, Shepherd herself made an 'error of judgment':

On that late April day, after some halcyon weather, a sudden snow storm blew up. It snowed all night – thick heavy snow that lay even under the next day's sunshine. We were going to the Dubh Loch of Ben a' Bhuird, with no intention of a summit, and I had taken no precautions against exposure; I had expected neither frosty wind nor hot sun to play havoc with my skin, nor had I had till then any experience of strong light upon snow. After a while I found the glare intolerable; I saw scarlet patches on the snow; I felt sick and weak. My companion refused to leave me sitting in the snow and I refused to defeat the object of his walk, which was to photograph the loch in its still wintry condition; so I struggled on, with his dark handkerchief veiling my eyes – a miserable blinkered imprisonment.[37]

The description of being blinded by snow makes for uncomfortable reading, not least because of Shepherd's self-admonitory remark that her discomfort 'might have [been] avoided had I remembered that snow can blow out of a warm sky': this is a lesson painfully learned.[38] In Shepherd's writing, though, true learning – like hill-walking – is arduous. True knowledge of the mountains is only possible through the suffering of the body brought on through the relentless motion of the feet. Without this suffering, though, it would have been impossible for Shepherd to write.

In her explorations of the rivers and inside spaces of the mountains, Shepherd often left paths behind, choosing to pursue instead unmarked routes which bore no trace of pedestrian traffic. 'Eye and foot acquire in rough walking', Shepherd wrote in *The Living Mountain*, 'a co-ordination that makes one distinctly aware of where the next step is to fall.' This knowledge becomes so intuitive that the feet learn to position themselves without conscious thought; Shepherd recounts one occasion when racing down a heather-clad hillside, her body independently avoided two adders, leaving her 'to consider with amused surprise the speed and sureness of my own feet'.[39]

While Shepherd took considerable pleasure in such 'rough walking', the following of paths also played an important part in how she understood the mountains, and her place within them. Robert Macfarlane has written of paths as 'offering not only means of traversing space, but ways of feeling, being and knowing',[40] while Rebecca Solnit describes them as 'a record of those who have gone before, and to follow them is to follow people who are no longer there'.[41] Both ideas seem to be at work in the meaning Shepherd found in the Cairngorms' paths:

> Up on the plateau nothing has moved for a long time. I have walked all day, and seen no one. I have heard no living sound. Once, in a solitary corrie, the rattle of a falling stone betrayed the passage of a line of stags. But up here, no movement, no voice. Man might be a thousand years away.
>
> Yet, as I look round me, I am touched at many points by his presence. His presence is in the cairns, marking the summits, marking the paths, marking the spot where a man has died, or where a river is born. It is in the paths themselves; even over boulder and rock man's persistent passage can be seen, as at the head of the Lairig Ghru, where the path, over brown-grey weathered and lichened stones, shines as red as new-made rock. It is in the stepping-stones over the burns, and lower in the glens, the bridges.[42]

Shepherd is alone, and is yet in the company of numberless others who have trodden the routes visible from her lofty vantage point, whose marks on the rock have remained visible long after they passed. It is a kind of haunting, though a companionable one; the landscape is littered with the physical traces of people perhaps now dead, but those traces are evidence of people's lives and experiences. Shepherd's isolation is therefore only partial; total separation from other humans may not be possible where there are paths, which serve as links between not only places, but people, and which cross not only space but time.

Paths could also serve as links between different realms of experience. Shepherd recounts how one snowy day she found herself 'companioned' on the path, not by humans leaving traces of their footsteps, but by the tracks of animals and birds, laid down in the hours since the snow stopped. The presence of these tracks transforms the space from an 'empty world' into a populous one in which humans and animals comfortably and amicably co-exist.[43] That morning, Shepherd was able to see evidence of a 'hare bounding, a hare trotting, a fox dragging his brush, grouse thick-footed, plover thin, red deer and roes'.[44] These creatures are fellow path-makers and path-followers, and as a result, there is a sense of empathy in Shepherd's writing that enables human experience to come close to animal, and vice versa. This was an important aspect of 'companioned' walking. For Shepherd, 'The perfect hill companion is the one whose identity is, for the time being, merged in that of the mountains, as you feel your own to be', so that distinctions between animal or human, living being or rock, cease to matter.[45]

In 1940, not long before *The Living Mountain* was likely begun, Nan Shepherd wrote to Neil Gunn about his two latest novels, *Wild Geese Overhead*, published the year before, and *Second Sight*, which had just appeared.[46] She had enjoyed both, but had particularly loved the latter

Not because of the theme, or any consideration of its
implications: but because of the uncanny way you enter
my breathing and living and seeing and apprehending.
To apprehend things – walking on a hill, seeing the light
change, the mist, the dark, being aware, using the whole of
one's body to instruct the spirit – yes, that is a secret life one
has and knows that others have. But to be able to share it,
in and through words – that's what frightens me. The word
shouldn't have such power. It dissolves one's being. I am no
longer myself but part of a life beyond myself when I read
pages that are so much the expression of myself. . . . you can
take movements of being and translate them out of themselves into words. That seems to me a gift of a very high and
rare order.[47]

Shepherd was in awe of Gunn's ability to 'share' the
'movements of being' that are the core of human existence,
to articulate the 'secret life' within each of us. In *The Living
Mountain*, she would match his accomplishments. Here she
would succeed in 'sharing' through her prose an understanding
of what it is to come to truly know a place, to walk knowledge
into oneself, to 'discover the mountain in itself'.[48] Such
knowledge was a gift, and *The Living Mountain* serves in
part as an acknowledgement of all that walking with the
mountains has given to Shepherd, the most precious of all
being 'a life of the senses so pure, so untouched by any mode
of apprehension but their own' that the individual is finally
able to encounter what Shepherd called 'the total mountain'.[49]

It is perhaps the greatest gift of Shepherd's writing that
she outlines how our experiencing, feeling, walking selves are

the means by which we gain insight into the inner mysteries both of the world and of human existence, that 'The more one learns of this intricate interplay of soil, altitude, weather, and the living tissues of plant and insect . . . the more the mystery deepens.'[50] The pursuit of mystery sustained Shepherd throughout her life, despite old age and infirmity. Confined physically by the failing of her body as well as the walls of her nursing home in Banchory, Shepherd's mind continued to roam, finding magic in the 'ordinary world' that brought joy in her last months.[51] Even at the end, she persisted in living 'all the way through'. Asked by Jessie Kesson whether she believed in an afterlife, Shepherd replied, 'I hope it is true for those who have had a lean life.' For herself, though, her own life 'has been so good, so fulfilling'.[52] It was a life lived with as much as in the hills of Aberdeenshire, and which ended in sight of those life-long friends.

IT WAS OCTOBER in the Cairngorms, and overnight a hoar frost had glazed grass and tree with a smooth, shrouding ice that scattered the tentative early morning sun into shards. Those faster with their boots and bags stood with their hands in their armpits, or jumped up and down while others fumbled with their laces, chilled fingers clumsy in the freezing air. Ready at last, we set off at a brisk pace, the cold making us eager to be on the move. Overhead the sky was a perfect blue, the colour as sharp as the air. We planned to walk to Derry Lodge, and from there to ascend Derry Cairngorm and Beinn Mheadhoin, 'the middle hill', whose Gaelic name recognizes the mountain's position at the centre of the Cairngorms massif even as it belies its considerable steepness. Hidden between the two peaks lay Loch Etchachan, its deep waters nestling snugly in the tight bowl of Coire Etchachan, where it is watched over by some of the highest mountains in Britain. If there is a place that can be considered the heart of the Cairngorms, it is Coire Etchachan, where routes to all points of the compass cross. But even on that perfect autumn day, bright lit by a chilled sun, it was a barren heart made of grey rock that had been sliced by water where it had not been smashed by ice. We fled from it, upwards, eager for a wider, shallower field of vision that did not force us to look deep into the earth, or ourselves.

When Nan Shepherd stood on that same spot during a summer eighty years before, her reaction could not have been more different. We were afraid to be exposed to the mountain's insides, to feel enclosed, perhaps even entombed by the place, but Shepherd found in this confined space a snugness that was both revelatory and comforting. The mountain became, for a time, a fortress, with its 'soaring barricade' of 'towering mountain walls' enclosing loch, landscape and woman. Perhaps if I'd have had her words to comfort me, I would have found the courage to enjoy the uncomplicated brutality of the place, but our acquaintance was a year away, and I was afraid.

When I next walked the mountains of the Cairngorms, it was with Shepherd in mind, and in my rucksack. It was my 35th birthday, and I had chosen to climb Bynack More. Like Coire Etchachan, it had been, for Shepherd, a place of interiorities, a place where she found she could access the cold elemental heart of the Cairngorms. I walked to the Barns of Bynack after reaching the mountain's summit, eager to see the rock-house she had described and to climb the staircase and to look out of the window as she had done: I would take temporary possession of a grand home made from stone, I thought, and play at being laird of the mountain. What I found was a towering eminence of black rock, all smooth sides and curves like a child's drawing of a cloud made hardly real, penetrated on the northern side only superficially by a few mossy clefts. The startling, lively green of the vegetation made a pleasing contrast with the dour sheen of the stone beneath, but such colour is only possible in the presence of water: any attempt to climb these slits would result in a potentially lethal slip on the edgeless rock. Only one cleft in the Barns was dry on that cloudless day: a huge schism that, from the south, looked to have cleaved the giant rock almost in two. But even this seemed dangerous to me – while the up scramble might have been possible, I had less confidence in my ability to get down again. Less brave than Shepherd, I was forced to enjoy the Barns from the outside, and to take what solace I could from the 'startling view' on my return to Bynack More's summit cairn, the preserve of 'beginners' and 'the talking tribe' who know no better.

In the years since I walked Bynack More, I have continued to try to understand the pull of the mountain interior that so thrilled and drew Nan Shepherd, but I am no match for her. Instead, it seems I must make do with the mountains' surfaces: boulders, heather, ski tracks, cotton grass, scree, summit cairn, scattering of sunlight off quartz, 'tang' of mountain height. It is enough.

EIGHT

Anaïs Nin

Yesterday I began to think of my writing – life seeming insufficient, doors closed to fantasy and creation. I had written a few pages now and then. This morning I awoke serious, sober, determined, austere. I worked all morning on my Father book. Walked along the Seine after lunch, so happy to be near the river. Errands. Blind to cafés, to glamor, to all this stir and hum and color of life, which arouses such great yearnings and answers nothing. It was like a fever, a drug spell. The avenue des Champs-Elysées, which stirs me. Men waiting. Men's eyes. Men following. But I was austere, sad, withdrawn, writing my book as I walked.

Anaïs Nin, diary entry for 30 October 1935

Anaïs Nin, the diarist, essayist and novelist, spent much of her life walking the streets of the cities in which she lived, and walking her writing into being. Born in France in 1903 to Spanish and Cuban–Danish musician parents, Nin's early years were peripatetic, with frequent moves between Havana and numerous European cities to further her father's musical career. She reached maturity in New York, though, where she went with her mother and siblings following her father's desertion of his family when she was eleven. It was here that Nin learned English – the language in which she would come to be most comfortable as a writer – and where she first began to wander on foot. The streets of New York provided much for a girl of Nin's imaginative powers who, even as an adolescent, was developing a keen observational eye which she was eager to deploy. Aged sixteen and walking with her school friend Frances, Nin wrote how

> First we walked from 112th Street to 77th Street . . . We walked fast and there weren't many people on Broadway at that time of day. About 6 we came out of the theatre and once again walked up Broadway . . . and this time Broadway was full of people of every kind. That's what I want to try to describe.[1]

New York, with its bustling, jostling crowds and packed streets, was an ideal training ground for a writer-in-the-making for whom people – and the glimpses of their lives that city-living provided – were of greatest interest. Walking the streets, Nin had discerned early, brought her effortlessly into fleeting contact with the richness, variety and strangeness of people's everyday existences. In her diary for 30 March 1919, she attempted to describe the flock of fashionably dressed and promenading women she encountered, though her first recourse in her journal was to pictures rather than words: the diary contains a small sequence of finely observed sketches of women's clothes on slender, partially realized human figures. Finding images inadequate to contain and convey the essence of what she saw, Nin followed these drawings with a written description in which she demonstrates a level of worldly cynicism that seems surprising in one so young, but which brings a knowing humour to her assessment of the scene:

> We saw all those ladies walking with little tiny steps. They almost all looked like painted dolls. Each was surrounded by several men and they looked terribly artificial. The more extravagantly they were dressed, the more attention they got from the opposite sex, which would stop walking to admire them. Some of the men stroll around on the street corners and stand there to watch the people go by. Then when a 'lady' comes along, they follow her. It was all very funny and very dumb at the same time.[2]

The entire episode hinges on Nin's subtle observations of the complex interactions between various types of walking and various types of watching. Only language is capable of capturing the mechanics of the relationship between the two – Nin's static sketches cannot record the movement on which these social interactions depend. The fashionable 'ladies' advertise, through their affected and ineffective walking – they cannot have gone far using 'little tiny steps' – their femininity and their desirability. At the same time, the men perform their masculinity and virility by prowling on street corners and following the women who walk past them. But running below all of this is Nin's own walking, and Nin's own observations. It is by walking that she is able to watch these men and women, but she is apparently a different kind of walker: the observer of this scene walks while being herself immune from the predatorial behaviour of the men. This would be a hallmark of both Nin's walking and writing – she rarely experienced any sense of risk. Instead, her work uses a detached observational mode, with Nin a confident and disinterested witness to the varied and messy life to be found on the busy streets of America and Europe.

Having reached adulthood in New York, it was in Paris, where Nin moved in late 1924, aged 26 and newly married, that she began to really hone her observational writing. It was also a city with which Nin fell quickly and powerfully in love. Barely six months after arriving, Nin's literary development had already become contingent on her relationship with the city and its many moods, which frequently mirrored or shaped her own. This relationship was developed and maintained as Nin roamed the streets at all times of day and night. The city's creative energy electrified her diary writing:

> The fever has begun again. Thoughts about everything are burning me, and on top of this, in the usual sequence, the desire to write. So I am working again to the tune of my Parisian life.
>
> This Parisian life, I am convinced now, is a constant source of irritation to me. Why? I don't know. Deeply, beyond the surface glow, I feel the impurities of it keenly. Towards nine o'clock . . . I awake to the sounds of the street, [and] a quiet enjoyment fills me . . . I walk to the windows to open the shutters, and lean over the iron railing to question the weather. If it is sunny, I am drawn outside, irresistibly. Avenue d'Iéna is wide and clean and aristocratic, and I walk up to the Étoile in the delicate shadow of lacy

trees. In the corner I breathe more deeply because the air is heavy with the scent of cut flowers on their stand . . .

Paris is like a giant park, riotous in coloring, festive in its fountains and flowers, glorious in its monuments. When I stand at the top of the Champs-Elysées, with its chestnut trees in flower, its undulations of shining cars, its white spaciousness, I feel as if I were biting into a utopian fruit, something velvety and lustrous and rich and vivid.[3]

The sensuousness of the description threatens to overwhelm the reader, with the final sentence nearly overrun by the cumulative force of all the 'ands' with which Nin attempts to capture the corporeality of Parisian life. Every sense is engaged here, though smell and touch are particularly important – Paris becomes plum-like, ripe, dripping and juicy, as the writer seems to 'take in' the city as both intellectual and physical nourishment. But the ways in which space is conceptualized is also significant, with Nin's description of how depth interacts with colour to delineate the physical bounds of the city particularly acute. The cumulative effect of all of these physical perceptions, enabled through multiple corporeal contacts with the city, is to bring Nin into the creative 'fever' state in which she is able to write.

Nin would live in or near the city for nearly sixteen years, walking its boulevards and haunting its cafés, wandering between her favourite bookshop in Montparnasse and choice strolls along the Seine, or walking through the city's parks and avenues. She walked the city in all weathers and in all lights, revelling in the violence of a winter storm, 'the kind that strikes your face', as much as the heat of the Parisian summer.[4] She frequently walked alone, though she would also stroll with lovers, particularly Henry Miller, and, occasionally, her husband. With the outbreak of the Second World War, however, Nin was forced to flee France and return to New York, something she regretted enormously. Though necessary, Nin's removal from Paris was a bereavement which grieved her for years: finally reunited years after the end of the war with the furniture she had abandoned in Paris, Nin could not bear to look at it and sold it all without hesitation.

Throughout her time in Paris, and in the numerous other cities Nin would call home during her itinerant life, she maintained a detailed diary in which she documented how she moved and felt and lived in urban spaces. By 1966 – with another eleven years of diary-writing to come before her death from cancer – her diary spanned 150 volumes which filled 'two five-drawer file cabinets in a Brooklyn bank vault'.[5] Writing, at times, nearly 100,000 words a year in her journals, Nin's diary-keeping was almost obsessively copious.[6] Her journal documents, among other things, the importance of walking to Nin's life, from its function as a mechanism to manage her emotional health, to the role it played in her writing, to its involvement in the ways in which she expressed and experienced her sexuality. For Nin, city walking offered creativity, escape, fantasy, pleasure and solace. 'When I'm sad', she wrote in 1935, 'I sometimes tire my sadness away by walking. I walk until I am exhausted. I give myself a *fête des yeux* [feast for the eyes]. I look at every shop window. Rue Saint-Honoré, rue de la Boétie, rue de Rivoli, avenue des Champs-Élysées, Place Vendôme, avenue Victor-Hugo.'[7] Anaïs Nin, who would become internationally famous for her diary, was brought into being as an author by city walking; the shape of the streets was captured in her journals, but was learned through her feet.

THERE IS NO doubting the importance of city walking to Nin's development as a writer, nor to her understanding of her own self. Readers of Nin's journals can observe over the passing of the years the ways in which her alertness to detail, and her sympathy with the people and places she encountered in her walks, contributed to her growing confidence both as an author and as a woman. On 27 April 1934, for instance, while on a visit to London to meet the writer Rebecca West, Nin wrote how 'I find myself walking the streets . . . fascinated by houses, windows, doorways, by the face of a bootblack, by a whore, by the dreary rain, by a gaudy dinner at the Regents Palace, by Fitzroy's Tavern.'[8] The observer's eye is indiscriminate, finding interesting subjects in any and all things, both high status and low. Over the next few days Nin revelled in the creative richness of London's streets, writing the next week how she walked 'the streets happy, meditating my new book', because doing so enabled her 'to know many people', to 'possess a map of realities' that was more authentic, more significant, than any municipal street plan could ever be.[9] Nin did not walk with a map, but walked to create a map, one that charted not geographical mundanities but the metaphysical wonders of people's lived experiences, the glimpses of people's lives.

Most histories of urban walking discount the possibility of women experiencing the streets in the ways Nin's diary records, or even of there being women's accounts of walking the streets at all. Instead, books have concentrated on the phenomenon of the male urban wanderer, a figure made iconic by French writers of the nineteenth century including Honoré de Balzac and Charles Baudelaire. The latter described the milieu of the male stroller, the *flâneur*, in an essay in the Parisian newspaper *Figaro* in 1863:

> The crowd is his element, as the air is that of birds and water of fishes. His passion and his profession are to become one flesh with the crowd. For the perfect flâneur, for the passionate spectator, it is an immense joy to set up house in the heart of the multitude, amid the ebb and flow of movement, in the midst of the fugitive and the infinite. To be away from home and yet to feel oneself everywhere at home; to see the world, to be at the centre of the world, and yet to remain hidden from the world – impartial natures which the tongue can but clumsily define. The spectator is a prince who everywhere rejoices in his incognito. The lover of life makes the whole world his family, just like the lover of the fair sex who builds up his family from all the beautiful women that he has ever found, or that are or are not – to be found; or the lover of pictures who lives in a magical society of dreams painted on canvas. Thus the lover of universal life enters into the crowd as though it were an immense reservoir of electrical energy. Or we might liken him to a mirror as vast as the crowd itself; or to a kaleidoscope gifted with consciousness, responding to each one of its movements and reproducing the multiplicity of life and the flickering grace of all the elements of life.[10]

Baudelaire's description is intensely male, from the analogies to the pronouns. There are, however, evident similarities between the delineation of the stroller outlined here and the powerful experiences in Paris and London that Nin documented as a woman walking the streets; Nin was also in her 'element' in a crowd, especially if she could remain detached from its business, though she was aware, as Baudelaire was, of the contradictions inherent in being both present and absent from the human bustle of the city street. And it was certainly not an exclusively male experience to feel the 'electrical energy' of city walking: Nin's prose hums with it. Nor was Nin a peculiar case – other women, too, haunted the streets of Europe and the United States in the nineteenth and twentieth centuries, finding there freedom and purpose. Despite this, there has been little acknowledgement that women participated in urban culture as *flâneurs*, or even as *flâneuses*, with just one or two exceptions. Lauren Elkin's 2016 book *Flâneuse*, for instance, laments how it is only men's accounts of walking in cities that are read, so that 'Our most ready-to-hand sources for what the streetscape looked like in the nineteenth century are male, and they see the city in their own ways.'[11] The experiences of a very small proportion of the population have formed the models for understanding human interactions with and in the city. Our views of who walks in our cities have been, and continue to be, understood solely through men's accounts, even though women like Nin, but also Jean Rhys, George Sand, Kate Chopin, Virginia Woolf and others, were just as active in utilizing their urban experiences for creative purposes.

The absence of women's experiences from studies of the city, or of city walking, has in part been the result of assumptions about what it was socially possible – or permissible – for women to do. Most accounts of walking in the city see urban walking as extremely dangerous for women because of a perceived risk of sexual assault, and the additional possibility that, historically at least, a respectable woman walking the streets might be mistaken for a prostitute – the archetypal 'streetwalker'.[12] However, such assumptions are often erroneous, and have done little more than perpetuate old-fashioned gender stereotypes. Rebecca Solnit, for example, notes that 'A man of the streets is only a populist, but a woman of the streets is, like a streetwalker, a seller of her sexuality.'[13] For Lauren Elkin, while 'We can talk about social mores and restrictions' that might have had an impact on women's walking in the city, 'we cannot rule out the fact that women were there'. Instead, Elkin insists, 'we must try to understand what walking in the city meant to them'.[14] And this means recognizing women's presence in urban spaces, and understanding how they experienced city streets as walkers and as women.

For Nin, the city was a complex place in which sexual violence was certainly a possibility, but this possibility was, for her, much less important than the opportunities she found for both sexual and creative self-expression: Nin's journals outline a very different relationship between streetwalker and street dangers, and between woman-walker and the city, than those allowed in most accounts of women in urban spaces. In the extract from Nin's diaries quoted at the beginning of this chapter, for instance, the terse two-word sentences acknowledging the presence of men on the street – 'Men waiting. Men's eyes. Men following' – would certainly seem to be full of threat, not least because these men are described solely in terms of eyes and actions; there is no consciousness in those eyes, no individual who can be identified, no internal world that can be understood, no person who might be held to account for his conduct. But while Nin acknowledges the men's presence, their gaze and their actions are unable to penetrate into *her* internal world, which is focused not on them, but on the act of 'writing' her book 'as she walks'. Whatever danger these men might seem to pose, or might be assumed to pose, Nin's experience is not one of being threatened.

Key to Nin's confidence is an acute awareness of her own sexual power and appetites, an awareness which was articulated in explicit detail in the diaries from the late 1920s onwards. In 1923 Nin married Hugh 'Hugo' Guiler, an American-born son of Scottish parents, whom Nin met and married in New York. While Nin wrote frequently how her marriage to Hugo was an essential part of her emotional life, that he was 'a refuge, a soft, dark, secure hiding place', she also acknowledged in her diaries that she found their relationship sexually unsatisfactory to her sexual needs: Hugo was, she wrote, 'in everything else sensitive, to this completely blind'.[15] Not long after, Nin began to engage in a range of extra-marital sexual adventures which included orgies, experiments with homosexuality and parallel affairs with up to five men at a time: for a period in the 1930s, she was in committed relationships with three men – Guiler, Henry Miller and Antonin Artaud – each of whom believed she was living and sleeping only with him. Nin's diaries document dozens, perhaps hundreds, of affairs, and outline an apparently perpetual sensitivity both to her sexual attractiveness and sexual arousal. Her sexuality determined in various ways how and to what purpose Nin walked the city, with implications for her work as a writer. Nin enjoyed sex and revelled in her ability to seduce and to charm both men and women, and in the midst of one of her more involved affairs – with Gonzalo Moré – she recorded in her diary how, as a result of their relationship,

> I feel vibrations through all my senses at the bodies and faces I see on the streets; it is the moment when I am sensitive and open to every leaf, cloud, wind gust, the eyes around me . . . Growing lighter and purer, walking dispossessed, as with June, walking without hat, underwear, stockings, walking poor to better feel reality, to be nearer, to be less enveloped, protected, to be purified.[16]

Walking the streets of Paris in this hyper-aroused state seems to create within Nin an almost-orgasmic connection with everything she encounters, whether that is a 'body' or a 'leaf'. These sensations are enhanced by the state of partial dress, with little by way of underwear, that Nin describes as 'walking poor', enabling her to access even more sensations, or 'vibrations'. On the one hand, the idea that walking can bring the human and the natural into closer proximity is a familiar trope of Romantic walker-writers, but here there is a sensuality to this proximity that verges on the pansexual, a circumstance from which she is taking evident physical pleasure. It follows that it is not possible for those surroundings to contain anything, or anyone, that is sexually threatening. Nin's assertive, sexual self-confidence places her in a powerful position in what becomes an intoxicatingly sensual relationship between the writer, the city and her walking of its streets.

Nin's self-possession developed in tandem with her awareness of her sexual desirability (and her knowledge of how to exploit it). Earlier in her life, her diary entries were more tentative about her existence as a sexual being, and more fearful of men when she walked in the city. As a teenager, Nin wrote several times about how she was afraid of the male students she encountered on her walks in New York. Aged sixteen, she recorded that, on a beautiful walk near Central Park with her friend Frances, they came across 'many young men carrying books, students, no doubt'. For the rest of the walk, the young Nin 'lowered' her eyes 'whenever we met them', 'as I am accustomed to do'.[17] A decade later in 1929, Nin wrote of another, rather more threatening encounter, though the development of her literary abilities transforms the experience into something rather more complex:

When I walk alone, quickly, because it is cold, in these sad streets of Paris with their fog-colored houses, my eyes seek the lights, crude artificial lights, illuminating drugstores, hotwater boys, toothbrushes, dancing on soaps; endlessly circling Michelin tyres; burning in red darts down the dark stairs of the Métro; jumping and skipping for the Revue de Paris; shining white on imitation jewelry. All in black, I follow the lights. I glance critically at the shop windows. A young man stops me; a burned-up face, burned-up with cheap living, a handsome face, lined before its time, with eyes that have seen everything. He smiles a smile that whips you with its humiliating lucidity, certain of its charm. 'Tu est trop jolie pour te promener seule'. [You are too pretty to walk alone.] I decide to cross the street. I look to the right, and to the left, swiftly. I step forward. But a taxi, which has been parked, suddenly backs out. It touches me, barely. The young man pulls me back in time, without a smile, without a word. I dart across the street again, walk without looking at the shops.[18]

The account begins as a record of Parisian street life, with the observer magpie-like in her attraction to brightness. The mundane is rendered bizarre by the evening light, the tyres transformed from black rubber into burning red darts of flame descending towards the subway, which is itself transfigured into something like hell. The present tense enables readers to feel like they are walking with the observer through the city's colourful wonders, but it also ensures that when the narrator encounters the 'burned-up man', we too feel threatened. The effect is that when he, 'wordless' and unsmiling, pulls the observer away from the taxi, it feels like an assault – forceful, coercive and devoid of human connection. In this silent and ambiguous encounter, Nin creates a sense of danger – the man's familiarity is unsettling, his intentions impossible to determine – but there is also a sense of narrative distance. The observer has had time to see that the taxi 'has been parked' for a while at least, and events proceed sequentially through decision, action and consequence. While this makes sense in the earlier part of the passage, when the observer is moving at walking pace through streets that unfold lineally, the involvement of multiple actors in the second half makes such a simple progression less plausible. Nin evokes a disturbing moment of sexual and physical vulnerability for the solitary woman walker, but it is a moment that has had narrative order imposed upon it: the literary sits awkwardly with the experiential, and makes it impossible to determine the boundary between truth and narrative, and between threat and creative encounter.

For Nin, there was an important link between sexual experience, sexual confidence and the development of her literary voice, all of which were bound up with the ways in which she walked through the city. In the diary entry she wrote in London in 1934, she documented how 'Only the watchfulness of the men cuts my wings, because I feel I could be easily swayed and I don't want a banal adventure. Or maybe I'm just a coward. My imagination runs amok, but I can't yield to the passerby's interest.'[19] It is not sexual threat that here 'cuts the wings' of the observer, but awareness of her own sexual desires. This woman is not the passive prey of the men who gaze upon her, but is, in fact, an equally sexual being making definite choices about the types of physical encounters she seeks. To acknowledge the presence of the men is not to make herself a victim of their sexual urges, but of her own: it would be a 'banal adventure', not a sexually exciting or satisfying one. This, in Nin's writing, is the fundamental standard by which encounters with men are to be judged: pleasure, not danger. However, what Nin most required was 'Solitude', because that, she felt, was 'the true expression of myself. As I walk for hours alone, I accept myself, I accept what I am. I no longer censure myself, nor will I let others censure me. Obedience to the mystery, which the journal seeks only to describe, no longer to explain.'[20] Independent of others' judgements or desires, Nin's sexual and literary selves were free to take shape on the city's streets.

It was walking the Parisian streets that enabled Nin's decision to 'accept herself', and to make a determination to resist the judgements of others upon her: pedestrianism opened up for Nin new possibilities about how she saw herself, and how she wished to be seen by others. Walking also helped Nin understand what she sought to achieve as a writer. On foot, she came to understand that what she wished to do was 'describe' the 'mystery' of her existence, rather than to offer any explanation for or of it, and that the best means of achieving this aim was through her diaries. As she matured as a writer and as a woman, she became increasingly aware of the complex network of connections between what she did, how she moved and who she was.

One of the fruits of this increasing awareness was the story 'The Labyrinth', published as part of *Under a Glass Bell*, a small collection of short stories printed by Nin's own press in 1944. After many years of frustration at her failure to attract the notice of the literary establishment, Nin with this collection finally found both critical and commercial success: the first edition sold out within three weeks.[21] She succeeded in fusing 'life and art, fact and imagination',[22] and her readers found themselves enchanted by tales that were 'half short stories, half dreams'.[23] 'The Labyrinth' takes as its starting point the moment in Nin's life when, aged eleven, she began to write a diary; from this biographical fact, Nin creates a Surrealist fairy tale, a coming-of-age story set in a landscape where the intangible and the undefinable are made manifest. Words and feelings take on physical form, and paper is inscribed just as easily by the narrator's feet as by her pen. The story opens with the narrator entering, Alice-like, into a dream world unbound by physical laws:

> I was eleven years old when I walked into the labyrinth
> of my diary. I carried it in a little basket and climbed the
> moldy steps of a Spanish garden and came upon boxed
> streets in neat order in a backyard of a house in New York.
> I walked protected by dark green shadows and followed a
> design I was sure to remember. I wanted to remember in
> order to be able to return. As I walked, I walked with the
> desire to see all things twice so as to find my way back into
> them again.[24]

In this place, the metaphorical becomes real, and the distinction between the imaginative and the factual collapses. Here, walking functions both as a physical act and as a figurative device which stands in at various times for writing, living and experiencing. Walking also serves as both memory and map, and becomes a vessel which is able to contain all the ideas and knowledge needed to navigate this peculiar terrain. The landscape is one where the distinction between beginning and ending is uncertain, and where even the boundaries of the labyrinth are unclear; only on foot can the narrator come to any knowledge of the place. Walking is simultaneously metaphor and process.

As the narrator moves through this Wonderland-like place, words themselves start to twist, shifting between the abstract concrete from signifiers of meaning to physical surfaces upon which the narrator is able to walk. Abruptly, these surfaces become vertical rather than flat, and the narrator finds herself 'walking up a stairway of words', before realizing that she is not, in fact, walking at all, but simply retreading the word 'pity'.[25] 'I was walking on the word pity pity pity pity pity pity,' she says, but 'When the word was the same, it did not move, nor did my feet.'[26] Communication, Nin reminds us, is a physical act, and requires movement (of mouth, tongue, feet) if it is to be successful. Emotions and experiences, too, take on solid form and become the labyrinth through which the narrator walks. Words become an 'escalator', moving the narrator forwards until she finds that 'I was walking on my rebellions, stones exploding under my feet.' Sorrow and grief become obstacles, causing the narrator's feet to slip 'on accumulated tears' like 'the slippery silt of river banks', before rising up to become the walls of the labyrinth itself, nightmarish in their tangibility: 'I touched rock-crystal walls with white foaming crevices, white sponges of secret sorrows set in a lace of plant skeletons. Leaves, skins, flesh had been sucked of their juices, and the juices and sap drunk by the crevices, flowing together through the river bed of stillborn desires.'[27] The water imagery continues, with the narrator now struggling for footing as she traverses 'gangways, moats, gangplanks' before she finds herself 'suspended between earth and sea, between earth and planets'.[28] Shadows, footprints and echoes are all 'left behind' in this strange in-between place, all three serving as poignantly temporary markers of a momentary human presence: a walker is only ever just passing through.[29]

The story climaxes with the narrator walking into a 'white city' made of a 'honeycomb of ivory-white cells' – a sepulchral beehive – with 'streets like ribbons of old ermine'.[30] Buildings are held together by a mortar mixed with 'sunlight, with musk and white cotton', pale luxuries fit to partner the ivory and the ermine. But the city is actually made not of ivory or ermine, nor of musk or cotton, but of paper. From her contemplation of the city's various textures, the narrator is 'awakened by a sound of paper unrolling':

> My feet were treading paper. They were the streets of my own diary, crossed with bars of black notes. Serpentines of walls without doorways, desires without issues. I was lost in the labyrinth of my confessions, among the veiled faces of my acts unveiled only in the diary . . . My feet touched the leaves of intricate flowers shriveling, paper flowers veined with the nerves of instruments.[31]

It is not the hand wielding the pen that is able to 'unveil' the acts contained by the diary, but the feet which are walking the 'streets' that are both text and life, both paper and tears. Mapping this internal landscape of dreams and imaginings can only be accomplished on foot.

Nin's 'labyrinth' was internal and external, hers and humanity's, and exploring it required real and imagined walking. At times she felt 'like a fugitive from the mysteries of the human labyrinth' she was trying to understand through her writing, but determined that 'The outer world is so overwhelmingly beautiful that I am willing to stay outside, day and night, a wanderer and a pilgrim without abode.'[32] Nin was particularly keen on this kind of 'wandering' when she was in company with one of her lovers. The couple would walk the city streets – typically at night, though certainly not always – and at these times Nin wrote of her feelings of wild exhilaration, of being intensely present in the moment in a way that brought her profound happiness. One day with Henry Miller, for instance, she described how

> Saturday was magical. I had an errand to do, and Henry began his trick of following me until Hugh's return. We wandered through the city like two southerners, two conva-lescents, he said, very close, very soft, very sentimental . . . Nowhere else do I find this magic, this beautiful, complete present. Together the moment becomes infinite.[33]

Nin craved the 'magic' wrought by walking with a lover, but most special of all was the 'magic' of walking with a new lover. Even imagining this was intoxicating to Nin. Tiring of Henry Miller, she was, by 1935, on the hunt for someone different. In her diary, she wrote 'I am in love walking down Villa Seurat in the red Russian dress and white coat, in love with the world and the one who is coming, who is on his way, the one who will travel with me.'[34]

In the summer of 1936, Nin determined on making the Peruvian artist and Communist Gonzalo Moré her newest lover, and the trajectory of their affair was directly shaped by their city walks. At the beginning of their liaison, Nin wrote how

> At nights through the streets, kissing, smelling . . . I am ensorcelled by his beautiful dark face, his vehemence, his poetry. He creates as we walk, between kisses, a white pas-sion, which he subtly, perversely intensifies by denial. He won't take me.

Through the ugly city we walk blindly. It is the middle of
the night and we are sitting by the river . . . We are so drunk
on kissing we reel through the streets.[35]

While Nin walked with many of the men in her life, walking
with Moré seems to have had a particular significance for her.
Her diary of this period is littered with accounts of varied wanderings during which the exploration and enjoyment of her
feelings for Moré came to be overlaid onto her understanding
of Paris, with each informing the other. Moré and Nin walked
through 'villages of ragpickers and gypsies' at the edge of the city,
'Little villages of shacks' in which were housed 'All the leftovers
of the city, the odds and ends, the rags, broken pipes . . . detritus'
both inanimate and human.[36] They walked so far so often that
Nin's feet began to hurt her, but the result was joyous.[37] One
morning, six months into the affair, Nin described awakening
'Overflowing with energy, courage'. Driven by the power of
this sensation, she writes, 'I take my diary and walk the streets.
I plot with Gonzalo. I fall into a reverie.' On foot, reflective,
she determines that 'The time to act has come, and man awakes
first. I have to catch up.'[38] Walking the city with Moré fostered
a new kind of creative energy brought about not only by the
novelty of a new lover, but the different parts of Paris she was
now exploring. These areas were sometimes quite removed from
the elegant boulevards Nin had previously haunted, but the thrill
of walking in these at times insalubrious places, 'Through the
marketplaces, the whorehouses, the abattoirs, the butcher shops,
the scientific laboratories, hospitals, Montparnasse' brought
such creativity that Nin felt herself able to 'walk with my dream
unfurled and lose myself in my own labyrinths'.[39]

Walking Paris as Moré's lover added a significant new element in how Nin conceptualized and understood the city. In addition to finding its rough and derelict corners a powerful catalyst for her literary creativity, she also began to view the city in terms of the relationships she had conducted there. By this time, Nin had lived in Paris for over a decade, and existed within what she would later term a vast 'spiderweb' of connectivity, not only as a result of her own numerous liaisons, but of her husband's professional activities as a banker and artist, the presence of her family and their social circle, and her own network of platonic acquaintances.[40] These various social spheres jostled for space in the Paris of Nin's memory so that the streets of this imagined city became uncomfortably crowded. A year into her affair with Moré, Nin wrote how

> Gonzalo and I walked back through the Bois, passed le boulevard Suchet, where I first visited [Otto] Rank [her therapist and former lover], passed Boulevard Suchet studio. At seven we parted at the Passy subway station. At seven Hugh and Horace [Guicciardi, a solicitor friend of Hugh's] were bicycling through the Bois while I walked back along the rue de Passy to the little restaurant on the rue Boulainvillier, where Henry and I used to eat when we stayed in the rue des Marronniers.[41]

A sequence of near-misses and an account of lives lived in parallel, Nin's diary entry describes a city permanently populated by lovers real and remembered so that every space is occupied: there is very little room here between lives or experiences, and it seems inevitable that at some point, some of them will crash into each other. For all the danger and strain of so full a city – and so full a memory – Nin's experiences as a walker in Paris are significantly enriched because every street, every café, is overlaid repeatedly with memories and loves.

These memories would sustain Nin through the years of the Second World War and her exile in America. Towards the end of her affair with Moré, who had also fled to New York, Nin was able to find solace in being able to overlay a happier past onto a less certain present:

> Gonzalo and I are still walking the streets together . . .
> We still sit at cafés together, we still lament having no shelter to make love, and have to content ourselves with furtive caresses stolen with the anxiety that Hugh might come, but we are not walking the streets of the present, but of the past, an echo of an early passion, its human echo, a once-shared passion, a flame with enduring reverberations. We are not sitting at today's cafés, but at an extension of the Paris cafés.[42]

Nin came to conceive of the streets of Paris as repositories for her recollections of those she had loved, so that walking, as it had been for Dorothy Wordsworth a century earlier, became a form of memory.

As a walker, Nin was able to transform the world in which she lived in astonishing ways: she had the ability, honed while she walked Paris and New York, to reimagine the city as a series of interconnected lives giving shape to, and being shaped by, the streets on which they were experienced. She could also conceive of walking as a kind of bodily inscription in which the path is the page, in a world where we can touch and hold all the thoughts we have ever had. The diaries and fiction which emerged from Nin's walking gave form to these impossible worlds and enabled others to enter those strange places. As a walker-writer, the rules of the ordinary, physical world did not apply to Nin. Instead she was able to escape 'in space, fluid, beyond all walls, all doors', to a place only her feet, with the help of her imagination, knew how to find.[43]

I WAS LIVING IN BOSTON when I found Anaïs Nin. Having read a passing reference about her city walking, I searched her out in Harvard's Widener Library, where I pulled book after book of hers from the shelves. I walked home that day the 2 miles from Harvard Square to my rooms with Nin's writing in my hands, intrigued by how her imaginative powers were rooted in her walks across New York and Paris. I had never really attended to the pleasures of strolling among people whose lives I could only guess at. Cities to me had usually meant fears of attack and, in the U.S., anxiety about being perceived as peculiar for preferring to walk. Boston, however, was a perfect city for a novice *flâneuse*; not only are visitors encouraged to experience the city on foot, but even the locals avoid driving on Boston's hellish roads.

For a few weeks, then, I wandered the city at all times of day and night with a feeling of safety. I strolled along Boston's famous harbour just after dawn and stood looking out to the Atlantic, where I imagined home was just over the horizon. I drifted through the Common, watching the hustlers. I picked up the Freedom Trail that links Boston's historical sites and dipped in and out of the crowds as the feeling took me. I delighted in seeing so many people out on the streets, so many women. With some I exchanged glances, others a nod of the head. These moments of connection seemed some kind of acknowledgement of a shared purpose. We were streetwalkers, and these were our streets to walk.

NINE

Cheryl Strayed

In the vision I'd had of myself ten years before, I felt sure I'd have published my first book by now. I'd written several short stories and made a serious stab at a novel, but I wasn't anywhere close to having a book done. In the tumult of the past year it seemed as if writing had left me forever, but as I hiked, I could feel that novel coming back to me; inserting its voice among the song fragments and advertising jingles in my mind. That morning in Old Station . . . I decided to begin.

Cheryl Strayed, *Wild*

The Pacific Crest Trail is one of the most arduous walks in North America. It runs for 2,650 miles from the Mexican border north to Canada, following the various mountain ranges that separate the West Coast of the United States from the country's arid interior, and climbing at its highest point to more than 13,000 feet. Those wishing to walk the whole route in a season are recommended to allow a good five months, carefully timed to avoid the worst of the late winter snows in the Sierra Nevada, while arriving in the north before the onset of the next mountain winter. The logistics involved in attempting to 'through-hike' – the act of walking long sections of the trail or the whole thing – are daunting. The trail stays away from large settlements, and it would be impossible for hikers to carry all the food, clothes, water and other equipment they would need. Instead, they must post supply parcels to themselves to be held at post offices or general stores near the trail, which they collect as they walk. Even so, few people complete the whole trail each season. Of those who have so far managed the full distance, approximately one-third have been women.

Cheryl Strayed set out alone to walk part of the Pacific Crest Trail (PCT) in 1995 when she was 26, after the collapse of her marriage, the death of her mother and a dalliance with drugs. Over three months she covered a distance of 1,100 miles across two sections of the trail, a journey recounted in her memoir *Wild*, published in 2012. A movie of the same title, starring Reese Witherspoon, appeared in 2014. Strayed decided to hike the PCT alone, with no previous experience of long-distance walking, because she picked up a guide book by chance:

> I would walk that line, I decided – or at least as much of it as I could in about a hundred days. I was living alone in a studio apartment in Minneapolis [Minnesota], separated from my husband, and working as a waitress, as low and mixed-up as I'd ever been in my life. Each day I felt as if I were looking up from the bottom of a deep well. But from that well, I set about becoming a solo wilderness trekker. And why not?[1]

Strayed's naive optimism is hopelessly misplaced, and will likely rankle with any experienced walker who knows the difficulties of long-distance trekking. But at the root of Strayed's bombast is not ego, but a desperation to find an identity with which she can be comfortable. Having been, by her own account, 'so many things already', from a 'loving wife' to 'an adulteress', a 'beloved daughter' to 'an aspiring writer who hopped from one meaningless job to the next while dabbling dangerously with drugs and sleeping with too many men', she aspires at the beginning of her journey to become 'a woman who walks alone in the wilderness for eleven hundred miles'.[2] Such a person is to be admired rather than condemned, celebrated rather than pitied. Such a person might even be comfortable with herself.

The means of acquiring this identity, Strayed quickly discovers, is through pain, desperation and despair. Entirely unprepared for the rigours of the PCT, Strayed encounters considerable physical suffering almost from the moment she sets off. However, the pain that results from her ignorance becomes, as she walks further and further, a form of purification: by walking until her feet bleed, Strayed scourges herself, expunging with suffering all the shitty things she has done to herself and others. Through the act of walking the Pacific Crest Trail, Strayed comes to believe she can change.

From the start, near Mojave in southern California, it is clear that Strayed's hike will be no idyllic stroll – will bear no resemblance to the walks of Dorothy Wordsworth, Virginia Woolf and certainly not Nan Shepherd. Closest is Elizabeth Carter and her love of vagabonding across the countryside, but even that kind of walking falls far short of what Strayed was about: it was to be brutal and brutalizing. Finding herself alone in the parking lot of a grubby motel, carrying nothing but what she will take on the hike, she feels 'suddenly exposed, less exuberant than I had thought I would', having failed to imagine during the six months of planning the desolation of beginning.[3] A few days later, in the initial stages on the trail, Strayed recalls, 'I'd thought I'd weep tears of cathartic sorrow and restorative joy each day of my journey. Instead, I only moaned, and not because my heart ached. It was because my feet did and my back did and so did the still-open wounds all around my hips.'[4] Many of these wounds are caused by the inadequate kit purchased by the inexperienced Strayed, which she fails to test before starting on the PCT despite being 'firmly advised' to make a 'trial run'.[5] Instead, Strayed packs her rucksack for the first time the morning of her first day, cramming into it an exhausting and frankly bewildering array of equipment.

Strayed describes working her way through what she calls 'the mountain of things, wedging and cramming and forcing them into every available space of my pack until nothing more could possibly fit'.[6] Her plans to use her five bungee cords 'to attach my food bag, tent, tarp, clothing sack, and camp chair' to the outside of the bag come unstuck when she realizes how much more will need to be housed there: sandals, camera, mug, candle lantern, trowel, keychain, thermometer.[7] And on top of all this, Strayed is also to carry 'two 32-ounce [950-ml] plastic water bottles and a dromedary bag capable of holding 2.6 gallons [1 l] of water', as there is little fresh water to be found on the PCT itself.[8] The water alone weighed, Strayed calculates, 11 kg (24½ lb) – a debilitating weight for anyone, never mind a novice walker hiking the hot, dusty, undulating PCT.

With everything packed at last, Strayed is ready to set off:

> I put on my watch, looped my sunglasses around my neck by their pink neoprene holder, donned my hat, and looked at my pack. It was at once enormous and compact, mildly adorable and intimidatingly self-contained. It had an animate quality; in its company, I didn't feel entirely alone. Standing, it came up to my waist. I gripped it and bent to lift it.
>
> It wouldn't budge.[9]

In the film version of *Wild*, this scene is played for laughs: the petite Reese Witherspoon's frame is comically dwarfed by that of a monstrous backpack she cannot lift – at least, until she straps herself into it on the floor before deadlifting its vast weight to vertical. Whatever humour is in the scene is quickly cancelled out, however, by the realization that, rather than rethink or repack, Strayed is walking out of the door bearing this bag, bent double, determined to walk the PCT with it. Instead of rearranging the load (or, even better, ditching a pile of stuff), Strayed tightens the hip straps in a desperate attempt to make the bag less terrible to bear by redistributing some of the weight from her shoulders. The bag feels 'pretty awful', but being totally ignorant of hiking with kit, Strayed assumes that 'this was how it felt to be a backpacker.'[10]

Throughout Strayed's account, though, the physical suffering – which abates only marginally as the miles pass – has an importance that transcends comedy or tragedy. Indeed, at times it serves as a peculiar sort of protection. Early on, it prevents Strayed from being afraid: of unknown creatures; of what she has undertaken; of being in the wilderness alone; of being alone in the wilderness as a woman. Later, she finds that as she becomes inured to her pain, she also gains emotional toughness. A week or so into her journey, Strayed writes,

> It had begun to occur to me that perhaps it was okay that I hadn't spent days on the trail pondering the sorrows of my life, that perhaps by being forced to focus on my physical suffering some of my emotional suffering would fade away. By the end of that second week, I realized that since I'd begun my hike, I hadn't shed a single tear.[11]

This hardening is not at the expense of the capacity to feel emotional pain or grief. Rather, the intensity of those feelings is reduced by the intensity of the physical discomfort. Strayed's grief at her mother's death is not removed, but sublimated by pain from a sense of overwhelming loss into something approaching acceptance. In this way, as Strayed walks through wildflowers that remind her of her outdoorsy childhood, she writes, 'I felt the presence of my mother so acutely that I had the sensation that she was there': on the trail Strayed finds companionship with the dead, rather than feeling abandoned by those she has lost.[12]

Bodily experiences are at the heart of Strayed's account of her time on the PCT: all that her mind is capable of, she says, is playing a 'nonsensical loop' of jingles and adverts from some sort of bizarre 'mix-tape radio station' to accompany the relentless trudging.[13] There is little, as a result, to document beyond the physical. Having a female body, though, means Strayed's experiences are different from most of those who publish accounts of what it means to be a human walking, though they are not different to many of those who actually walk. As Strayed makes clear, while it was unusual for a woman to walk the PCT solo, many women did walk it; and it was also unusual, it should be remembered, for men to walk the trail alone. Greg, a fellow 'through-hiker' who overtakes her on the trail in California, highlights Strayed's distinctiveness by informing her that since starting at the southern end of the trail near the Mexican border, 'You're the only solo woman I've met so far out here and the only one I've seen on the register.'[14] At her first supply point at Kennedy Meadows, the woman behind the counter hands over the only package that has arrived with 'a girl's name on it'.[15] Here, among six men who have also gathered at Kennedy Meadows, Strayed is forced to consider for the first time the significance of status as a woman walker. Described by one of the men as 'the only girl in the woods', Strayed becomes aware that she is 'alone with a gang of men'. Her response, which she feels is borne out of 'necessity', is to 'sexually neutralize the men I met by being, to the extent that was possible, one of them'.[16] Rather than experiencing this as a threat to her body, however, for Strayed, the threat is posed to her sense of identity – her sense of herself as a particular kind of woman.

Initially it seems necessary for Strayed to negate herself, by becoming 'one of the guys', and therefore less female. However a significant shift in Strayed's thinking occurs. To feel safe on the trail, Strayed does not have to turn herself into a man, but accept herself as a different type of woman. Rather than being forced to 'inhabit' a more masculine identity, Strayed, now that she has become a walker, is no longer able to adopt the feminine identities she had previously worn as if they were costumes. All that is left is a single identity, one that is showing its 'grubby face to the whole wide world' for the very first time. It is the identity of a woman 'who walks alone in the wilderness' – the sort of woman Strayed herself had wished to be.

As Strayed walks further and further along the PCT, her identity as a woman of the wilderness – hardened, tough, determined – becomes more firmly embedded. And it is not just an internal transformation, but a change inscribed into her body. Three weeks in, Strayed finds herself in a motel following a decision to bypass the High Sierra mountains because of unseasonably late snows. In front of a mirror for the first time in a fortnight, Strayed is startled by what she sees:

> I did not so much look like a woman who had spent the past three weeks backpacking in the wilderness as I did a woman who had been the victim of a violent and bizarre crime. Bruises that ranged in color from yellow to black lined my arms and legs, my back and rump, as if I'd been beaten with sticks. My hips and shoulders were covered with blisters and rashes, inflamed welts and dark scabs where my skin had broken open from being chafed by my pack. Beneath the bruises and wounds and dirt I could see new ridges of muscle, my flesh taut in places that has recently been soft.[17]

The violence done to the body of this solitary woman walker has been inflicted entirely by herself, by walking the trail. As such, it is thrilling, not frightening, and there is a sense of pride in Strayed's account at not only having suffered it, but having endured it – even thrived under it. Emerging from beneath the bruises and scabs, in a kind of particularly brutal metamorphosis, is a muscular, strong, vital body. Not that the transformation is yet complete. Miles later, just over the border into Oregon, Strayed again sees herself in a mirror after a long period on the trail. She is leaner again, with 'my hair lighter than it had been since I was a little girl', though her body is nothing like that of a little girl's, with its '100-percent-muscle ass and thighs.'[18] The changes to Strayed's body are wrought by the 'scorching cure' of the trail, purging her of anything extraneous until all that is left is distilled, essential strength.[19]

So fundamental are these changes that they alter the internal geography of Strayed's body to the point that it is no longer familiar to her:

> Mid-afternoon, I felt a familiar tug inside me. I was getting my period, I realized. My first on the trail. I'd almost forgotten it could come. The new way I'd been aware of my body since beginning my hike had blunted the old ways . . . The smallest inner reverberations were obliterated by the frank pain I always felt in the form of my aching feet or the muscles of my shoulders and upper back that knotted and burned so hard and hot that I had to pause several times an hour to do a series of moves that would offer a moment of relief.[20]

The physiological signs of impending menstruation might be the same as they were in her old life, but Strayed's understanding of this once-familiar experience is transformed as a result of the physical demands of the PCT. Her period is demoted to a 'small inner reverberation', whose cramps or abdominal discomfort are trivial when compared with the shrieking muscles being shredded by the trail. Now inhabiting a body in which 'the only thing to think about' is 'whatever was the physically hardest', Strayed experiences her own internal world anew.[21]

Her description also forces the reader to understand a different internal view – the embodied perspective of a woman. By reading only accounts of walking written by men, such matters must rarely, if ever, have assumed any importance in our understanding of what it means to walk. But menstruation and its associated sensations – cramping, a change in mood, altered energy levels and the physical sensation of bleeding steadily and continuously for days at a time – must have been, and surely are, regularly felt by the many, many women for whom walking has mattered. Strayed's experience of walking is frequently informed by her understanding of herself as an embodied woman, and while her increasing physical strength is evident to those she meets, it makes the most impression on the women she encounters. Like Dorothy Wordsworth and Sara Hutchinson in Scotland entering into a house where only grieving women are present, Strayed as a woman walker is able to access, and give voice to, experiences that are unavailable to men.

Forced off the trail once again, this time by a combination of snow, slow progress and inadequate supplies, Strayed is given food and a shower by a stranger, Christine, because Strayed is a lone woman, and Christine is impressed by her courage. A mother of two teenage daughters, Christine sees in Strayed qualities she wishes for her children. 'I'd love it if they did something like you're doing,' she says to Strayed, 'If they could be as brave and strong as you.'[22] Two girls who subsequently give Strayed a ride back to the trail are similarly admiring, and it is perhaps no coincidence that it is while Strayed is in the company of women that her thoughts turn to her mother, whose presence at this moment she feels 'so acutely', it almost takes her breath away.[23]

A few days later at Belden Town, Strayed meets Trina and Stacy, both of whom have been on the PCT for two or three days. Strayed has met plenty of men on the trail, many of whom she befriends, but, she writes, 'At last I'd met some women on the trail! I was dumbfounded with relief as we exchanged in a flurry the quick details of our lives.'[24] In contrast with her encounters with men, Strayed describes feeling an immediate sense of camaraderie with these women, though why she should feel 'relief' at meeting them goes unexplained, at least directly. A little later she writes that she had 'been savoring the company of the women all day, grateful for the kinds of conversation that I'd seldom had since starting the PCT'.[25] As a woman among women, Strayed is able to enjoy a companionship different from any she has previously known as a walker. Her sense of 'relief' might well be because, for once, she is with people whose physical experiences and inner lives mirror her own.

However, while Strayed finds strength and friendship in the company of women and in the changes to her body, the femaleness of Strayed's experience is, on one occasion, a distinct disadvantage. Despite widely held views about women's sexual vulnerability if they head outside on their own

– views articulated by Strayed early on in her account – none of the other women in this book write of experiencing a clear physical threat from men. Strayed's description of a meeting with two men in Mount Jefferson Wilderness in Oregon is, therefore, more shocking because it is so unusual, both in the context of her own experiences – where the male hikers are to a man friendly and kind – and more broadly. The encounter begins innocuously enough, with two hunters coming into a clearing where Strayed is about to set up camp, and asking for water. Now an experienced woodswoman, Strayed teaches the men how to use her water purifier, but they quickly break it through carelessness. From here the sense of threat grows quickly, with Strayed finding herself made uncomfortable by the way one of the men is 'openly appraising my body'.[26] The men then turn all that has made Strayed strong and resilient against her, claiming that they cannot believe 'a girl like you would be all alone up here. You're way too pretty to be out here alone, if you ask me,' and objectifying the strong female body she has created by discussing Strayed in the abstract: '"She's got a really nice figure, don't she?" the sandy-haired man said. "Healthy, with some soft curves. Just the kind I like."'[27]

At this point she lies to the men about walking further and the men head off in the opposite direction to the great relief not only of Strayed but of her reader. As she recovers from the adrenaline spike, 'letting the knot in my throat unclench', she reassures herself that 'They'd been obnoxious and sexist and they'd ruined my water purifier, but they hadn't done anything to me.'[28] She sets camp and changes her clothes, but then one of the men returns. Strayed has encountered dangerous animals on the trail – a black bear early on, a rattlesnake

– but this is the first time she describes having to manage a predator who might attack. 'Terrified' by the man's presence, Strayed feels as though she has 'come across a mountain lion and I'd remembered, against all instinct, not to run. Not to incite him with my fast motions or antagonize him with my anger or arouse him with my fear.'[29] All the wildlife, all the wilderness, that Strayed has encountered are less dangerous to her than this man in this moment. He has watched Strayed undress and, as he continues his sexual harassment, all that she has achieved – all the internal and external strength she has built – threatens to collapse to nothing. Inside her mind, she describes hearing 'a great clanging', which is the devastating 'realization that my whole hike on the PCT could come to this. That no matter how tough or strong or brave I'd been, how comfortable I'd come to be with being alone, I'd also been lucky.'[30] Instead of the ability to walk unassaulted being a right, the man's presence turns personal safety into a matter of good fortune. And 'if my luck ran out now, it would be as if nothing before it had ever existed, that this one evening would annihilate all those brave days.'[31] At stake here is not just the vulnerability of Strayed's female body, but the identity she has created for herself, and which is now an integral part of that self. Rape would violate her physically, but it would obliterate her mentally. It would erase Strayed as she has come to know herself.

At the moment of crisis, however, Strayed is 'saved' by the return of the man's companion. The two men leave together, though not without a parting threat from the predatory man, who raises his can of Pepsi in a mock toast: 'Here's to a young girl all alone in the woods,' he says.[32] While the physical danger is no longer present, the psychological effects prove longer-lasting. Half-hearted attempts at self-reassurance proving ineffective at calming her, Strayed bolts despite it being nearly dark:

> I shoved my tent back into my pack, turned off my stove, dumped the almost-boiling water out into the grass, and swished the pot in the pond so it cooled. I took a swig of my iodine water and crammed my water bottle and damp T-shirt, bra, and shorts back into my pack. I lifted Monster [Strayed's name for her bag], buckled it on, stepped onto the trail, and started walking northward in the fading light. I walked and I walked, my mind shifting into a primal gear that was void of anything but forward motion, and I walked until walking became unbearable, until I believed I couldn't walk even one more step.
>
> And then I ran.[33]

She eventually stops and pitches tent, though she continues to feel frightened and anxious for a time afterwards. Eventually, though, the rhythms of walking the trail take the sharpness off the memory of what happened, the 'scorching cure' of the PCT again proving effective at forcing the mind to consider the current moment rather than lingering on past traumas.

Strayed's hike on the PCT was not ultimately defined by what happened in Mount Jefferson Wilderness. Instead, she writes about the 'pure, unadulterated' joy she feels as she walks towards the end point of her hike, and about the easy companionship she finds on the trail earlier in Oregon. She even discovers a strange comfort in the unrelenting physical hardships forced upon her by the trail, which mean that 'Even after all this way, with my body now stronger than it had ever been and would likely ever be, hiking on the PCT still hurt.'[34] At the end of her walk, on the bridge over the Columbia River south of Portland in Oregon, Strayed comes to realize that her life from this point will be shaped and defined by what she has just done. And only in the telling of the story of her hike on the PCT, Strayed writes, can the full meaning of her experience 'unfold inside of me', a 'secret' that is 'finally revealed' years later.[35] It's a story Strayed first tells her children, sat on the bridge where she found herself at the end of the trail to be a woman walker: strong, capable, independent and free.

I HAD SPENT much of the three weeks I'd been in Los Angeles staring, love-struck, at the mountains that hemmed in the city to the north. The only walking I'd managed so far was a warm and over-populated hike up Mount Hollywood (which at least meant I'd been able to tick off the obligatory selfie with the Hollywood sign), a sweaty scramble up Runyon Canyon further west in Hollywood and a great deal of pavement pounding between Pasadena and San Gabriel. What I'd not been able to do was to escape the concrete confines of the sprawling city. I had decided not to hire a car during my stay in order to use my feet in this famously car-obsessed megapolis, but I had not reckoned on my mountain-love. Although the lower slopes of the San Gabriel mountains are just about accessible by public transport from the city – if you count a 3.6 mile walk to the Metro station, a thirty-minute train ride and a twenty-minute walk to the trailhead as accessible – the wilder walking of Los Angeles county ironically requires a vehicle.

It was by luck that I came across the Sierra Club's website. A Google search of 'LA walking clubs' was my last-gasp attempt to avoid paying ninety-odd dollars for two days' car hire to facilitate a walking weekend. Several pleading emails to various club officials yielded the information that I should apply to the Pasadena branch, and a couple more begging letters brought me in touch with Don Bremner, one of the Pasadena walk leaders, who happened to be organizing a walk that weekend from Mount Wilson. It was agreed that if I could get a taxi to the car share point at La Cañada Flintridge on the northern edge of the Los Angeles basin, Don would get me to the walk start and would drop me back home afterwards. Early on the Saturday morning, I arrived at the designated meet point to be greeted by Dave Taylor, another walk leader, and Don, whose handshake was warm and firm, and whose lean limbs and rangy frame suggested a gait that would eat up miles.

Rarely have I been more excited for a walk, and as Don's slightly knocked-about car whisked us up the Angeles Crest Highway into the hills, my excitement turned to exhilaration. We climbed rapidly, passing flocks of intrepid cyclists pedalling hard up the relentless gradient, and in a matter of minutes, 60 or 70 miles of conurbation, with a glint of ocean to the west, were laid out seemingly flat below us.

Our destination, Mount Wilson, is a prominent peak above Los Angeles: in part because it is one of the highest mountains in the eastern San Gabriels at nearly 6,000 feet, but also because of the transmitter masts that bristle along the summit ridge like spines. Fourteen of us disgorged from the small fleet of cars that had brought us to the trailhead just below the rash of masts. Immediately, the route took us down into chaparral and pines. It was a little cool in the deep shade, for this was January, and we were 5,500 feet above sea level for all that it was California, but the path wound pleasingly down into the woodland. The soil in the Los Angeles area is loose and fine, especially when it is dry; and it has been very dry here, I was told, for nearly a decade. At times the path, or 'tread', as Don called it, had partially given way, leaving little more than a foot's width of shifting, unstable soil for us to walk on, dangerously high above rock-littered ravines. I skipped over these sections as if the path were covered in hot coals, keen to trust my body weight to the ground as few times as possible. I had just days before discovered I was pregnant with my first child, and my sense of risk had shifted as rapidly as my physiology. A slick river bed caught me by surprise; all the streambeds we had passed had been dry, and my mind was focused on the next heart-stoppingly narrow section of path. At the last moment, I remembered to look out for a loose wire and caught hold just as my balance was about to tip me down a large and slimy rock shelf.

Soon afterwards, the terrain changed, and we were walking on paths that actually deserved the name. Now, without the anxiety about whether the ground was going to give way, I was able to look about me. The trail contoured around the hillside, weaving in and out of gulches and gullies, always descending. Suddenly the trees dropped away, and we were treated to our first views of the distant mountains. On the horizon was one snow-capped peak – this was Mount Baldy, I was told – the highest mountain in the San Gabriels at over

10,000 feet. Ordinarily in January the whole range (including our own Mount Wilson) would have been covered in snow, but in only one winter of the last five had the traditional snows appeared. While this was an appalling indictment of the effects of climate change on the area, we benefited that day by being able to walk because of the unseasonably warm weather.

The path clung to the hillside well above a nexus of wooded valleys for a mile or more before dropping us back into the forest just above Valley Forge Camp Ground, where we stopped for lunch. We sat in the sun on benches so high that even Don, all 6 ft 5 in. of him, could swing his legs like a boy. Chatting gaily, we shared our packed snacks of fruit and chocolate before beginning our climb towards the walk end at Red Box. Almost immediately, we were enveloped once more by the trees. Here I saw sycamores with broad five-fingered leaves and oaks which yielded the largest acorns I had ever encountered: if there were squirrels with mouths large enough to store those giant fruits, I was disinclined to meet one. I was also perplexed by what appeared to my northern European eyes as a peculiarly a-seasonal landscape: the oaks and sycamores had shed their leaves, and the ghostly pale bare branches of some kind of birch glowed eerily in the forest shade; but for the manzanita, yucca and other mountain plants, this was prime growing time, and their vibrant green spoke more of mid-summer than late January. The shade produced by the vegetation was welcome though, as the air temperature pushed somewhere north of 20°C (68°F) and I hauled myself up the surprisingly sustained climb back up the mountain. The final section was up a winding, sandy staircase which broke through the canopy and brought the full heat of the sun onto my sweating back, but it also brought the breeze. All of a sudden, I was at the top, and as my body paid down its oxygen debt, my eyes wandered again to the far horizon, and the peaks of the Pacific Crest in the distance.

TEN

Linda Cracknell
and a Female Tradition

The writing of any story is mostly re-writing . . . I think
of it as a repeated walk; a loop with varieties or diversions.
Revisiting our own memories is like this too. We subtly
reconstruct them as we go, so that our life stories are less
like photographic, objective reality and more like an act
of imagination, re-invented over and over.

Linda Cracknell, *Doubling Back*

For many women who walked, including Dorothy
Wordsworth, Nan Shepherd, Anaïs Nin and Linda
Cracknell – a writer living in the Tayside town of Aberfeldy
– going over the same ground brings into being a connection
between present and past selves, and between these selves
and the future. By virtue of walking a path that endures
beyond the limits of human lifespans, we can inhabit the
same space as our selves-that-were, and keep the path open
for the selves-to-come. For Cracknell (and for Shepherd,
and Nin, and for Wordsworth before them), retreading a
path also enables the creation of a sympathetic connection
between individuals that is powerful enough to reach across

time. In 2014 Cracknell published a book, *Doubling Back*, whose purpose was to explore the power and significance of the bond created through rewalking routes laden with past importance. There are dangers, though, in retracing steps and seeking to walk over previous ways: memories of a teenage love affair begun during a week's walking around Boscastle in Cornwall feel, for the older Cracknell, fragile and tenuous when contrasted with the sharp, bright edge of the present. Cracknell returns to the village thirty years after her first visit 'with a soft tread', eager to avoid destroying earlier memories in the process of creating new ones, 'fearful of shattering dreams' by walking too heavily on the paths of the past.[1] However, going back, it turns out, does not destroy the wonder or the vitality of these earlier times. Instead, Cracknell experiences something of the walker's wonder when, on turning to look back at where you started, you realize just how far your feet have been able to carry you. In retracing her steps, Cracknell is able to see, for the first time, 'a clear pathway between that 17 year old who was learning to draw and paint and the woman who writes in 2008'. She observes that 'We are not so different. I've not outgrown . . . my passion for paths and for walking as well as for literature': the present self is just further along the way.[2]

But the main concern of Cracknell's walking is not to reconnect with her youthful self, but to find ways to connect with those who have gone. Over the course of her book, she explores routes traced by those who are dead, with whom she seeks through walking to create empathy. In these walks, Cracknell looks to tread 'those paths that beat with a human resonance', and to learn to use her own body as a means 'to re-tell someone's story' in order to find something of those who have been lost.[3] For Cracknell, and for Dorothy Wordsworth and other women walkers, the pedestrian body becomes a conduit through which past, present and future are connected. The physical self is a medium through which time, stories, lives, all intersect. For Cracknell, this is particularly important because one of the paths she retraces was walked by her father, the man who helped give life to her body, but who died of cancer when she was a young child.[4] For this man Cracknell has no name, having grown up without him since 'before I had much language', but through walking in his footsteps, she is gradually able to come to some understanding of who he had been. Those footsteps lead Cracknell to the Alps, where her father climbed as a student at Oxford while a member of the Oxford University Mountaineering Club. Surrounded by the high, sparkling peaks which he ascended, she is able to imagine her father as an Alpine raconteur, the 'life and soul of the party' camping in the mountains, and as Cracknell herself climbs Finsteraarhorn she comes, by covering the same terrain, to bring her father back to some sort of life.[5] She envisages him, 'in this three weeks or so of adventure before his "grown-up" life began, feeling viscerally alive as he breathed the fine Alpine air'.[6] Half a century later it is Cracknell herself who feels herself supremely alive as she walks: using the body her father gave her, she gives life to him in turn.

Walking in the Alps enables Cracknell to form this resonant and valued tie to her father – to regard with fondness 'that meeting place of deep ice' within which her life and his now intersect – because she too imprints her presence on the mountain terrain in the same way.[7] Yet there are differences between his walking and hers, between their physical realities. For one, Cracknell finds that there is no comparison between the mountain apparel of the 1950s and the clothes modern walkers and climbers are expected to want to protect their bodies from weather and risk:

> His mountain photographs feature equipment made of canvas, wool and hemp. When I prepared myself by looking at a few websites about alpine climbing gear, I was quite overwhelmed by recommendations for lightweight crampons, clothing made from Windstopper, Polartec Powershield, Schoeller Dryskin Extreme, etc. I decided to make do with a 20-year-old ice axe, borrowed crampons, wool leggings under summer-weight walking trousers.[8]

Sitting awkwardly somewhere between the 1950s and the 2000s, Cracknell's equipment is both better and worse than that used by her father on his journey through the Alps, but whereas he was a committed and experienced Alpinist, used to the terrain and the equipment required to navigate it safely, his daughter is making do and borrowing. Hers will be by necessity a limited experiment in Alpinism. Nor, Cracknell finds, does she share her father's love of the very highest peaks, admitting to questioning her desire to climb so high where the 'fearful implications' of injury and death are the Alpinist's constant companions.[9] Cracknell confronts the reality that his body is not hers – that his life is not hers – a fact which is demonstrated by her strong preference for 'the lower ways and passes where lives still linger, where green things grow'.[10] Walking in the Alps serves to move Cracknell both closer to and further away from her father, a sensation given physical form for her by the sweep of the mountain's glaciers over which they have both now walked: her father's footprints are a long distance 'downstream' from her in the ice, having 'drifted' over the half-century since he stood in the snow.[11] Yet having walked over the glacier herself, Cracknell too has left footprints that will also move, in time, down the valley, making of the ice a 'great . . . meeting place' of lives otherwise sundered.[12]

Walking and writing are, for Cracknell, both fundamentally empathetic activities. Literature connects 'us to the lives of others', she writes, and it has evident parallels with pedestrianism: walking '"in someone else's shoes" . . . and on their paths connects one to their stories'.[13] This is central to Cracknell's attempts to connect with the father she long ago lost. But she is also conscious of the importance of walking to her own creative practice, where it enables her to 'think better on the move, think more creatively . . . Attentive to both inner and outer landscapes', and so Cracknell also seeks to follow other women for whom walking mattered in order to connect her story to theirs.[14] The first is Jessie Kesson, the Scottish novelist, poet and BBC Radio playwright, who lived, for a time in the 1930s, above Loch Ness at Achbuie. A friend of Nan Shepherd's in later life, Kesson wrote frequently about her experiences wandering the hillsides above the Great Glen in a number of her novels as well as her radio plays. These wanderings enabled Kesson to find solace in the land after a year's incarceration in a mental hospital following a chaotic childhood. Walking for Kesson was a means of reconnecting with herself, something she learned as a young child while on the move with her much-loved but troubled mother. Later Kesson would write that

> The first eight years of my childhood were spent in a small room in a city tenement. My mother, country born and bred, was alienated from her family, so that springs and summers were spent wandering through the highways and byways of her Morayshire roots. We haunted that wide landscape. Rarely able to afford public transport my feet became as tough as new leather.
>
> Most people have a specific destination in mind on their weekend journeyings. A point to their travels, a stately home, a garden open to the public, an acquaintance whom they might 'drop in on' in the passing. Not us. Never us. The countryside itself was the magnet that drew us.[15]

Kesson 'haunted' the landscape around Achbuie too for the six months that she lived there, 'boarded out', as Cracknell records, to live with 'an elderly woman on her croft'.[16] There Kesson was able to 'ramble freely', with no walls to contain her.[17] Not needing a destination to wander, she simply walked where she would, and, as a result, Cracknell finds that 'The visceral thrill of the place in springtime pulses through her writing in different genres ever after.'[18] Kesson wove her experiences above Loch Ness into a number of writings, from magazine pieces to poems. In them she explores the physical qualities of the place with a minuteness of attention that suggests how thoroughly she had come to 'learn' the place through her walking:

A high hill-slope nine miles west of Inverness. It is curious –
up there where one is surrounded by crags, deep gulleys and
all the sterner stuff that goes to make a hill – to find Springs
so profuse, and green, and gentle. It would be hard to find
one bit of brown earth on that hillside in April, for bracken,
rightly called 'lovely curse' by Highland folk, spreads like a
vast, young, strong plantain, and all through the bracken,
in countless multitudes, cluster primroses that are thick and
yellow and smelling like spice.

The hill is composed of red rock, and in clear, Spring
sunlight the rocks glow like fire.

It is so high up that you feel as if in any moment you
might topple into Loch Ness below. They say the loch is
bottomless and treacherous, yet, on calm days, it is, as
Coleridge writes 'a painted ocean'.

Spring in the hills would confront the greatest artist with
too vast a panorama. I doubt if he could ever capture it. For
Spring there is more than colour; it is music and scent. The
burns literally hum down the hillside, the trees have rhythm
in their shaking. The smell of Spring in the hills is a blend-
ing of peaty thickness, bracken-mould, flowers' spicyness,
and clean, quick purge of the wind. Down in the hollows
anenomes, bereft of smell, gleam in pale patches.[19]

Like Harriet Martineau in the Lake District eighty years
before, Kesson found in the hills a new freedom, a release from
physical confinement. And like Martineau, Kesson celebrated
and internalized this freedom by walking in a place in which
life could now expand, so that, in Kesson's case, she became
attuned to the unique 'rhythm' of each tree's susurration.

It is in spring that Cracknell comes to Achbuie, eager to bring herself into some sort of contact with Kesson's 'powerful influence', to 'share her exuberance' for life and for walking.[20] On the hillside above Loch Ness, Cracknell begins to imagine a young Kesson romping across the landscape, its 'precipitous pathways of loose rock' offering danger and challenge to her and to the young children who followed Kesson about.[21] As Cracknell herself explores this place, these imaginings become more substantial, so that the landscape becomes haunted in an eerie echo of Kesson's characterization of her early wanderings. Climbing higher onto the moor, Cracknell writes,

> The wind carved down the lochside, and the bare birches rang maroon against a clear sky. Deer poured uphill on winter-dusky heather whose wiry stems snapped at my bootlaces. I kept turning, wondering whose step it was that caught at the back of mine, half expecting to find a line of children in a giggling retreat.[22]

But it is by imagining herself into Kesson's feelings, as she walked for the first time on this hillside after her release from hospital, that Cracknell populates the place. The spring air buzzes with sound, from the 'Birdsong bubbles' to the 'buzzard-mewls', to the 'Soft unexplained pops' which 'rise from the grass', just as it did when Kesson trod the ground here: the seventy years between the two are erased by the infinitely recurring spring symphony.[23]

> I imagine Jessie Kesson stepping from the deadened enclosure and stale air of the mental hospital into this cacophony

of sound and the sense of elevation. Coming from a regimented institution with every thought and activity crowded by other lives, this could hardly have failed to provoke her free spirit and to animate her feet in exploration. Perhaps it recalled her to those barefoot walks with her mother and a sense of inhabiting again her wild self.[24]

Cracknell is also attentive to the 'music' of the place and seeks to know the hillside as Kesson did by composing a detailed aural topography that is sensitive to the subtle variations in tone and sound. Descending from the high moorland, Cracknell searches for the exact way Kesson came down from the croft. Once 'Sure of Jessie's route down the burn', Cracknell retraces the older woman's steps down secretive and cunning paths:

> I cross the burn, follow the lane a little south, wondering where Jessie would have found the next part of her descent. And there, between one burn and the next is a gate and a path marked by a scattered line of brown leaves, leading down between trees. It is unremarked on the map and delights me with the soft secrecy of its way. Here there is soprano birch leaf and the bronzy tenor of the first clusters of oak leaves.[25]

Cracknell is willing to use her body as Kesson did, to use ears and mind to listen with attention and discrimination to the mellifluous and multi-tonal 'music' of the burns. Consequently, she moves beyond mere imagination to reanimation by bringing to life once more the sensations and experiences enjoyed by Kesson. At the end of her walk, Cracknell feels like she has 'brushed shoulders with a character' in the 'green song-tunnels beside the burn'.[26] For a time, Cracknell's use of her body – from her feet to her ears – is able to recreate something of Kesson's physical presence.

Coda

I first walked the Birks of Aberfeldy on an overcast and drizzling January afternoon a few years ago. The previous summer I had gobbled up all the Munros in nearby Glen Lyon in one exhausting sitting, but in October a disc in my back, between my L5 and S1 vertebrae, had given way in spectacular fashion and, after four months of intensive recovery, I had only just been cleared by my physiotherapist to start gentle hill-walking again. The Birks seemed perfect: an hour's amble up a beautiful wooded glen would give an attractive walk with little strain for my back and would leave plenty of time for a hot chocolate at one of the lovely cafés in town. There were, though, other reasons, besides physical necessity, to walk the Birks. Having read Dorothy Wordsworth's account of her experience there when touring Scotland with her brother, and Linda Cracknell's loving descriptions, I was eager to not only experience the walk for myself but to see whether treading in their steps brought me the same sense of connection that Cracknell experienced on Jessie Kesson's hillside above Loch Ness: I was looking to 'brush shoulders' with the characters I had been reading and thinking about for so long. Certainly the presence of Dorothy Wordsworth at the Birks was significant for Cracknell – a great deal more so than that of Robert Burns, the much more frequently remembered chronicler of the area's beauty, whose visit is commemorated by a statue. Coming abruptly upon the newly installed monument complete with ready-made faux verdigris, Cracknell is appalled by its crass celebration of the man instead of his poetry. In response, she recalls Dorothy Wordsworth's visit in 1803. 'I like to picture her walking here', she writes, 'with her stooped gait and tanned face. Instead of the birches she remarked on the planted laburnums', which, for Wordsworth, surpassed anything else she had seen in autumn for colourful beauty.[1] 'Dorothy's words haven't earned her a statue,' Cracknell tartly concludes.[2]

As I read and reread both Wordsworth's journals and Cracknell's writing, I had been moved by Cracknell's evocation of how meditation and memory rippled across time to bring together two women who walked the same ways over and over again. As I walked the Birks, I had them both in my mind – what they thought as they walked, how they felt – but I didn't manage to achieve any sense of direct connection with either mind. It had certainly been enjoyable reflecting on other women's experiences there and comparing my own, but I failed to experience any kind of empathetic bond.

A year before, I had been in the Lake District walking with a group of friends, scholars who wrote about the Wordsworths and the literature of the Lake District. We decided to traverse the ridge above Thirlmere from Raise to Grisedale Tarn before moving down to Grasmere. Although we had not discussed it explicitly, we all enjoyed the idea of walking the hills that the Wordsworths walked, and doing so in fellowship. We

began from St John's in the Vale, from where we would climb
to the ridge. We had hoped for the opportunity to reflect on
the literary history of our walk, but as we ascended out of
the quiet valley to begin our traverse, we began to encounter
not just one or two, but dozens and dozens of other people.
On every hill and at every pass, we could see that people had
made tracks as broad as any major road: there was nowhere
that did not bear the signs of people passing in their hundreds,
perhaps thousands. We walked quickly over Helvellyn and
made for the relative quiet of the descent past Dollywaggon
Pike to Grisedale Tarn, hopeful for some respite of the crowds.
As we approached the water, I thought again about Dorothy
and William Wordsworth saying farewell to their brother
John for the last time at that exact place and once more tried
to imagine the grief felt by Dorothy each time she returned
after John's death. But however hard I attempted to forge the
kind of bond written of with such power by Cracknell and
Shepherd, Nin and Woolf, I could not call the Wordsworths
into the landscape. I tried to imagine them stood at the water's
edge; I tried to imagine what Dorothy might have worn the
day she saw her brother for the last time, but I couldn't: the
sober colours of their handmade clothes could not compete in
my mind with the bright shades of Goretex cascading down
the hillsides around me.

My failure at Grisedale and at the Birks troubled me for
a time. But as this book has progressed, and as I have walked
with more and more women writer-walkers in my mind, their
experiences and writings have fizzed in my brain, overflowing
at times onto the people I have been walking with. In this way,
whole hours on the hills have been taken up by me talking

about Anaïs Nin's Parisian wanderings, or describing Sarah Stoddart Hazlitt's physical strength, or arguing about Nan Shepherd's characterization of the Cairngorms. Now, every time I go for a walk, whether it's on a path they took, or one that I've adopted as a favourite, or a brand new route, I take them all with me: they are as essential to my walking as my waterproof jacket and boots, and I pack them as carefully. I find I am conscious now of myself as a *woman* walker, and of the rich cultural heritage that attaches to that description. I am increasingly aware of how much more frequently I talk with other women walkers when I am alone as a woman walker, than when I walk in a group, or with my husband, and I understand that these encounters have something in common with the experiences of Dorothy Wordsworth, Joanna Hutchinson, Stoddart Hazlitt and Ellen Weeton. My path is now 'companioned', to borrow Nan Shepherd's lovely phrase, by these women-wanderers.

THERE ARE DOZENS and dozens more women who loved and wrote about their walking, from the eighteenth-century playwright Hannah More, to the cross-dressing novelist George Sand in the nineteenth, to the short-story-writer Katherine Mansfield in the twentieth century, to Rebecca Solnit, Clare Balding, Raynor Winn and Kate Humble in the twenty-first. Women have always walked, first from necessity and later, as society gained more leisure time, for pleasure. Women writers too have, for hundreds of years, found walking to be essential to their creative processes, and to their sense of self. Walking has served a variety of purposes – purposes as varied as the women themselves. It has been a means of communing with the dead (Wordsworth, Cracknell), of defying convention (Carter), of self-discovery (Stoddart Hazlitt, Strayed), of relief (Weeton, Kesson), of stepping beyond the self (Nin, Shepherd), of escaping personal difficulties (Stoddart Hazlitt, Weeton, Kesson, Woolf, Nin). And for the many hundreds of other women writers who have walked over the centuries, it has served more purposes besides. Of course, women have experienced restrictions on their ability to walk, including the constraints of domestic and childcare responsibilities as well as perceptions of safety and vulnerability, but these restrictions did not stop women from walking, though they shaped their experiences on foot. However, assumptions about what women could and could not do have sometimes been used to justify a continued failure among those who have written about the significance of walking to even *look* for women's accounts. These assumptions, and the omission of women from the literature of walking, can no longer be justified. For women walkers, their literary creativity is bound to walking just as tightly, and just as profoundly, as men's. But women move differently, see differently and write differently about their experiences. To deny the existence of their accounts is to deny ourselves our own history.

APPENDIX

In this book I have chosen writers for my chapters according to a fairly strict set of criteria. While they had, of course, all to be walkers, I was looking for writers who actively reflected on their pedestrianism, or who found in their walking something that contributed to their understanding of themselves as authors and as people: walking, for inclusion in this book, had to intersect with other areas of these writers' lives in ways which has a significant impact on their work. This approach, I hope, has illuminated the complex and varied roles played by walking in several women's lives, and that our understanding of their work has been enriched by considering them as walkers. However, there have been hundreds, perhaps thousands, of women walkers over the centuries, and no single book can hope to cover them all, or to convey the richness of each woman's experience. In this appendix, then, I offer some suggestions for reading by other women who walked, or who have published about women's walking. Some of these women fictionalized their walking; others walked often but wrote about it infrequently; but for all of them, walking played an important part in their lives and in their writing.

Austen, Jane (1775–1817)

Elizabeth Bennet is perhaps the best-known of Austen's many celebrated heroines, but her disregard for fashionable social rules is flagged in *Pride and Prejudice* by Austen's description of her as a walker. Austen herself was a keen pedestrian around her home in Chawton in Hampshire, though she found the muddy winter lanes an impediment. Austen seems not to have written any sustained account of her walking, but her letters outline her rambles round her Hampshire home. See *Jane Austen's Letters*, ed. Deirdre Le Faye (Oxford, 2011).

Balding, Clare (b. 1971)

TV and radio presenter Clare Balding has hosted for many years a long-running and much-loved radio show called *Ramblings* (www.bbc.co.uk), and has also written about her walking in *Walking Home: Great British Adventures . . . And Other Rambles* (London, 2015).

Bodichon, Barbara (1827–1891)

Born into an unconventional family (her parents were radicals, Unitarians and unmarried), Bodichon was granted as a young woman a sum of money on which she could live. Such financial independence was rare, and it helped Bodichon pursue what would be a lifelong commitment to women's education and rights, culminating in the establishment of Girton College, Cambridge. She was an ardent walker, though the wonderful story that she strode through continental Europe on walking tours with her friend Jessie Parkes in hobnailed boots and cut-off skirts appears, unfortunately, to be apocryphal. Bodichon wrote of her other travels in works including *An American Diary, 1857–8*, ed. Joseph W. Reed Jr (London, 2018).

Brontë, Charlotte (1816–1855), Emily Brontë (1818–1848) and Anne Brontë (1820–1849)

All three Brontë sisters walked frequently across the moors around their Yorkshire home in Haworth, with numerous critics arguing that the women drew on their experiences on foot to craft their fiction. *Wuthering Heights* (1847, Emily Brontë) especially is read as emerging from its writer's intimate knowledge with the high Yorkshire land in all weathers. Charlotte Brontë's letters are perhaps the best source of information about the walking habits of the three women – in them she describes walks at home, walks while abroad and walks undertaken for companionship and in memory. Unfortunately, few personal papers belonging to Anne or Emily Brontë survive. See Charlotte Brontë, *Selected Letters*, ed. Margaret Smith (Oxford, 2007), and *The Brontës: A Life in Letters*, ed. Juliet Barker (London, 2016).

Campbell, Ffyona (b. 1967)

Campbell is a professional long-distance walker. Her achievements include crossing the U.S., Australia and the continents of Africa and Europe. She wrote about her experiences on these various journeys in three books, *On Foot through Africa* (London, 1995), *The Whole Story* (London, 1996) and *Feet of Clay: On Foot through Australia* (London, 1999).

Chopin, Kate (1850–1904)

An American short story writer and novelist, many of Chopin's stories hinge on the act of walking: the women in her work, trapped by circumstances, or marriage, tend to find walking the mechanism by which they are able to leave their old worlds behind. Chopin herself was a keen walker, and on her honeymoon in 1870, she walked extensively in a number of European cities, sometimes alone. Later in life, she took to walking the streets of St Louis, Missouri, or New Orleans, Louisiana, early in the morning, unaccompanied and sometimes eccentrically dressed. Her most famous novel is *The Awakening* (1899), in which walking plays a crucial role. More of her writings, including the short stories which initially brought Chopin fame, can be enjoyed in *A Kate Chopin Miscellany*, ed. Per Seyersted and Emily Toth (Oslo, 1979).

Farjeon, Eleanor (1881–1965)

Most famous as a children's writer – she won three major awards during a lengthy and celebrated career – Farjeon was also close friends with the poet Edward Thomas, with whom she would go tramping in the early twentieth century. She wrote of their relationship in the part-biographical, part-memoir book *Edward Thomas: The Last Four Years* (Sutton, 1997).

Kesson, Jessie (1916–1994)

A novelist, playwright and radio producer, Kesson worked across a range of genres as a writer. Much of her work, in all modes, was inspired by her experiences living and working in the Highlands of Scotland, especially near Inverness. Born to a mother who later became a prostitute, Kesson was taken into an orphanage and subsequently worked in domestic service before a breakdown prompted a year-long stay in hospital. As she recovered, Kesson was sent to live with an elderly woman on a croft above Loch Ness. She later became a friend of Nan Shepherd's. Kesson wrote a number of novels, including *The White Bird Passes* (Edinburgh, 2003) and *A Glitter of Mica* (Edinburgh, 1998). She also wrote about walking and the countryside, especially in *A Country Dweller's Years: Nature Writings*, ed. Isobel Murray (Edinburgh, 2009).

Mansfield, Katherine (1888–1923)

Born in Wellington in New Zealand, Mansfield left her native country for Britain aged nineteen. She began writing and publishing in New Zealand, but it was in Britain that she found fame as a short story writer. Walking was an important part of Mansfield's life, and served as balm during periods of difficulty and distress. Being on foot also helped Mansfield remember her home and her brother, who was killed in the First World War. Her walking is documented most clearly in *The Journal of Katherine Mansfield* (London, 2006).

Mitchell, Emma (currently active)

Mitchell's book *The Wild Remedy* (London, 2018) explores the importance of walking in nature in maintaining good mental health. Mitchell recounts her ramblings during which she made detailed observations and drawings of the natural world.

More, Hannah (1745–1833)

Poet, playwright, novelist and teacher, Hannah More in late life suffered extremely from ill health, but in her thirties and forties, she was an ardent walker, enjoying rambles in the countryside around Bristol, as well as longer walks. It was on a walking tour with William Wilberforce that More persuaded her friend to become involved in the growing movement to abolish the slave trade in Britain, an event recorded by Wilberforce in his journal. More's experiences are recorded in a number of letters (www.hannahmore.co.uk).

Radcliffe, Ann (1764–1823)

One of the most popular novelists of the later eighteenth century, Radcliffe earned a fortune through her gothic tales, including *The Mysteries of Udolpho* (1794). She also walked, and published an account of her journey through the Lake District: *Observations during a Tour to the Lakes of Lancashire, Westmoreland, and Cumberland*. A new and affordable edition, edited by Penny Bradshaw, has recently been published by Bookcase of Carlisle (2014).

Rhys, Jean (Ella Gwendolyn Rees Williams, 1890–1979)

Born in Dominica, Rhys came to Britain aged sixteen. During the 1910s and 1920s Rhys lived a peripatetic life in Britain and Europe, walking to Paris at one point. Rhys lived in the city for a while, but subsequently moved to a number of European cities with her journalist husband. Walking, especially in Paris, was important to Rhys both as a writer and as a woman, and it was in the city that her literary career took off in earnest with the publication of *Voyage in the Dark* in 1934.

Sagner, Karin (currently active)

Sagner's book, *Women Walking: Freedom, Adventure, Independence* (New York, 2017) features numerous works of art depicting women on foot from the eighteenth century to the present day.

Sand, George (Amantine Lucile Aurore Dupin, 1804–1876)

A French novelist and memoirist, Sand was a keen walker, especially on the streets of Paris. Her memoirs do not give enormous detail about her walking, but do explain how she sometimes dressed as a man in order to pass more freely round the city. She also considered a good pair of boots important for a walker. See *Story of My Life: The Autobiography of George Sand*, ed. Thelma Jurgrau (New York, 1991).

Shelley, Mary Wollstonecraft (1797–1851)

Like her mother, Mary Wollstonecraft, Mary Shelley travelled extensively in Europe. As a teenager, she journeyed through France and Italy with her lover, the poet Percy Bysshe Shelley, visiting many important cultural sites. While in Europe, Mary Shelley began to find her voice as a writer, and started work on what would be her most famous story, *Frankenstein* (1818). Before her debut novel appeared, Mary Shelley published an account of her continental journey, *History of a Six Weeks Tour* (London, 1817), documenting her travels.

Solnit, Rebecca (b. 1961)

Solnit's *Wanderlust* (London, 2002) is one of the few histories of walking written by a woman. While its theorization of women's walking has been important in the development of this book, *Wanderlust* is also important as a record of Solnit's own walking in northern California and beyond.

Stewart, Alexandra (b. 1896)

Born in Glen Lyon in Perthshire before the arrival of the motor car, Stewart recounts in *Daughters of the Glen* (ed. Innis Macbeath, 1986) a childhood spent on foot. Much of this walking was with a purpose – simply travelling along the glen involved walking. But Stewart speaks too of walking for pleasure, and of simply walking for the sake of walking, with no particular destination in mind. Stewart's long intimacy with the beauties of the Glen enable her to bind together in her account history, social change, the realities of rural life in Highland Scotland and the importance of coming to know the land by walking it.

Thompson, Flora (1876–1947)

A postmistress for much of her life, Flora Thompson walked miles each day as part of her work. These experiences helped shape her writing, especially the *Lark Rise to Candleford* trilogy, originally published in 1939 (Oxford, 2011), which is set in rural Oxfordshire at the turn of the twentieth century.

Winn, Raynor (currently active)

A former farmer, Winn and her husband became homeless. Winn writes of the two seasons she and her husband spent walking the

South West Coast Path with just a tent and a small amount of money in *The Salt Path* (London, 2018).

Wollstonecraft, Mary (1759–1797)

Before meeting her lover Gilbert Imlay, Wollstonecraft had worked as a governess, and later a literary reviewer and polemicist, publishing *A Vindication of the Rights of Men* and *A Vindication of the Rights of Woman* in 1790 and 1792, respectively. In these texts, she argued for radical political and social reform. In the mid-1790s Wollstonecraft undertook a journey to Scandinavia, then a little-visited and little-known place. Accompanied only by her infant daughter Fanny, Wollstonecraft there undertook secret work on behalf of Imlay, an American citizen. While in the north, Wollstonecraft undertook numerous walks, often at times of great emotional distress (her relationship with Imlay was collapsing at the time). She published a record of her experiences in *Letters Written During a Short Residence in Sweden, Norway and Denmark* in 1796.

REFERENCES

Setting Off

1 Thomas de Quincey, *The Collected Writings of Thomas de Quincey*, ed. David Masson (London, 1896), p. 242.
2 Figures taken from Morris Marples, *Shanks's Pony: A Study of Walking* (London, 1959).
3 William Wordsworth, Preface to *Lyrical Ballads* [1800], ed. Michael Gamer and Dahlia Porter (Peterborough, ON, 2008), p. 175.
4 Rebecca Solnit, *Wanderlust: A History of Walking* (London, 2002), p. 123.
5 Carole Cadwalladr, 'Frédéric Gros: Why Going for a Walk Is the Best Way to Free Your Mind', *The Guardian*, www.theguardian.com, 20 April 2014
6 Elizabeth Carter to a friend, n.d., in *Memoirs of the Life of Elizabeth Carter*, by Montagu Pennington (London, 1809), p. 106.
7 Elizabeth Carter to Catherine Talbot, 24 June 1763, in *Memoirs*, p. 275.
8 De Quincey, *The Collected Writings of Thomas de Quincey*, p. 239.
9 Dorothy Wordsworth to unknown recipient, April 1794, in *The Letters of William and Dorothy Wordsworth: The Early Years 1787–1805*, ed. Ernest de Selincourt, rev. Chester L. Shaver (Oxford, 1967), vol. I, p. 113.
10 Dorothy Wordsworth to Aunt Crackenthorpe, 21 April 1794, ibid., p. 117.
11 Sarah Stoddart Hazlitt, 'The Journals of Sarah and William Hazlitt, 1822–1831', ed. William Hallam Bonner, *The University of Buffalo Studies*, XXIV/3 (1959), p. 208.

12 Ellen Weeton, *Miss Weeton's Journal of a Governess*, ed. J. J. Bagley, 2 vols (Newton Abbott, 1969), vol. II, pp. 33–4.

13 Sarah Stoddart Hazlitt, *The Journals of Sarah and William Hazlitt 1822–1831*, p. 208.

14 Robert Macfarlane, *The Old Ways* (London, 2012), p. 24.

15 Harriet Martineau, *Autobiography*, 2 vols (Boston, MA, 1877), vol. I, pp. 1146–7.

16 Virginia Woolf, journal entry for Saturday 27 February 1926, in *The Diary of Virginia Woolf*, vol. III: *1925–1930*, ed. Anne Olivier Bell and Andrew McNeillie (London, 1981), pp. 62–3.

17 Macfarlane, *The Old Ways*, p. 24.

18 Anaïs Nin, diary entry for 3 August 1937, in *Nearer the Moon: From a Journal of Love: The Unexpurgated Diaries of Anaïs Nin* (London, 1996), p. 76.

19 Anaïs Nin, diary entry for 19 February 1920, in *Linotte: The Early Diary of Anaïs Nin, 1914–1920* (San Diego, CA, 1978), p. 445.

20 Anaïs Nin, diary entry for 7 August 1931, in *Linotte: The Early Diary of Anaïs Nin*, vol. IV: *1927–1931* (San Diego, CA, 1985), p. 455.

21 Nin, diary entry for 13 October 1927, in *Linotte: Early Diary of Anaïs Nin*, vol. IV: *1927–1931*, p. 25.

22 Nin, diary entry for 3 August 1937, in *Nearer the Moon*, p. 76.

23 Nan Shepherd, *The Living Mountain* [1977] (Edinburgh, 2011), p. 4.

24 Cheryl Strayed, *Wild: A Journey from Lost to Found* (London, 2013), p. 95.

25 Linda Cracknell, 'Stepping Out, Stepping In', blog entry for 30 January 2015 on Walkhighlands, www.walkhighlands.co.uk, accessed 22 August 2017.

26 Alexandra Stewart, *Daughters of the Glen*, ed. Innis Macbeath (Aberfeldy, 1986), p. 17.

27 Ibid.

28 Linda Cracknell, 'Mother Nature's Recipes', blog entry for 30 October 2015 on Walkhighlands, www.walkhighlands. co.uk, accessed 22 August 2017.

29 Solnit, *Wanderlust*, p. 234.

30 Ibid., p. 245.

31 Robert Macfarlane, 'Introduction' to *The Living Mountain*, by Nan Shepherd, p. xvii.

1 Elizabeth Carter

1 Elizabeth Eger, *Bluestockings: Women of Reason from Enlightenment to Romanticism* (Basingstoke and New York, 2012), p. 7.
2 Norma Clarke, *Dr Johnson's Women* (London, 2001), p. 33.
3 Elizabeth Carter to Catherine Talbot, 24 May 1744, in *A Series of Letters between Mrs. Elizabeth Carter and Miss Catherine Talbot*, 4 vols (London, 1809), vol. I, pp. 58–9.
4 Elizabeth Carter to Elizabeth Montagu, 13 March 1759, in *Letters from Mrs. Elizabeth Carter to Mrs. Montagu, Between the Years 1755 and 1800*, 3 vols (London, 1817), vol. I, p. 27.
5 Elizabeth Carter to Elizabeth Vesey, 30 October 1763, in *Letters between Mrs. Elizabeth Carter and Miss Catherine Talbot*, 4 vols (London, 1809), vol. III, pp. 227–8.
6 Elizabeth Carter to Elizabeth Vesey, 23 September 1783, in *Letters between Mrs. Elizabeth Carter and Miss Catherine Talbot*, vol. IV, pp. 333–4.
7 Elizabeth Carter to Elizabeth Montagu, 2 July 1762, in *Letters from Mrs. Elizabeth Carter to Mrs. Montagu*, vol. I, pp. 166–7.
8 Elizabeth Carter to Catherine Talbot, 5 August 1748, in *A Series of Letters between Mrs Elizabeth Carter and Miss Catherine Talbot*, vol. I, p. 287.
9 Elizabeth Carter to an unknown correspondent, undated, in *Memoirs of the Life of Elizabeth Carter* by Montagu Pennington (London, 1809), p. 26.
10 Elizabeth Carter to Elizabeth Montagu, 30 May 1772, in *Letters from Mrs. Elizabeth Carter to Mrs. Montagu*, vol. II, pp. 134–5.
11 Clarke, *Dr Johnson's Women*, p. 26.
12 Ibid.
13 Ibid., p. 27.
14 Elizabeth Carter to Elizabeth Vesey, 30 September 1779, in *Letters between Mrs. Elizabeth Carter and Miss Catherine Talbot*, vol. IV, pp. 233–4.
15 Elizabeth Carter to Elizabeth Vesey, 25 July 1779, in *Letters between Mrs. Elizabeth Carter and Miss Catherine Talbot*, vol. IV, pp. 226–7.
16 Elizabeth Carter to Elizabeth Montagu, 12 October 1769,

in *Letters from Mrs. Elizabeth Carter to Mrs. Montagu*, vol. II, pp. 47–8.

17 Elizabeth Carter to Elizabeth Vesey, 4 December 1764, in *Letters between Mrs. Elizabeth Carter and Miss Catherine Talbot*, vol. III, p. 249.

18 Elizabeth Carter to Catherine Talbot, n.d., in *Letters between Mrs. Elizabeth Carter and Miss Catherine Talbot*, vol. I, pp. 192–3.

19 Clarke, *Dr Johnson's Women*, p. 36.

20 Elizabeth Carter to Catherine Talbot, 2 June 1753, in *Letters between Mrs. Elizabeth Carter and Miss Catherine Talbot*, vol. II, p. 120.

21 Elizabeth Carter to Elizabeth Montagu, 26 October 1774, in *Letters from Mrs. Elizabeth Carter to Mrs. Montagu*, vol. II, p. 286.

22 Pennington, *Memoirs of the Life of Elizabeth Carter*, p. 489.

23 Elizabeth Carter to Elizabeth Vesey, 26 July 1763, in *Letters Between Mrs. Elizabeth Carter and Miss Catherine Talbot*, vol. III, p. 224.

24 Elizabeth Carter to Catherine Talbot, 13 July 1743, in *Letters between Mrs. Elizabeth Carter and Miss Catherine Talbot*, vol. I, pp. 35–6.

25 Elizabeth Carter to Catherine Talbot, 13 July 1750, in *Letters between Mrs. Elizabeth Carter and Miss Catherine Talbot*, vol. I, pp. 351–2.

26 Elizabeth Carter to Catherine Talbot, 29 October 1747, in *Letters between Mrs. Elizabeth Carter and Miss Catherine Talbot*, vol. I, pp. 231–2.

27 Pennington, *Memoirs of the Life of Elizabeth Carter*, p. 489.

28 Elizabeth Carter to Elizabeth Vesey, 6 October 1786, in *Letters between Mrs. Elizabeth Carter and Miss Catherine Talbot*, vol. IV, p. 367.

29 Pennington, *Memoirs of the Life of Elizabeth Carter*, p. 73.

30 Elizabeth Carter to Elizabeth Montagu, 24 June 1785, in *Letters from Mrs. Elizabeth Carter to Mrs. Montagu*, vol. III, pp. 240–1.

31 Pennington, *Memoirs of the Life of Elizabeth Carter*, p. 336.

32 Elizabeth Carter to Elizabeth Montagu, 24 July 1779, in *Letters from Mrs. Elizabeth Carter to Mrs. Montagu*, vol. III, p. 106.

2 Dorothy Wordsworth

1 Dorothy Wordsworth to Jane Pollard, 23 May 1791, in *The Letters of William and Dorothy Wordsworth: I. The Early Years 1787–1805*, ed. Ernest de Selincourt, rev. Chester L. Shaver (Oxford, 1967), pp. 46–7.

2 William and Dorothy Wordsworth to Samuel Taylor Coleridge, 24 and 27 December 1799, in *The Letters of William and Dorothy Wordsworth: The Early Years*, p. 277.

3 Pamela Woof, Introduction to *The Grasmere and Alfoxden Journals*, by Dorothy Wordsworth (Oxford and New York, 2002), p. xiii.

4 Dorothy Wordsworth, entry for Wednesday 14 May 1800, 'Grasmere Journal', *Grasmere and Alfoxden Journals*, p. 1.

5 Ibid.

6 Dorothy Wordsworth, entry for Friday 16 May 1800, 'Grasmere Journal', pp. 2–3.

7 Dorothy Wordsworth, entry for Monday 2 June 1800, 'Grasmere Journal', p. 7.

8 Dorothy Wordsworth, entry for Sunday 31 January 1802, 'Grasmere Journal', pp. 60–61.

9 Lucy Newlyn, *William and Dorothy Wordsworth: 'All in Each Other'* (Oxford, 2013), p. 6.

10 Rebecca Solnit, *Wanderlust: A History of Walking* (London, 2002), p. 68.

11 Dorothy Wordsworth, entry for Tuesday 10 November 1801, 'Grasmere Journal', p. 37.

12 Dorothy Wordsworth, entry for Thursday 4 March 1802, 'Grasmere Journal', p. 74.

13 Dorothy Wordsworth to Lady Beaumont, 11 June 1805, in *The Letters of William and Dorothy Wordsworth: The Early Years*, pp. 598–9.

14 Robert Macfarlane, *The Old Ways* (London, 2012), p. 27.

15 Dorothy Wordsworth, *Recollections of a Tour Made in Scotland*, ed. Carol Kyros Walker (New Haven, CT, and London, 1997), p. 55.

16 Ibid., p. 184.

17 Solnit, *Wanderlust*, p. 168.

18 Samuel Taylor Coleridge, *Coleridge's Notebooks: A Selection*, ed. Seamus Perry (Oxford, 2002), p. 31.

19 Dorothy Wordswoth, *Recollections of a Tour Made in Scotland*, p. 75.

20 Dorothy Wordsworth, 'Journal of My Second Tour in Scotland', in *Journals of Dorothy Wordsworth*, 2 vols, ed. Ernest de Selincourt (London, 1959), vol. II, pp. 366–7.

21 Ibid., pp. 365–7.

22 Ibid., pp. 391–2.

23 Ibid., p. 392.

24 Dorothy Wordsworth to Jane Marshall, 10/12 September 1800, in *The Letters of William and Dorothy Wordsworth: The Early Years*, p. 294.

25 Dorothy Wordsworth to Catherine Clarkson, 13 November 1803, *The Letters of William and Dorothy Wordsworth: The Early Years*, p. 420; Dorothy Wordsworth to Catherine Clarkson, 16 April 1805, in *The Letters of William and Dorothy Wordsworth: The Early Years*, pp. 584–5.

26 Dorothy Wordsworth, entry for Sunday 9 September 1820, in 'Journal of a Tour to the Continent', vol. II, pp. 260–61.

27 Ibid., p. 263.

28 Dorothy Wordsworth, entry for Thursday 23 August 1820, in 'Journal of a Tour to the Continent', vol. II, p. 190.

29 Dorothy Wordsworth, entry for Sunday 9 September 1820, in 'Journal of a Tour to the Continent', vol. II, p. 259.

30 Susan M. Levin, *Dorothy Wordsworth and Romanticism* (New Brunswick, NJ, and London, 1987), p. 104.

31 Tim Ingold and Jo Lee Vergunst, eds, 'Introduction' to *Ways of Walking: Ethnography and Practice on Foot* (Aldershot and Burlington, VT, 2008), p. 1.

32 Dorothy Wordsworth, *Journal of My Second Tour in Scotland, 1822: A Complete Edition of Dove Cottage Manuscript 98 and Dove Cottage Manuscript 99*, ed. Jiro Nagasawa (Tokyo, 1989), p. 410.

33 Dorothy Wordsworth, *Journals of Dorothy Wordsworth*, vol. II, p. 405.

34 Newlyn, *William and Dorothy Wordsworth: 'All in Each Other'*, p. 275; Ernest de Selincourt, ed., *The Letters of William and Dorothy Wordsworth: The Later Years, 1821–1853*, rev. Alan G. Hill, 4 vols (Oxford, 1978–88), vol. II, p. 448.

35 Newlyn, *William and Dorothy Wordsworth: 'All in Each Other'*, p. 292.

36 Dorothy Wordsworth, 'Thoughts on My Sick-bed' (1832), www.rc.umd.edu, accessed 26 July 2018.
37 Ibid.

3 Ellen Weeton

1 Ellen Weeton, *Miss Weeton's Journal of a Governess*, vol. II: *1811–1825*, ed. J. J. Bagley (Newton Abbott, 1969), p. 388.
2 Ibid.
3 Ibid., p. 389.
4 Ibid.
5 Ibid.
6 Ibid., pp. 390–91.
7 Ibid., p. 390.
8 Ibid., p. 391.
9 Ibid.
10 Ibid., p. 392.
11 Ibid., pp. 392–3.
12 Ibid., p. 393.
13 Ellen Weeton, *Miss Weeton's Journal of a Governess*, vol. I: *1807–11* (Newton Abbott, 1969), p. 3.
14 Morris Marples, *Shanks's Pony: A Study of Walking* (London, 1959), p. 98.
15 Weeton, *Miss Weeton's Journal of a Governess*, vol. I: *1807–1811*, pp. 168–9.
16 Weeton, *Miss Weeton's Journal of a Governess*, vol. II: *1811–1825*, p. 45.
17 Weeton, *Miss Weeton's Journal of a Governess*, vol. I: *1807–11*, pp. 272–4.
18 Ibid., pp. 313–4.
19 Marples, *Shanks's Pony*, p. 98.
20 Weeton, *Miss Weeton's Journal of a Governess*, vol. II: *1811–1825*, pp. 24–5.
21 Jean-Jacques Rousseau, *Confessions of a Solitary Wanderer* (Oxford, 2016), p. xx.
22 Weeton, letter to Miss Ann Winkley, 15 June–5 July 1812, in *Miss Weeton's Journal of a Governess*, vol. II: *1811–1825*, p. 26.
23 Ibid, p. 28.
24 Ibid.
25 Ibid. pp. 28–9.

26 Ibid. p. 29.
27 Rebecca Solnit, *Wanderlust: A History of Walking* (London, 2002), p. 234.
28 Ibid., p. 50.
29 Weeton, *Miss Weeton's Journal of a Governess,* vol. II: *1811–1825,* p. 25.
30 Ibid., pp. 32–3.
31 Ibid., p. 34.
32 Ibid. p. 154.
33 Ibid.
34 Ibid., p. 176.
35 Ibid., p. 369.

4 Sarah Stoddart Hazlitt

 1 Sarah Stoddart Hazlitt, entry for Friday 17 May 1822, *The Journals of Sarah and William Hazlitt, 1822–1831*, ed. William Hallam Bonner, The University of Buffalo Studies, XXIV/3 (1959), p. 208.
 2 Stoddart Hazlitt, entry for Sunday 19 May 1822, 'The Journals of Sarah and William Hazlitt, 1822–1831', p. 208.
 3 Ibid.
 4 Stoddart Hazlitt, entry for Monday 20 May 1822, 'The Journals of Sarah and William Hazlitt, 1822–1831', p. 208.
 5 Ibid.
 6 Stoddart Hazlitt, entry for Friday 24 May 1822, 'The Journals of Sarah and William Hazlitt, 1822–1831', p. 210.
 7 Stoddart Hazlitt, entry for Friday 31 May 1822, 'The Journals of Sarah and William Hazlitt, 1822–1831', pp. 213–4.
 8 Stoddart Hazlitt, entry for Saturday 1 June 1822, 'The Journals of Sarah and William Hazlitt, 1822–1831', p. 214.
 9 Ibid.
10 Stoddart Hazlitt, entry for Sunday 2 June 1822, 'The Journals of Sarah and William Hazlitt, 1822–1831', p. 216.
11 Stoddart Hazlitt, entry for Saturday 1 June 1822, in 'Journals of Sarah and William Hazlitt, 1822–1831', p. 215.
12 Ibid., p. 216.
13 Stoddart Hazlitt, entry for Monday 3 June 1822, 'The Journals of Sarah and William Hazlitt, 1822–1831', p. 219.
14 Ibid., p. 220.

15 Stoddart Hazlitt, entry for Tuesday 4 June 1822, 'The Journals of Sarah and William Hazlitt, 1822–1831', p. 221.
16 Stoddart Hazlitt, entry for Thursday 6 June 1822, 'The Journals of Sarah and William Hazlitt, 1822–1831', p. 221.
17 Stoddart Hazlitt, entry for Thursday 18 July 1822, 'Journals of Sarah and William Hazlitt, 1822–1831', p. 251.

5 Harriet Martineau

1 Harriet Martineau to William Johnson Fox, 19 February 1840, in *Collected Letters of Harriet Martineau*, 5 vols, ed. Deborah Anna Logan (London, 2007), vol. ii, p. 44.
2 See Alison Winter, *Mesmerized: Powers of Mind in Victorian Britain* (Cambridge, 1998); Winter offers a comprehensive history of mesmerism.
3 Harriet Martineau to Edward Moxon, 28 September 1844, in *Collected Letters*, vol. ii, p. 333.
4 Deborah Anna Logan, 'Introduction' to vol. ii of *Collected Letters*, p. viii.
5 Harriet Martineau, *Autobiography*, 2 vols (Boston, MA, 1877), vol. i, pp. 481–2.
6 Letter from Macready to Harriet Martineau, 25 March 1846, quoted in Martineau, *Autobiography*, vol. ii, p. 387.
7 Harriet Martineau to Helen Bourn Martineau, 28 June 1821, in *Collected Letters*, vol. i, p. 2.
8 Harriet Martineau to Helen Bourn Martineau, 19 October 1824, in *Collected Letters*, vol. i, p. 26.
9 James Martineau, 'Biographical Memoranda', quoted in *Collected Letters*, vol. i, p. 28, fn 1.
10 Harriet Martineau to Helen Bourn Martineau, 3 August 1824, in *Collected Letters*, vol i, pp. 24–5.
11 Martineau, *Autobiography*, vol. i, p. 98.
12 Ibid., p. 507.
13 Harriet Martineau to Richard Monckton Milnes, 18 June 1845, in *Collected Letters*, vol. iii, p. 13.
14 Ibid., p. 14.
15 Harriet Martineau to Henry Crabb Robinson, 24 June 1845, in *Collected Letters*, vol. iii, p. 15.
16 Martineau, *Autobiography*, vol. i, p. 132.

17 Ibid., p. 488.
18 Ibid.
19 Ibid.
20 Harriet Martineau to Helen Bourn Martineau, 12 May 1825, in *Collected Letters*, vol. I, p. 31.
21 Harriet Martineau to Helen Bourn Martineau, 9 April 1827, in *Collected Letters*, vol. I, p. 46.
22 Harriet Martineau to Henry Crabb Robinson, 6 October 1844, in *Collected Letters*, vol. II, p. 336.
23 Harriet Martineau to Richard Monckton Milnes, 27 October 1844, in *Collected Letters*, vol. II, p. 337; Harriet Martineau to William Johnson Fox, 30 January 1845, in *Collected Letters*, vol. III, p. 2; Harriet Martineau to Miss Fenwick, early summer 1845, in *Collected Letters*, vol. III, p. 12.
24 Harriet Martineau to H. G. Atkinson, 7 November 1847, in Martineau, *Autobiography*, vol. I, p. 540.
25 Harriet Martineau, *How to Observe Morals and Manners* (New York, 1838), p. 57.
26 Ibid., pp. 54–5.
27 Ibid., p. 54.
28 Martineau, *Autobiography*, vol. I, p. 482.
29 Ibid., p. 494.
30 Ibid., p. 503.
31 Ibid., p. 512.
32 Ibid., p. 513.
33 John Keats, 'On First Looking into Chapman's Homer', www.poetryfoundation.org, accessed 9 April 2020.
34 Harriet Martineau to H. S. Tremenheere, 6 July 1846, in *Collected Letters*, vol. III, p. 64.
35 Harriet Martineau to H. S. Tremenheere, 10 July 1846, in *Collected Letters*, vol. III, p. 67.
36 Harriet Martineau to Richard Cobden, 12 July 1846, in *Collected Letters*, vol. III, p. 68.
37 Martineau, *Autobiography*, vol. I, p. 513.
38 Harriet Martineau, 'A Year at Ambleside', January, in *Harriet Martineau at Ambleside, with 'A Year at Ambleside', by Harriet Martineau*, by Barbara Todd (Carlisle, 2002), p. 47.
39 Ibid., pp. 47–9.
40 Ibid., pp. 49, 50.
41 Ibid., pp. 69–70.

42 Ibid., p. 70.
43 Alexis Easley, 'The Woman of Letters at Home: Harriet
    Martineau and the Lake District', *Victorian Literature
    and Culture*, xxxiv/1 (March 2006), p. 305.
44 Harriet Martineau, *A Complete Guide to the English Lakes*
    (Windermere, 1855), p. 51.
45 Ibid., p. 57.
46 Ibid.
47 Easley, 'The Woman of Letters', p. 302.
48 Martineau, *A Complete Guide*, p. 58.
49 Ibid., pp. 63–4.
50 Ibid., pp. 64–5.
51 Easley, 'The Woman of Letters', p. 302.
52 Martineau, *A Complete Guide*, pp. 150–51.
53 Ibid., p. 153.
54 Harriet Martineau to Mr Allen, 16 December 1854,
    in *Collected Letters*, vol. iii, pp. 338–9.
55 Deborah Anna Logan, Introduction to *Collected Letters*,
    vol. iv, p. vii.
56 Harriet Martineau to Lord Carlisle, 1 January 1856,
    in *Collected Letters*, vol. iv, p. 1.

6 Virginia Woolf

 1 Virginia Woolf, 8 August 1917, *The Diary of Virginia Woolf*,
    vol. i: *1915–1919*, ed. Anne Olivier Bell (Harmondsworth,
    1979), p. 41.
 2 Virginia Woolf, *Street Haunting: A London Adventure* [1927]
    (n.p., 2012), p. 21.
 3 Virginia Stephen to Violet Dickinson, 4 August 1906, in
    *The Flight of the Mind: The Letters of Virginia Woolf: Volume
    One 1888–1912*, ed. Nigel Nicolson and Joanne Trachtmann
    (London, 1975), p. 234.
 4 Virginia Stephen to Violet Dickinson, 16 April 1906,
    in *Letters*, p. 221.
 5 Virginia Stephen to Clive Bell, 19 August 1908, in *Letters*,
    p. 356.
 6 Woolf, 3 November 1918, *The Diary of Virginia Woolf*, vol. i:
    1915–1919, p. 214.
 7 Ibid., p. 35.

8 Virginia Woolf, 28 March 1930, *The Diary of Virginia Woolf*, vol. III: *1925–1930*, ed. Anne Olivier Bell and Andrew McNeillie (London, 1981), p. 298.

9 Virginia Woolf, 25 October 1920, *The Diary of Virginia Woolf*, vol. II: *1920–1924*, ed. Anne Olivier Bell and Andrew McNeillie (London, 1980), p. 72.

10 Woolf, 10 November 1920, *The Diary of Virginia Woolf*, vol. II: *1920–1924*, p. 73.

11 Woolf, 18 August 1921, *The Diary of Virginia Woolf*, vol. II: *1920–1924*, pp. 132–3.

12 Woolf, 15 August 1924, *The Diary of Virginia Woolf*, vol. II: *1920–1924*, p. 310.

13 Woolf, 11 May 1920, *The Diary of Virginia Woolf*, vol. II: *1920–1924*, p. 36.

14 Virginia Stephen to Clive Bell, 26 December 1909, in *Letters*, p. 416.

15 Woolf, 3 January 1918, *The Diary of Virginia Woolf*, vol. I: *1915–1919*, pp. 94–5.

16 Woolf, 7 January 1920, *The Diary of Virginia Woolf*, vol. II: *1920–1924*, pp. 3–4.

17 Woolf, after 26 July 1926, *The Diary of Virginia Woolf*, vol. III: *1925–1930*, p. 102.

18 Woolf, 22 August 1929, *The Diary of Virginia Woolf*, vol. III: *1925–1930*, p. 248.

19 Virginia Woolf, 2 October 1934, *The Diary of Virginia Woolf*, vol. IV: *1931–1935*, ed. Anne Olivier Bell and Andrew McNeillie (London, 1982), p. 246.

20 Woolf, 31 May 1927, *The Diary of Virginia Woolf*, vol. III: *1925–1930*, p. 186.

21 Woolf, 15 August 1924, *The Diary of Virginia Woolf*, vol. II: *1920–1924*, p. 301.

22 Woolf, *Street Haunting*, p. 5.

23 Ibid., pp. 6–7.

24 Ibid., p. 14.

25 Ibid., p. 21.

7 Nan Shepherd

1 'Scots Women Writers' by 'Cynthia', *The Scotsman*, 14 November 1931.

2 Nan Shepherd to Neil Gunn, 15 September 1931, NLS DEP209 Box 19 Folder 7.

3 Jessie Kesson to Nan Shepherd, 18 July 1980, NLS MS27438.

4 Robert Macfarlane, 'Introduction' to *The Living Mountain*, by Nan Shepherd [1977] (Edinburgh, 2011), p. xiii.

5 Ken Morrice to Nan Shepherd, 26 December 1977, NLS MS27438.

6 Shepherd, *The Living Mountain*, p. 15.

7 Ibid., p. 106.

8 Macfarlane, 'Introduction' to *The Living Mountain*, p. xxxiii.

9 Ibid., p. xxxi.

10 Shepherd, *The Living Mountain*, p. 6.

11 Ibid.

12 Ibid., pp. 6–7.

13 Ibid., pp. 78–9.

14 Ibid., p. 8.

15 Ibid.

16 Ibid., p. 9.

17 Ibid., pp. 11–12.

18 Ibid., p. 16.

19 Ibid.

20 Ibid.

21 Ibid., p. 4.

22 Ibid., pp. 22–3.

23 See Genesis 2:19–23.

24 Shepherd, *The Living Mountain*, pp. 27, 28.

25 Ibid., pp. 26, 29.

26 Nan Shepherd to Neil Gunn, 2 April 1931, NLS DEP209 Box 19 Folder 7.

27 Nan Shepherd to Neil Gunn, 24 February 1948, NLS DEP209 Box 19 Folder 7.

28 Shepherd to Neil Gunn, 2 April 1931, NLS DEP209 Box 19 Folder 7.

29 Nan Shepherd, 'The Hill Burns', NLS DEP209 Box 19 Folder 7.

30 Robert Macfarlane, *The Old Ways* (London, 2012), p. 192.

31 Shepherd, *The Living Mountain*, pp. 37–8.

32 Shepherd, Preface to *The Living Mountain*, pp. xli, xlii.

33 Shepherd, *The Living Mountain*, p. 40.

34 Ibid., p. 29.

35 Ibid., p. 33.

36 Nan Shepherd, 'Snow', from *In the Cairngorms* [1934] (Cambridge, 2014), p. 43.
37 Shepherd, *The Living Mountain*, p. 35.
38 Ibid., p. 36.
39 Ibid., p. 13.
40 Macfarlane, *The Old Ways*, p. 24.
41 Rebecca Solnit, *Wanderlust: A History of Walking* (London, 2002), p. 72.
42 Shepherd, *The Living Mountain*, p. 76.
43 Ibid., p. 30.
44 Ibid., pp. 30–31.
45 Ibid., p. 14.
46 Robert Macfarlane writes in his introduction to the text that while 'precise information about the composition . . . is hard to come by', it was 'written mostly during the closing years of the Second World War'. See Macfarlane, 'Introduction' to *The Living Mountain*, p. xii.
47 Nan Shepherd to Neil Gunn, 14 May 1940, NLS DEP209 Box 19 Folder 7.
48 Shepherd, *The Living Mountain*, p. 108.
49 Ibid., p. 105.
50 Ibid., p. 59.
51 Nan Shepherd to Barbara Balmer, quoted in Macfarlane, 'Introduction' to *The Living Mountain*, p. xxxii.
52 Nan Shepherd to Jessie Kesson, quoted in Robert Macfarlane, Foreword to *In the Cairngorms* by Nan Shepherd, p. xvi.

8 Anaïs Nin

1 Anaïs Nin, diary entry for 30 March 1919, in *Linotte: The Early Diary of Anaïs Nin, 1914–1920* (San Diego, CA, 1978), p. 213.
2 Ibid.
3 *Anaïs* Nin, diary entry for 6 May 1925, in *The Early Diary of Anaïs Nin*, vol. III: *1923–1927* (Boston, MA, 1983), p. 142.
4 Nin, diary entry for 27 February 1925, in *The Early Diary of Anaïs Nin*, vol. III: *1923–1927*, p. III.
5 Rupert Pole, Introduction to *The Journals of Anaïs Nin*, vol. VI: *1955–1966*, by Anaïs Nin (London, 1977), p. xi.
6 Deirdre Bair, *Anaïs Nin: A Biography* (New York, 1995), p. 110.
7 Anaïs Nin, diary entry for 18 September 1935, in *Fire: From 'A*

Journal of Love': The Unexpurgated Diary of Anaïs Nin, 1934–1937 (San Diego, CA, New York and London, 1995), p. 147.

8 Anaïs Nin, diary entry for 27 April 1934, in *Incest: Unexpurgated Diaries 1932–1934* (London and Chicago, IL, 1992), p. 325.

9 Nin, diary entry for 4 May 1934, in *Incest*, p. 327.

10 Charles Baudelaire, *The Painter of Modern Life and Other Essays* (London, 1995), p. 9.

11 Lauren Elkin, *Flâneuse: Women Walk the City in Paris, New York, Tokyo, Venice and London* (London, 2016), p. 9.

12 See, for instance, Matthew Beaumont's *Nightwalking: A Nocturnal History of London* (London, 2015).

13 Rebecca Solnit, *Wanderlust: A History of Walking* (London, 2002), p. 176.

14 Elkin, *Flâneuse*, p. 11.

15 Quoted in Bair, *Anaïs Nin: A Biography*, p. 65.

16 Nin, diary entry for 23 July 1936, in *Fire*, p. 266.

17 Nin, diary entry for 1 April 1919, in *Linotte: The Early Diary 1914–1920*, p. 214.

18 Nin, diary entry for 9 January 1929, in *Linotte: The Early Diary of Anaïs Nin*, vol. IV: *1927–1931* (San Diego, CA, 1985), p. 151.

19 Nin, diary entry for 27 April 1934, in *Incest*, p. 325.

20 Ibid., p. 196.

21 See Elizabeth Podniek's Introduction to the Swallow Press edition of *Under a Glass Bell* (Athens, GA, 2014), p. ix.

22 Ibid., p. x.

23 Edmund Wilson's review in the *New Yorker*, quoted by Nin in *The Early Diary of Anaïs Nin*, vol. III: *1923–1927*, p. 10.

24 Anaïs Nin, 'The Labyrinth', in *Under a Glass Bell*, p. 45.

25 Ibid., p. 46.

26 Ibid.

27 Ibid.

28 Ibid., p. 47.

29 Ibid.

30 Ibid., pp. 47, 48.

31 Ibid.

32 Anaïs Nin, *Diary of Anaïs Nin*, vol. V: *1947–55*, ed. Gunther Stuhlmann (New York and London, 1974), p. 51.

33 Nin, diary entry for 27 May 1933, in *Incest*, pp. 175–6.

34 Nin, diary entry for 24 July 1935, in *Fire*, p. 115.
35 Nin, diary entry for 5 July 1936, in *Fire*, pp. 250–51.
36 Nin, diary entry for 11 September 1936, in *Fire*, p. 296.
37 Nin, diary entry for 23 August 1936, in *Fire*, p. 289.
38 Nin, diary entry for 18 December 1936, in *Fire*, pp. 350–51.
39 Nin, diary entry for 3 January 1937, in *Fire*, p. 370.
40 Anaïs Nin, diary entry for 16 June 1937, in *Nearer the Moon: From a Journal of Love: The Unexpurgated Diaries of Anaïs Nin* (London, 1996), p. 40.
41 Nin, diary entry for 1 May 1937, in *Nearer the Moon*, p. 29.
42 Anaïs Nin, diary entry for 29 January 1946, in *Mirages: The Unexpurgated Diaries of Anaïs Nin, 1939–1947* (Athens, OH, 2013), p. 336.
43 Nin, diary entry for 8 February 1938, in *Nearer the Moon*, p. 211.

9 Cheryl Strayed

1 Cheryl Strayed, *Wild: A Journey from Lost to Found* (London, 2013), pp. 4–5.
2 Ibid., p. 5.
3 Ibid., p. 30.
4 Ibid., pp. 84–5.
5 Ibid., p. 33.
6 Ibid., p. 41.
7 Ibid.
8 Ibid., p. 40.
9 Ibid., p. 42.
10 Ibid., p. 44.
11 Ibid., p. 92.
12 Ibid., p. 90.
13 Ibid., p. 85.
14 Ibid., p. 88.
15 Ibid., p. 102.
16 Ibid., p. 111.
17 Ibid., p. 129.
18 Ibid., pp. 245–6, 249.
19 Ibid., p. 193.
20 Ibid., p.164.
21 Ibid., p. 193.

22 Ibid., p. 148.
23 Ibid., p. 151.
24 Ibid., p. 168.
25 Ibid., p. 173–4.
26 Ibid., p. 285.
27 Ibid.
28 Ibid., p. 286.
29 Ibid.
30 Ibid., pp. 286–7.
31 Ibid., p. 287.
32 Ibid.
33 Ibid., p. 288.
34 Ibid., p. 307.
35 Ibid., p. 311.

10 Linda Cracknell and a Female Tradition

1 Linda Cracknell, *Doubling Back: Ten Paths Trodden in Memory* (Glasgow, 2014), p. 24.
2 Ibid., p. 35.
3 Ibid., p. 98.
4 Ibid.
5 Ibid., p. 136.
6 Ibid., p. 137.
7 Ibid., p. 133.
8 Ibid., p. 138.
9 Ibid., p. 144.
10 Ibid.
11 Ibid., p. 153.
12 Ibid.
13 Ibid., pp. 52, 53.
14 Ibid., p. 12.
15 Jessie Kesson, article in *Country Living* (April 1990), quoted by Isobel Murray in *Jessie Kesson: Writing her Life* (Edinburgh, 2000), p. 53.
16 Cracknell, *Doubling Back*, p. 41.
17 Ibid.
18 Ibid.
19 Jessie Kesson, *Country Dweller's Year 10*, quoted by Isobel Murray in *Jessie Kesson: Writing Her Life*, p. 119.

20 Cracknell, *Doubling Back*, p. 41.
21 Ibid., p. 42.
22 Ibid.
23 Ibid., p. 46.
24 Ibid., p. 47.
25 Ibid., p. 48.
26 Ibid., p. 50.

Coda

1 Linda Cracknell, *Doubling Back: Ten Paths Trodden in Memory* (Glasgow, 2014), p. 243.
2 Ibid., p. 242.

FURTHER READING

Bagley, J. J., ed., *Miss Weeton's Journal of a Governess*, 2 vols
    (Newton Abbott, 1969)
Bair, Deirdre, *Anaïs Nin: A Biography* (New York, 1995)
Beaumont, Matthew, *Nightwalking: A Nocturnal History of London*
    (London, 2015)
Birkett, Dea, *Off the Beaten Track: Three Centuries of Women
    Travellers* (London, 2004)
Bonner, William Hallam, 'The Journals of Sarah and William
    Hazlitt, 1822–1831', *University of Buffalo Studies*, xxiv/3 (1959),
    pp. 172–281
Carter, Elizabeth, *Letters from Mrs. Elizabeth Carter to
    Mrs. Montagu*, 3 vols (London, 1817)
—, *A Series of Letters between Mrs. Elizabeth Carter and
    Miss Catherine Talbot*, 4 vols (London, 1809)
Clarke, Norma, *Dr Johnson's Women* (London, 2001)
Coleridge, Samuel Taylor, *Coleridge's Notebooks: A Selection*,
    ed. Seamus Perry (Oxford, 2002)
Coverley, Merlin, *The Art of Wandering: The Writer as Walker*
    (Harpenden, 2012)
Cracknell, Linda, Blogs for Walkhighlands, www.walkhighlands.
    co.uk
—, *Doubling Back: Ten Paths Trodden in Memory*
    (Glasgow, 2014)
De Quincey, Thomas, *The Collected Writings of Thomas de Quincey*,
    ed. David Masson (London, 1896)
Easley, Alexis, 'The Woman of Letters at Home: Harriet
    Martineau and the Lake District', *Victorian Literature
    and Culture*, xxxiv/1 (March 2006), pp. 291–310

Eger, Elizabeth, *Bluestockings: Women of Reason from Enlightenment to Romanticism* (Basingstoke and New York, 2012)

Elkin, Lauren, *Flâneuse: Women Walk the City in Paris, New York, Tokyo, Venice and London* (London, 2016)

Harrison, Melissa, *Rain: Four Walks in English Weather* (London, 2016)

Humble, Kate, *Thinking on My Feet: The Small Joy of Putting One Foot in Front of Another* (London, 2018)

Ingold, Tim, and Jo Lee Vergunst, eds, *Ways of Walking: Ethnography and Practice on Foot* (Aldershot and Burlington, VT, 2008)

Levin, Susan M., *Dorothy Wordsworth and Romanticism* (New Brunswick, NJ, and London, 1987)

Macfarlane, Robert, *The Old Ways* (London, 2012)

Marples, Morris, *Shanks's Pony: A Study of Walking* (London, 1959)

Martineau, Harriet, *Autobiography*, 2 vols (Boston, MA, 1877)

—, *Collected Letters of Harriet Martineau*, 5 vols, ed. Deborah Anna Logan (London, 2007)

—, *A Complete Guide to the English Lakes* (Windermere, 1855)

—, *How to Observe Morals and Manners* (New York, 1838)

Mort, Helen, et al., eds, *Waymaking: An Anthology of Women's Adventure Writing, Poetry and Art* (Sheffield, 2018)

Murray, Isobel, *Jessie Kesson: Writing her Life* [2000] (Glasgow, 2011)

Newlyn, Lucy, *William and Dorothy Wordsworth: 'All in Each Other'* (Oxford, 2013)

Nin, Anaïs, *Diary of Anaïs Nin*, vol. V: *1947–55*, ed. Gunther Stuhlmann (New York and London, 1974)

—, *The Early Diary of Anaïs Nin*, vol. III: *1923–1927* (Boston, MA, 1983)

—, *Fire: From 'A Journal of Love': The Unexpurgated Diary of Anaïs Nin, 1934–1937* (San Diego, CA, New York and London, 1995)

—, *Incest: Unexpurgated Diaries, 1932–1934* (London and Chicago, IL, 1992)

—, *The Journals of Anaïs Nin*, vol. VI: *1955–1966* (London, 1977)

—, *Linotte: The Early Diary of Anaïs Nin, 1914–1920* (San Diego, CA, 1978)

—, *Linotte: The Early Diary of Anaïs Nin*, vol. IV: *1927–1931* (San Diego, CA, 1985)

—, *Mirages: The Unexpurgated Diaries of Anaïs Nin, 1939–1947*
(Athens, OH, 2013)

—, *Nearer the Moon: From A Journal of Love: The Unexpurgated
Diaries of Anaïs Nin* (London, 1996)

Peacock, Charlotte, *Into the Mountain: A Life of Nan Shepherd*
(Cambridge, 2017)

Pennington, Montagu, *Memoirs of the Life of Elizabeth Carter*
(London, 1809)

Rousseau, Jean-Jacques, *Confessions of a Solitary Wanderer*
(Oxford, 2016)

Selincourt, Ernest de, ed., *Journals of Dorothy Wordsworth*, 2 vols
(London, 1941)

—, ed., *Journals of Dorothy Wordsworth*, 2 vols, 2nd edn
(London, 1959)

—, ed., *The Letters of William and Dorothy Wordsworth*, vol. I:
The Early Years, 1787–1805, rev. Chester L. Shaver
(Oxford, 1967)

—, *The Letters of William and Dorothy Wordsworth: The Later
Years, 1821–1853*, rev. Alan G. Hill, 4 vols (Oxford, 1978–88)

Shepherd, Nan, *In the Cairngorms* [1934] (Cambridge, 2014)

—, *The Living Mountain* [1977] (Edinburgh, 2011)

Simmons, Gail, *The Country of Larks: A Chiltern Journey in the
Footsteps of Robert Louis Stevenson and the Footprint of HS2*
(Chalfont St Peter, 2019)

Solnit, Rebecca, *Wanderlust: A History of Walking*
(London, 2002)

Stewart, Alexandra, *Daughters of the Glen*, ed. Innis Macbeath
(Aberfeldy, 1986)

Strayed, Cheryl, *Wild: A Journey from Lost to Found*
(London, 2013)

Taplin, Kim, *The English Path* (Ipswich, 1979)

Todd, Barbara, *Harriet Martineau at Ambleside, with 'A Year
at Ambleside', by Harriet Martineau* (Carlisle, 2002)

Weeton, Ellen, *Miss Weeton's Journal of a Governess, 1807–1811*,
ed. J. J. Bagley, 2 vols (Newton Abbott, 1969), vol. I

—, *Miss Weeton's Journal of a Governess, 1811–1825*, ed. J. J. Bagley,
2 vols (Newton Abbott, 1969), vol. II

Winn, Raynor, *The Salt Path* (London, 2018)

Winter, Alison, *Mesmerized: Powers of Mind in Victorian Britain*
(Cambridge, 1998)

Woolf, Virginia, *The Diary of Virginia Woolf*, vol. I: *1915–1919*, ed. Anne Oliver Bell (London, 1979)

—, *The Diary of Virginia Woolf*, vol. II: *1920–1924*, ed. Anne Olivier Bell and Andrew McNeillie (London, 1980)

—, *The Diary of Virginia Woolf*, vol. III: *1925–1930*, ed. Anne Olivier Bell and Andrew McNeillie (London, 1981)

—, *The Diary of Virginia Woolf*, vol. IV: *1931–1935*, ed. Anne Olivier Bell and Andrew McNeillie (London, 1982)

—, *The Flight of the Mind: The Letters of Virginia Woolf*, vol. I: *1888–1912*, ed. Nigel Nicolson and Joanne Trachtmann (London, 1975)

—, *Street Haunting: A London Adventure* [1927] (n.p., 2012)

Wordsworth, Dorothy, *The Grasmere and Alfoxden Journals*, ed. Pamela Woof (Oxford and New York, 2002)

—, *Journal of My Second Tour in Scotland, 1822: A Complete Edition of Dove Cottage Manuscript 98 and Dove Cottage Manuscript 99*, ed. Jiro Nagasawa (Tokyo, 1989)

—, *Recollections of a Tour Made in Scotland*, ed. Carol Kyros Walker (New Haven, CT, and London, 1997)

—, 'Thoughts on My Sick-bed' (1832), www.rc.umd.edu

Wordsworth, William, *Lyrical Ballads* [1800], ed. Michael Gamer and Dahlia Porter (Peterborough, ON, 2008)

ACKNOWLEDGEMENTS

Writing this book has been a joy. I have had the pleasure of meeting and talking to many people whose paths I've crossed over the seven years or so it's taken to walk this book into being. Most memorably, on the summit of Ben Cruachan, late in the afternoon and alone, a family from Birmingham took me in and walked with me all the way around the horseshoe and back to the road. There have been numerous other happenstance encounters that have shaped how I have thought about walking, what it means and why it matters, and I am grateful for each of these experiences.

As I come to offer long-overdue thanks, I realize how many of my friendships have been started or become dear on the move. I have enjoyed the company of Ewan Tait and Christine Tait-Burkard on many adventures in the Scottish hills, big and small, and am grateful for their kindness in letting me talk through the project on numerous walks over the last few years. Matt Sangster, Beatrice Turner, Philip Aherne and Helen Stark helped me craft the chapter on Dorothy Wordsworth while walking in the Lakes above Grasmere in the sunny autumn of 2014. Jo Taylor suggested I look at Harriet Martineau, and has been a cheerful companion on memorable walks in the Lakes, Somerset and the Yorkshire Moors. To Sarah Osmond Smith, Susan Anderson, Sarah Leonard, Shannon Draucker and Emily Knight – thank you for pointing me towards the Bluestockings and Elizabeth Carter, and for general LA cheer. I also benefited enormously from the supportive and generous feedback on the draft manuscript from Lesley McDowell at The Literary Consultancy. The Society of Authors offered useful advice at a crucial stage. David Watkins provided my book with a home. To him and the whole team at Reaktion, thank you for all you've done.

Michael Gamer, Dahlia Porter, Gabe Cervantes, Alan Vardy and Julia Carlson urged me at various points in our delicious annual coastal walks to more rigorous thinking about the project, and offered generous support in the form of critiques, beer and cream teas. Thank you also to Paul Lawrence, Stuart Orr, Jennifer and Martin Campbell, Diane Burn, Anousheh Fulford, Gemma Robinson and Gemma Burnside, with whom I have shared memorable walks in the Scottish Highlands and elsewhere. I am thankful to have rekindled my friendship with Cathy Clay in part through our shared love of walking. Her company has helped to feed my passion for the walkers' paradise of the Scottish Borders. Faye Hammill showed confidence in this project before I had any myself, and has been a champion to me for a number of years. Don Bremner of the Sierra Club, Los Angeles branch, and the other members of the walking group made me extremely welcome when I was desperate to escape the city. Walking with them helped ease the sadness of homesickness. To Toby Andrews, Sarrawat Rehman and Jenny Wilkinson, who started it all, thank you.

I am particularly grateful to Polly Atkin – lake-lover and tarn-swimmer – for seeing within my garbled half-idea for a book about walking something of importance and value. Her friendship over the years has been a blessing, as has that of Will Smith. My love of the Scottish mountains may never have taken hold without the supportive companionship offered by the members of the Glasgow Hillwalking Club and the Scottish Hillwalking and Activities Group, especially Helen Melone, Fiona Morrison, Patrick Cairns and Gillian McFall: walking with you gave me skills and confidence as well as very special memories.

I owe a significant debt to Tim Fulford, who has allowed me to walk with him for a decade, from our first walk together on Great Gable, to Helvellyn and Scafell Pike, the Cornish Coastal Path, Lochnagar and the hills above my house. He has listened patiently over many, many miles, as I tried to walk this book into shape; offered supportive criticisms of a number of drafts; and generously shared with me his deep knowledge of Romantic-era literature.

Parts of this book were written while I recovered from post-natal depression – indeed, the book was my recovery. I cannot say how grateful I am for the unwavering kindness and support of Linda Henderson; Julie, Natalie and the team at Nurture the Borders; and to Colette at PND Borders.

Acknowledgements

I express my thanks, too, for the work of the librarians at the British Library, London; the Houghton and Widener Libraries at Harvard University; the Huntington Library in Los Angeles; and especially the National Library for Scotland in Edinburgh. All have been patient with my questions and rummaging, and this book simply would not exist without them.

Permissions

INDEX